DEADLY SERVICE

MURDEROUS MAIDS, DEVIOUS HOUSEKEEPERS AND BUTLERS WHO KILL

KATE CLARKE

Non-Fiction
by the same Author

Murder At The Priory: The Mysterious Poisoning of Charles Bravo
(with Bernard Taylor) (Short-listed for the CWA's Gold Dagger Award)

Journal: Volume One (as Kate Paul)
(All subsequent volumes at the Mass Observation Archive
Special Collections/Sussex University Library)

Who Killed Simon Dale? & Other Murder Mysteries

The Book of Hay (local history)

In The Interests of Science: Adelaide Bartlett and the Pimlico Poisoning

Bad Companions

Lethal Alliance

Fatal Affairs

A Deadly Dilemma

Revised second edition

First edition published Carrington Press (2011)

ISBN: 978-0-9931806-6-8 (hardback)
ISBN: 978-0-9931806-9-9 (ebook)

Published by Mango Books
www.mangobooks.co.uk
18 Soho Square, London W1D 3QL

DEADLY SERVICE

Contents

Acknowledgements

My thanks to the following for their help and encouragement; Sasha and Anil Mahendra, Milly Eagle, Noelle Beales, Fred Bond, Andy Dixon, Jim Rogers, Frances Copping, Dorothy Allam, Anne Dewell, Anne Brichto, Derek Addyman, Molly Huddlestone and Paula Chihaoua.

I am especially grateful to Mark Ripper (M W Oldridge), Adam Wood and David Green for their invaluable contribution to this edition.

Permission to quote from *The Monster Butler* by Norman Lucas and Philip Davies was sought without response. Likewise permission to quote from Albert Pierrepoint's notes for his memoir, *Executioner: Pierrepoint*. In the event of permissions being granted after publication due acknowledgement will be included in any future printing.

Unless otherwise stated all quoted passages are from contemporary press reports.

Foreword

> Have you ever reflected for an instant on the deadly and justified hatreds and murderous – yes, murderous – desires that can seize us when, with a disdain that hurls us beyond the pale of humanity, we hear our masters crying out 'he has a servant's soul'… 'that's a servant's sentiment' whenever they want to describe something low and base? Well then, what do you expect us to become in such a hell?
>
> Octave Mirbeau, *Diary of a Chambermaid*

What is it that ignites and unleashes an uncontrollable fury, exposing the smouldering resentment in those who finally rebel against a life of servitude? Surprisingly perhaps, this type of killing is relatively rare and when one considers the degradation and exploitation experienced by generations of servants, it is remarkable indeed that so few have resorted to murder.

Surely it could not have been merely the fussy, ostentatious ways of Mrs Julia Thomas that drove the surly housekeeper, Kate Webster, in 1879, to push her down the stairs and then systematically cut up her body and boil the bits in the kitchen copper?

Could it be that the obsequious widow, Jane Cannon Cox, was so determined to maintain her luxurious lifestyle as companion to the wealthy Florence Bravo, that, in 1876, she was prepared to kill Charles, her mistress's new husband, with enough antimony to 'kill a horse'?

Is it really possible that something as innocuous as a broken iron unleashed such an orgy of violence in the incredible case of two maids, Christine and Léa Papin, who, in France in 1933, mercilessly beat their mistress and her daughter to death and literally scratched their eyes out?

It is difficult to believe that being given the sack in 1927 had so enraged the mild-mannered and kindly butler, Charles Houghton, that, after serving their breakfast the next morning, he calmly shot his two elderly employers, Ella and May Woodhouse, at point blank range before returning the gun to its usual place in the larder.

As for the dumpy chatter-box, Louisa Merrifield, she was finding it hard to manage on her low wages and husband 'Pop' Merrifield's old age pension. When, in 1953, her elderly employer rashly made a will bequeathing the couple her modest little bungalow in Blackpool, the greedy housekeeper helped her on her way by feeding her the occasional spoonful of rum, laced with rat poison.

In 1884, young John Lee made criminal history by cheating the hangman and becoming famous as 'The man they could not hang'. When his benefactress, Miss Emma Keyse, had decided to dock sixpence from his weekly wage, he was seen to be upset. He was even more annoyed when she asked him to forgo an early morning tryst with a young lady in order to rake the gravel paths. He killed the old woman, it was said, by knocking her senseless before cutting her throat to the bone. But was he the killer or was the perpetrator, in fact, the lover of his pregnant half-sister, the cook, Elizabeth Harris?

Roy Fontaine was a meticulous butler, a brilliant conman and an audacious jewel thief; a career criminal who murdered five people – his first victim was an ex-lover, David Wright, and in 1977, he killed and robbed his wealthy employers, Mr and Mrs Scott-Elliot. He went on to beat one of his accomplices, Mary Coggle, to death with a poker because she refused to hand over part of the loot - a luxurious fur coat and some very expensive jewellery. His final killing was that of his despised half-brother, Donald, with chloroform.

This book contains studies of seven extraordinary cases of servants who have killed their employers, revealing the frustration and inner turmoil fostered by insecurity, poverty or greed so urgent and compelling that they were driven to kill, each in a totally different way.

But in each case it achieved nothing. Kate Webster, Charles Houghton and Louisa Merrifield lost their lives on the gallows. One of the Papin sisters lost her sanity. Jane Cox, though never charged with the murder of Charles Bravo, lost Florence Bravo's friendship, her credibility and her job. As for John Lee, though he cheated death in one of the most bizarre incidents in criminal history, nevertheless wasted twenty-two years of his life in prison.

Finally, the incorrigible Roy Fontaine, convicted of five murders and incarcerated for the rest of his life, time enough to reflect on his extraordinary life and truly callous killings before dying in Kingston Prison, Portsmouth, on 16 September, 2002, aged 78.

Kate Webster
A Truly Appalling Crime

Between four and five o'clock on the afternoon of Tuesday, 4 March, 1879, a tall, gaunt woman turned the corner into Rose Gardens, Hammersmith - a street in West London that was at the time little more than a rough track flanked by rows of two-up, two-down working men's cottages. Though poor and grossly overcrowded, the district was, nevertheless, a respectable one, and its inhabitants formed a close-knit community, bound by a shared struggle for survival.

Kate Webster was no stranger to the street for she, too, had once lived there. Now, some six years later, she had come back to the area to visit old friends, Henry Porter and his wife, Ann, at No 10. She was carrying a black canvas bag, the sort of bag a woman might use to carry vegetables back from the market.

Only Mrs Porter was at home and at first she failed to recognise her visitor for the woman standing on her doorstep was wearing a finely-cut dress of black silk, a fur-trimmed jacket and a fancy bonnet with a feather in it. Around her neck was a gold watch and chain and on her fingers several expensive rings. It was not until the woman greeted her warmly with a familiar, 'How are you, mother?' that she realised who she was - a woman she once knew simply as Kate, a next-door neighbour and drinking companion. Though both Mrs Porter and her husband were later to deny that they knew about Kate's busy criminal life this seems doubtful. Living so closely together, without the luxury of privacy, they must have been aware that Kate was, even in her mid-twenties when they knew her, a seasoned jail-bird with a string of convictions behind her for fraud and theft.

She was born Katherine Lawler, in Killanne, near Enniscorthy, Ireland, in 1847. Raised in a Catholic farming family, she had married a sea-captain called Webster whilst still in her teens and they had four children, all of whom died in infancy. She said later that when her husband also died, she had turned to crime in order to survive. It is as well to remember, however, as subsequent events will show, that Kate was an habitual liar with little concept of truth, changing the details of her life many times to suit her current circumstances. She was sentenced to a brief term of imprisonment for theft in Ireland and on her release made her way to Liverpool to continue with her criminal activities.

During her subsequent career as a thief, she adopted a number of aliases - Webb, Shannon, Gibbs, Gibbons or Lawless - and occasionally reverted to her maiden name of Lawler. Her criminal speciality was robbing lodging houses. She seemed to have had no difficulty in finding rooms, having first presented herself as an honest and respectable woman in need of lodging. Once installed, she would wait her chance to rob the occupants before disappearing, only to turn up in another district to repeat the offence, time and time again. Her mode of life, therefore, made her a rolling stone, forever changing her territory once she became known to the local police.

In 1867, she served a four year prison sentence for larceny and a number of other charges, including prostitution. On her subsequent release, she headed for London and, according to a statement she made later, she attempted to make an honest living by taking work as a domestic servant whenever she could. It was in 1873 that she had first turned up at Rose Gardens, Hammersmith, taking lodgings next door to the Porters. They said later that, when they knew her, she was an out-of-work domestic and they believed her when, after five or six weeks, she said she was leaving to take up a position as a maid in a house in Norland Crescent, Notting Hill.

However, she was soon to return to her criminal ways and on 4 May 1875, at the Surrey Sessions, she was convicted of thirty-six charges of larceny, all committed in the Kingston area, and sentenced to eighteen months' imprisonment at Wandsworth Prison. Two years later, on 6 February, she was again convicted of felony and served a further twelve months in gaol.

After leaving the area, Kate had occasionally gone back to see Annie Porter, but when these visits eventually stopped they lost contact altogether. Until, that is, there came that knock on the door. Remembering Kate as rather shabbily dressed and generally down-at-heel, it was little wonder that Mrs Porter barely recognised her. Not only was she now well-dressed, she seemed much more self-assured, almost proud in her carriage, and although she was a strong, big-boned woman, the cut of her new clothes suited her well. She even spoke differently, although her Irish accent was still strong.

Keen to hear what had brought about such a remarkable change in her fortunes, Mrs Porter invited her in for tea. Kate had come prepared - from a pocket deep in the folds of her skirt she pulled a bottle of whiskey and the two women settled down to bridge the gap of the intervening years over a glass or two.

Shortly after six o'clock, Henry Porter - or Harry, as Kate liked to call him - came home from work and joined them. He was also intrigued by the change in Kate and the story she had to tell. Since they had last seen her, she told him, she had married again, her name was now Mrs Thomas, and she had a young son called Johnny. But, she confided, although she was a widow once more, she had been more than fortunate, for an aunt had recently died and left her a respectable house, one of a pair known as Vine Cottages, in Park Road, Richmond.

Harry Porter and his wife were impressed. My goodness, Kate, what a stroke of luck! To celebrate her good fortune, the lodger's daughter was sent out for half a pint of gin - all the characters in this story, Kate included, seem to have drunk copious amounts at every opportunity - and the friends settled down to chat in the tiny back parlour.

Little did they know that inside the innocuous looking shopping bag their guest had placed so carefully under the table by her feet, was the recently severed head of Mrs Julia Martha Thomas, neatly wrapped in brown paper.

By the time Kate rose to take her leave that evening it was nearly seven-thirty and dark outside. Annie Porter, already the worse for drink when Kate arrived that afternoon, had gone upstairs to lie down and Harry Porter, feeling especially magnanimous towards Kate after all the whiskey, gin and talk of old times, offered to accompany her to the railway station at Hammersmith, taking his fifteen year old son, Robert, to carry the bag. Despite her errant ways, Kate had been well-liked in the area and was remembered as a kindly neighbour. So it was with a camaraderie fuelled by alcohol that Kate and Harry Porter set off for the station, with young Robert trailing behind with the canvas bag, which he found surprisingly heavy. So heavy, in fact, that his father took it from him when they reached the Angel public house. Outside, they met twenty-two year old William, the Porters' other son, who worked close by. This was as good an excuse as any to have a glass of beer in the Angel before resuming their journey.

It didn't take them long to reach their next port of call, a public house called the Oxford and Cambridge, close to Hammersmith Bridge. Naturally, the trio found it impossible to pass its doors without popping in for another drink. Whilst in the bar, Kate told Porter that she had arranged to take the bag to a friend in Barnes. She suggested that he wait for her there as she wouldn't be gone more than half an hour. Declining his offer to go with her to carry the bag, she disappeared into the murky blackness of Hammersmith Bridge.

Twenty minutes later, she was back in the pub - minus the bag - showing Harry Porter and his son five gold rings. They were family heirlooms, she told them, a legacy from her sister who had recently died. She went on to show them some photographs - one, she said, was a picture of her father and another, a likeness of her dead sister.

As for the house at Richmond, she assured Harry, it was full of nice pieces of furniture, not rubbish but good quality stuff. But, she informed them, she had been unlucky with her lodgers and, as her father was very frail and on his last legs, she had decided to sell the house and its contents and go home to look after him. She would like Porter to find her an honest broker to deal with the sale. Rather a hypocritical proviso, one would have thought, for someone like Kate to stipulate. However, when Harry suggested she find someone in the Richmond area, which would make the transaction more convenient for everyone concerned, she dismissed the idea. She didn't know anybody in Richmond, she said, and would much prefer a broker recommended by Porter.

Despite Kate's reputation as a thief, the Porters seemed to believe her - or, perhaps, more to the point, they simply chose to accept her story and enquire no further. Harry Porter promised to sort something out and when Kate asked if young Robert could accompany her back to Richmond, Porter agreed on one condition - that the lad was back in Hammersmith in time to get to work at 5.30 am the next morning.

After finishing their drinks, Harry Porter walked as far as the railway station at Hammersmith and Kate and Robert boarded a train for Richmond, arriving at the newly-built station by the bridge. When they reached Vine Cottage they entered the house by the side door and Kate asked Robert to go inside ahead of her and light the gas lamps.

Once inside she showed him into the drawing room and gave him a glass of rum and had one herself. Clearly thrilled to be the possessor of such an elegantly furnished home, she ran her fingers along the keys of the piano declaring that it was a very fine instrument indeed. She also showed him two £5 notes, a Building Society Book and a Post Office Savings Book, all left to her, she said, by her sister. She asked him to count up the figures, presumably because despite being innumerate she was anxious to impress the boy with her newly-acquired assets.

A little later, she went upstairs and came back dragging a wooden box, bound with strong cord. She also fetched a carpet-bag full of meat, vegetables, tea and sugar from the kitchen, saying that, as she thought she might come back to Rose Gardens for the night, the food would come in handy. But the first priority, she said, was to deliver the wooden box to a friend who would be waiting for her at the far end of Richmond Bridge.

By this time it was nearly eleven o'clock yet, with the apparent complacency that marked the attitude of all Kate's familiars, Robert took the bag of provisions in one hand and helped her carry the heavy box with the other. Unfortunately, the handle on his side was broken so he had to grip the cord instead; this caused his knuckles to rub against the rough side of the box, making them quite raw. He was no doubt extremely thankful, therefore, when, once on Richmond Bridge, Kate made him put the box down on a bench in one of the five pedestrian recesses. Then she abruptly told him to go back the way they had come, towards the railway station and wait for her there.

The boy instinctively did as he was told and began to walk away but, perhaps because it was so late, the night was particularly dark and there were few people about, he hovered apprehensively in the next recess. Almost at once, he heard a splash as something hit the water below. A gentleman, who happened to be passing at the time, also heard it and stopped to peer over the parapet for a moment before hurrying on his way.

Almost immediately, Kate emerged from the darkness and joined Robert telling him that she had met her friend at the far end of the bridge as arranged and had handed over the box. Together, they hurried to the railway station only to find that the last train to Hammersmith had already gone. The boy tried to persuade a cabbie to take him home for two shillings but the fare was three shillings and neither he nor Kate had the extra twelve pence. Robert had no alternative but to go back with Kate to the house in Park Road, Richmond. They sat up drinking rum until well past midnight when Kate made him a make-shift bed on the floor of her bedroom.

The following morning, Wednesday 5 March, while the lad no doubt nursed a bad head, Kate was up bright and early to make his breakfast. Once he had eaten, Robert, carrying the provisions in the carpet-bag, hurried to catch the 7.05 am train to Hammersmith, already more than an hour and a half late for work.

At about the same time, less than a mile downstream, a coalman called Henry Wheatley was driving his cart along the banks of the Thames, near Barnes Bridge, when he spotted a wooden box that had been washed up by the tide and become stuck in the mud. Perhaps hoping he might find something of value he hauled it clear of the mud and cut the cords. Curious to see inside he gave the box, which had a hinged lid, a good kick. He was horrified, however, when the box burst open to reveal a mass of congealed flesh.

Convinced it was human and not animal meat he hurried to the police station at Barnes where he reported his find to the officer on duty. A local surgeon, Dr Adams, was immediately called and able to confirm that the contents of the box were, indeed, portions of human flesh, and, when pieced together at the mortuary, it formed almost the complete body of a woman. He estimated that the woman was probably in her thirties. The head and one foot, however, were missing. The colour and texture of the flesh, the doctor concluded, seemed to indicate that it had been boiled - except, that is, for part of the woman's thigh, which had been left in its raw state.

This horrendous find, dubbed 'The Barnes Mystery', was soon the subject of some sensational newspaper reports and during the days following the gruesome discovery several theories were proposed - one being that the body in the box was some sort of practical joke played out by medical students. But this was soon discounted as the dismemberment of the body had been so amateurishly done and with such disregard for any underlying anatomical structure. Another suggestion was that the whole thing was merely a macabre hoax thought up by an enterprising journalist. Some newspapers dwelt on a number of similar cases where dismembered bodies had been washed up on the banks of the Thames.[1]

Young Robert Porter, however, his knuckles still sore from the night before, didn't read about the grisly find until the following Sunday, 9 March. Nor had he mentioned helping Kate carry a box to anyone, not even to members of his family - it was, he thought, of no consequence and the incident had completely slipped his mind.

Meanwhile, later that morning, as the doctor probed the disgusting remains, Kate, neatly dressed in her fashionable clothes and a fancy bonnet, made her way to Rose Gardens to spend the day with her old crony, Annie Porter. Husband Harry was at work; he had been a painter and decorator with the same firm for twenty-five years and worked from 5.30 am to 6.00 pm each day, with a half-day on Saturdays.

For some reason, Kate seemed unwilling to spend the night alone in the house in Richmond and, probably worse for drink by the evening, she decided to stay the night with the Porters. She settled down to sleep on the sofa in the front parlour - in fact, she had little choice for, incredibly, the rest of the tiny cottage was jam-packed with the Porter family - Annie, Harry, their two full-grown sons, William and Robert - and the lodger, Emma Clark, her husband, and their young daughter - all these people squashed into four, very small, shabby, candle-lit rooms.

The following day, Thursday, 6 March, Kate reminded Harry Porter about his promise to find her a broker to buy the furniture at Richmond. About nine o'clock that evening he took Kate to the shop of a local greengrocer, Mr Brook, who had a sideline in moving furniture, but it was closed. Kate, again not wishing to spend the night alone at Richmond, asked Harry to come back with her so that she could show him the furniture. But Porter declined, promising to

1 There was a similar case in 1827 of a man's headless remains, also boiled, found near Waterloo Bridge. And in 1873, the remains of a woman were found scattered on the foreshore at Battersea - other parts of the same body were later found downstream at Greenwich and Rotherhide.

make the journey on the following Saturday, when he finished work at mid-day.

Sometime during the remainder of the evening with the Porters, during which there can be little doubt that a great deal of alcohol was consumed, Kate managed to persuade their son, William, to accompany her back to Richmond, although the exact purpose of the visit was never fully explained. What is known is that Kate, probably inebriated and unaccustomed to owning keys to property, left her purse and latch-key at the Porters' house. When they reached Vine Cottage she had to ask William to fetch a ladder and climb in through a window.

Whether or not young William spent the night with Kate was never fully established, but there is evidence that she, at least, was in residence early the next morning. Confirmation of this came from Annie Porter, who, finding the purse with the key inside, had brought it over to Richmond. It seems rather an unnecessary journey on Mrs Porter's part, unless, of course, she used the key as an excuse to check up on young William's whereabouts. Whatever her real reason, by the time she arrived, according to her recollection, between 8 and 9 o'clock in the morning, Kate alone was there to welcome her. There was no sign of William. Kate gave her friend some breakfast and proudly showed her around the house. Whilst Mrs Porter was there, a paper-boy passed the house, calling out a headline from the *Daily News*:

> Supposed murder; shocking discovery of human remains in a box found in the Thames.

Hearing this Kate said: 'I expect that's only a catch penny, but we might as well have a paper.'

With that, she went to the front gate and bought a copy. Later that day, the two friends returned to Hammersmith together and Kate spent the night on the Porters' sofa once more.

The following morning, Saturday, 8 March, Kate arranged to meet

Harry Porter at the house in Richmond at two-thirty so he could assess the value of the furniture. She then went to see her friend, Sarah Crease, who lived in Richmond, the wife of a boot-black. She worked as a Saturday cleaner for a Miss Loder and was also looking after Kate's young son, Johnny, for three shillings a week. Kate and the child's father, a man called Strong, had brought him to her on 13 January. Kate was, in fact, extremely fond of the boy and, despite her miscreant ways, she always ensured that he was well-cared for during her frequent terms of imprisonment. But for Mrs Crease she changed her story - there was no mention of an ailing father when she told Sarah she would come to fetch the child on 12 March - she would be sending him, she said, to her parents in Glasgow.

From there she hurried back to Vine Cottage where Harry Porter joined her. After a quick look at the furniture, he stayed in the house for more than three hours, drinking and gossiping with Kate. There was certainly something about her that men, and women for that matter, found compelling, for she seemed to find little difficulty in persuading her friends to fall in with her various schemes.

Whilst not exactly pretty, the effigy of Kate Webster that appeared in the 'Chamber of Horrors' at Madame Tussaud's Waxworks, was misleading for, according to *The Penny Illustrated Paper*, she was 'not as ill-favoured as she has been described. The obliquity of her eyes, however, gives her a sinister appearance; the mouth is very determined'.[2]

Another description of Kate, in *Lloyd's Weekly News*, indicates that she was 'rather above medium height, strongly, though not stoutly built, dark complexioned, with sharp, darkish eyes and a palish sallow face, the features being tolerably regular, neither showing refinement or absolute coarseness'.

Whatever it was that attracted Harry Porter, it was not until late in the afternoon that he accompanied Kate back to Hammersmith, where she again commandeered the sofa in the front parlour.

2 It was a deplorable fact that the effigy of Kate Webster, depicting such a sinister and thoroughly evil-looking woman was on display on the Easter Monday, shortly after the Magistrates' Hearing and before she was sent for trial.

The next morning, Sunday, 9 March, Kate continued to nag Harry Porter into finding her a broker. As a result he took her along the road to the Rising Sun, a small, two-roomed beer-house run by a Mr John Church and his wife, Maria. Kate said later that she knew 'Jack' Church very well when she lived in Rose Gardens six years before but he always denied it. It is possible that Kate was still operating as a part-time prostitute, which would explain Church's reluctance to admit a past liaison yet, at the same time, in the days following their introduction that Sunday, she soon had him dancing attendance on her and he spent a great deal of time in her company.

The next day, Monday, 10 March, a human foot, recently severed at the ankle, was found in a dung heap on some allotments in Twickenham. It was also the day on which Mr Hull, the coroner for West Surrey, opened the inquest on the remains in the wooden box. The enquiry was held at The Red Lion Hotel, in Barnes. Dr Adams was called to give evidence concerning his findings but the identification of the body remained a mystery. After hearing the doctor's evidence, the enquiry was adjourned pending further investigations.

On Tuesday, 11 March, Kate finally managed to get Jack Church over to Vine Cottage to look at the furniture. Needless to say, he admitted later that he, too, spent several hours alone with Kate, drinking and smoking. He was about forty-one at the time, sporting a sandy-coloured beard and whiskers. His hair, according to one newspaper report, was piled up high in a quiff at the front and he liked to wear tweed suits and a deerstalker hat.

Jack Church was an ex-soldier who, after buying himself out of the army in 1866, took a job as a coachman before buying the Rising Sun. He was considered to be a man of some means - he had at least £500 in a bank account - despite a weakness for brandy (which he didn't sell at his own hostelry), hard-drinking women and betting on horses. Whilst he was out gallivanting, it appears that his wife was quite happy to run the beer-house single-handed for she made no complaint and spoke highly of her husband.

As for Kate, she entertained Jack Church at her house in Richmond, revelling in her impersonation of Mrs Thomas, showing off her fine furniture to Church and even telling him that a portrait hanging over the mantelpiece in the drawing room was a likeness of her deceased husband, a Scottish solicitor. Church so enjoyed her company he was back at Vine Cottage on 12th, 13th, 14th and 15th March. Kate did find time, however, to collect her young son from Sarah Crease on the 12th and take him to Hammersmith, where Annie Porter had promised to look after him. On Sunday, 16 March, Jack Church, his wife and their seven year old daughter, accompanied by William Porter and a friend, went for a boat trip on the river. Kate also joined the party although Church later said that she had not been invited.

Yet the following day, Monday, 17 March, he was back at Vine Cottage, helping Kate to pack her belongings. He valued the furniture and effects at £68 and, as Kate said she had some pressing bills to pay, he gave her an £18 deposit to tide her over. Later that day Church splashed out £1 on a pair of earrings for Kate. His wife, Maria, had a similar pair and Kate had expressed a wish to have the same.

On Tuesday, 18 March, the inquest at Barnes was resumed and Dr Bond, a surgeon and lecturer in forensic medicine, who had examined the remains, was called to give evidence. He produced the severed foot found on the dung heap in Twickenham and confirmed that, in his opinion, it belonged to the other portions found in the box at Barnes. Unfortunately, as the headless body had still not been identified and no arrest had been made in connection with the case, the jurors had little option but to record an open verdict.

That same evening, shortly before seven, Jack Church and Harry Porter arrived to supervise the removal men. Whilst they were loading up one of the vans, the next door neighbour, Miss Elizabeth Ives, was watching them closely. In fact, she had spent a great deal of time recently, peering from behind her lace curtains at all the comings and goings next door. She wasn't just being nosy - she owned both cottages and had rented the other to a Mrs Julia Martha Thomas. She had last seen her neighbour planting flowers in the garden on the afternoon of Saturday, 1 March - which was more than two weeks ago. It was all very odd. She knew that Kate, that rather surly-looking and uncommunicative maid, was still there and, moreover, much to her disgust, she knew for a fact that several different men had been coming to the house at all hours. What on earth was going on? And where was Mrs Thomas?

Determined to find out, Miss Ives hastened down the garden path and spoke to one of the men. She demanded to know where the furniture was going and who had ordered its removal. She then asked for Mrs Thomas's new address. Seeing her and the man in conversation, Kate panicked, sure that her impersonation was about to be discovered. She hurried round to Miss Ives's front door and spoke to her. When Miss Ives demanded to know the whereabouts of Mrs Thomas, Kate seemed momentarily lost for words. She simply said, 'I don't know' before running back into the house, her face flushed and agitated. As she did so, Miss Ives threatened to make further enquiries and, when she returned half an hour later with the land agent in tow, Kate panicked, pulled on her coat, grabbed her bonnet and ran out of the house carrying several dresses and a hat box which she flung into the back of one of the vans. Hastily retrieving one of the dresses, made of black silk, she ran off towards the station at Richmond, leaving the removal men without a word of explanation.

As soon as Jack Church realised something was wrong, he quickly removed all the items of furniture already loaded into the vans and returned them to the house. The removal men objected strongly to this sudden change of plan and demanded the £4 removal fee but eventually settled for £3 for their trouble.

Arriving at the railway station, Kate straightway hailed a cab to Hammersmith and from there headed for the Rising Sun where she borrowed a sovereign from Mrs Church. This done, she ran to the Porters' house but found only young Robert at home and her child in bed. She ordered Robert to go upstairs and fetch the little boy so that she could take him to her relatives as planned. Robert dressed the sleepy child in his best knickerbocker trousers and pea-jacket and then carried him to the end of the street where a cab was waiting. Kate leaned over and whispered something to the cabbie; Robert waved goodbye to the boy as the cab moved off in the direction of

Hammersmith railway station.

From there, Kate caught a train to Kings Cross, where she and the boy boarded a train for Liverpool. Once there, she managed to secure a passage to Ireland on a coal-boat and on arrival in Enniscorthy, she sought out, not her mother, who was apparently still in the area, but her uncle, Mr Lawless, at his farm in Killanne.

Meanwhile, back in London, Jack Church was in a quandary. Having dismissed the removal men and returned home, the whole business continued to bother him. The deal had gone badly wrong and now Kate had disappeared. He had, moreover, lost his £18 deposit. Perhaps it was this that propelled him - with Harry Porter in tow - to Richmond the following evening, hoping to talk to Miss Ives. She was growing decidedly worried about the whereabouts of Mrs Thomas and, probably suspecting that, as friends of Kate, the men had been party to the dubious furniture transaction, she refused to speak to them and slammed the door in their faces.

All next day, Church worried and schemed. There was still no sign of Kate. She hadn't even bothered to get in touch with the Porters and the dresses from the van were still in his wife's wardrobe. It was whilst Mrs Church was looking through the pockets on Friday, 21 March, that she found various bits and pieces belonging to Mrs Julia Thomas. Amongst these was a letter from a lady called Mrs Menhennick, of Finsbury Park.[3]

Realising that Kate had fooled them all by masquerading as Mrs Thomas, Jack Church and Harry Porter decided to call on Mr Menhennick that same evening. Once the Menhennicks had described the lady they knew as Mrs Thomas - a religious, middle-aged woman who was petite, genteel and fastidious - they were left in no doubt that she and Kate Webster were *quite* different women. The sinister aspect of Kate's impersonation was just beginning to dawn on Church and Porter. Mr Menhennick was also worried about the whereabouts of the real Mrs Thomas and immediately dispatched a letter to her solicitor, Mr Hughes, which he received

3 Her daughter, thirteen year old Edith, had been staying with Mrs Julia Thomas for the four months prior to her employment of Kate Webster.

the following morning. Being unwell at the time, Hughes sent his brother over to Hammersmith to interview John Church.

After hearing the whole saga of Kate's sudden reappearance in Rose Gardens on 4 March, her assertion that her name was Mrs Thomas and that the house and its contents had been left to her, followed by her sudden flight when challenged, Mr Hughes decided to investigate. He visited the Rising Sun on Saturday, 22 March and sent for Harry Porter. After hearing further revelations about Kate and her supposed inheritance - and, perhaps, a little of her criminal past - the three men went straight to Richmond Police Station. Concerned by the story they had to tell, Inspector Pearman accompanied them to Vine Cottage and a cursory search was made.

It was at this point that one aspect of Jack Church's behaviour was extremely suspect. Once inside Vine Cottage he went straight to a cupboard in the front parlour and opened it. Still with his back to Inspector Pearman he said: 'Here's her gold watch and chain.'

There was no way of seeing whether the items came from the cupboard or from Church's pocket. It seems most likely that Kate had given him the watch, either as a gift or to sell for her, and he couldn't wait to get rid of it, lest it implicate him still further in what was now clearly, at the very least, a serious case of fraud.

Nothing else of interest was found on this first visit but the next day, Sunday, 23 March, Inspector Pearman called for a further interview with Jack Church at the Rising Sun. He subsequently sent for young Robert Porter and it was at this interview that he told the police about helping Kate with the wooden box on 4 March. He hadn't, he said, given it a thought until he'd heard his father reading about the inquest in the newspaper. He proceeded to tell the policeman everything that had happened that night concerning both the bag at Hammersmith Bridge and the box at Richmond Bridge.

He was taken later in the day to the mortuary where he identified the box in which the human remains had been found as the same one that he had helped Kate Webster carry across Richmond Bridge. The side without the handle (it was later found at Vine Cottage) which had caused his knuckles to bleed, made this a simple task.[4]

This evidence, the mysterious disappearance of Mrs Thomas and the finding of some charred bones in her house - a further search on 27 March revealed some bloodstains and a 'fatty substance' - led the police to finally issue a warrant for Kate Webster's arrest. The following description of her was circulated throughout the country:

> Wanted, for stealing plate &c, and supposed murder of mistress: Kate, aged about 32, 5ft. 5 or 6 inches high: complexion sallow: slightly freckled: teeth rather good and prominent. Usually dressed in dark dress, jacket rather long, and trimmed with dark fur round pockets: light brown satin bonnet: speaks with an Irish accent and was accompanied by boy, aged 5, complexion rather dark, dark hair. Was last seen in Hammersmith.

With her criminal record it didn't take the authorities long to trace Kate to her family home in Killanne. She was arrested on Friday, 28 March, at her uncle's house and taken to the jail at Enniscorthy. In the presence of two police officers from Scotland Yard, she was charged with the murder of Mrs Julia Martha Thomas, on or about 2 March, 1879, and in addition, for attempting to steal Mrs Thomas's furniture and effects.

Several newspapers carried articles describing her arrest, informing their readers that Kate did not panic or become violent when taken into custody. On the contrary, she offered no resistance whatsoever and appeared to be 'a most reticent and determined character'.

However, no sooner had Kate and the two London policemen boarded a train to Dublin than she asked: 'Is there any other person in custody for the murder? There ought to be; the innocent should not suffer for the guilty.'

Kate was taken to Dublin and later that evening transported to London. During the journey by steam-boat from Holyhead she insisted that it was Jack Church, the landlord of the Rising Sun, who

4 Young Edith Menhennick and Julia Thomas's friend, Mrs Mary Ann Kent, both identified the box as the one that was in a bedroom at Vine Cottage and used by Mrs Thomas to store her best bonnets.

had killed Julia Thomas and should have been arrested in her place.

When they reached Richmond Police Station, Kate repeated her allegation in a formal statement which was taken down in writing. On Sunday, 30 March, Church was called in ostensibly to identify Kate Webster and her statement was read to him - at the end of which, to his 'absolute amazement', he was arrested on a charge of murdering Mrs Thomas in conjunction with Kate. His initial reaction was to burst out laughing as though the idea that he was a murderer was preposterous and he later admitted to being 'utterly dumbfounded'. Both prisoners were locked in the cells and appeared before the Magistrates' Court the following day, 31 March.

Brought into the court by the two Scotland Yard detectives, both Kate and Church were charged with the wilful murder of Mrs Julia Thomas. *The Penny Illustrated Paper* described Kate's appearance in some detail, saying she was dressed:

> ...in a plum-coloured dress, black cloth jacket, edged with fur, and hat of French grey and brown, with feather. She carried on her arm the grey waterproof cloak she put on at the time of her arrest. The woman, though not of pleasant features, is decidedly not so coarse or ill-favoured as she has been described; but a certain obliquity of the eyes gives her at times a rather sinister appearance, which is not decreased by an expression about the mouth denoting great firmness and determination.[5]

Throughout the proceedings she 'scarcely moved a muscle' and appeared 'calm and indifferent'. She was 'pallid and somewhat haggard but there was no nervousness or physical prostration'.

The atmosphere was tense, however, for although Jack Church and Kate stood side by side in the dock she deliberately kept her head turned away from him. For his part, he showed no emotion as Kate's statement was read to the court.

In it, she insisted that she had known Jack Church on an intimate level for some seven years during which time he had often taken her out drinking in various public houses. And, said Kate, Church had killed her mistress, Mrs Thomas, on the evening of Monday, 3 March.

5 Kate may have been partially sighted in one eye.

The previous day, according to Kate, he had been drinking heavily at Vine Cottage and had suggested they rob and 'do away' with Julia Thomas. Kate had told him she would have none of this, and anyway, Mrs Thomas didn't keep any money in the house. He had then said:

> 'We would have her things, and go off to America together and enjoy it, as I am getting tired of my old woman.'

He did not leave until late that night. Furthermore, according to Kate, Jack Church had come to the house again on Monday 3 March and, masquerading as her brother, had taken tea with Mrs Thomas. Soon after, Kate expressed a wish to go and see her little boy - which, incidentally, she usually did on a Sunday afternoon - leaving, as far as she was concerned, the potentially murderous Church alone with her mistress.

'When I returned,' her statement went on, 'I noticed the light was turned down. I knocked three times at the door and, at the third knock, Church opened the door, when I saw Mrs Thomas lying on the mat in the passage, struggling and groaning.'

Jack Church, Kate said, had beckoned her in but she had been too frightened. Despite the fact that there was, she noticed, a policeman standing on the opposite side of the road, she allowed Church to grab her arm and pull her through the doorway. At this point, he had then threatened her with a knife if she told anyone that he had killed Mrs Thomas.

Her statement then detailed the days that followed - her handing over the corded box without knowing its contents - and finding blood on a carving knife in the kitchen at Vine Cottage. When Miss Ives became suspicious, Kate went on, and confronted the removal men, Church had given her his photograph and address (which were, in fact, found on her when she was arrested) and told her to go back to Ireland and wait for him while he 'brazened it out' - then they would go off to America together. Finally, Kate said this:

'I never laid a hand on Mrs Thomas, and had nothing to do with murdering her, but I knew Church had done it. All the money left in the house belonging to Mrs Thomas was a £5 note and thirty shillings. This note I changed at a fishmonger's in Richmond. Church and Porter were with me at the time. I intend to tell the whole truth, as I don't see why I should be blamed for what Church has done. I wouldn't accuse my greatest enemy of anything wrong, let alone a friend, which Church has been to me up till now.'

When the proceedings were resumed on Wednesday, 9 April, Church vehemently denied that he had known Kate before Harry Porter had introduced her on 9 March. This was confirmed by Porter himself. He also produced a cast-iron alibi for 3 March, the date on which Kate said he had killed Mrs Thomas. As luck would have it, there were several witnesses able to swear that Church was in an upstairs room at the Rising Sun all that evening; there was no way he could have been in Richmond that night. Church, the gambler was, indeed, a lucky man, for his imprudent attendance on Kate Webster had already led him to stand charged with murder - it could have also cost him his life.

Thrown into confusion when the lies she had told in her first statement were so clearly disproved, Kate made another statement on 10 April, which was subsequently read at the Magistrates' hearing that day. This time, she tried to incriminate Harry Porter as well and changed the date of the supposed murder of her mistress from Monday, 3 March to Sunday, 2 March. But Church was able to produce an equally sound alibi for that day as well and, after a further two days of rigorous questioning, the magistrates withdrew the murder charge against him and he was released on 17 April.

As for Harry Porter, he, too, was able to produce an alibi for both days and, whilst no charge was ever made against him, he spoke bitterly about being implicated in the first place. For some reason, when he was giving evidence at the Magistrates' Court on 17 April, recalling how Kate had greeted him when he came home from work and found her drinking in his back parlour, she burst out laughing. Two weeks earlier, seeing the vast crowds gathered outside the courtroom - despite the fact that she was mercilessly hissed and booed whenever she appeared in public - her somewhat dour expression softened into a smile.

The public, however, reserved their venom for Kate Webster only - the subsequent release of Jack Church was a popular one and there were scenes of great jubilation when Church returned to the Rising Sun. One newspaper said that the place was 'crammed up to the time of closing and hundreds of persons visited Rose Gardens during the evening without being able to gain admittance to the house.' Church had to scale the counter and push his way through the crowd several times to receive the congratulations of his friends in the road outside.

He was still not entirely off the hook, however, for when the Magistrates' hearing was resumed, Church was called to give evidence. When questioned about the nature of his relationship with Kate Webster, he implied that he had gone to Vine Cottage for business purposes only, nothing else.

At this, he was subjected to a torrent of verbal abuse from Kate.

'It is false, you scoundrel!' she screamed. 'You had me up stairs in bed, and took the brandy to make me drunk. Seven years ago you took my character. You know more about me than you do about your wife. You scoundrel, you.'

She said this 'in a most indignant manner' and turned to face Church, glaring at him with those fierce black eyes.

'Her voice,' one journalist noticed, 'was interrupted by sobs and trembled with excitement: and the witness seemed to quail before this sudden attack.'

A great many witnesses were examined in the weeks that followed and it was not until 16 May that Kate was finally committed to stand trial for the murder of Julia Thomas at the Central Criminal Court of the Old Bailey on Wednesday, 2 July, 1879.

The judge who presided over Kate Webster's trial was the Hon Mr Justice Denman. The Prosecution was led by the Solicitor General, Sir Hardinge Giffard, K.C.,on behalf of the Crown; he was assisted by Messrs Harry Poland and A L Smith. Defending Kate Webster, who pleaded, Not Guilty, to the charge of killing Julia Thomas, *'feloniously and willfully, and with malice aforethought'*, were Messrs Warner Sleigh and Keith Frith, whilst Mr Brindley watched the case on behalf of Jack Church, who was to appear as a prosecution witness.

Kate Webster was brought up from the cells beneath the Old Bailey to stand in the dock of Court Number One, the scene of so many great criminal trials - Drs Crippen, Pritchard and Palmer, John Reginald Christie, Edith Thompson and Frank Bywaters, Ruth Ellis and many more.

According to *The Daily Telegraph:*

> ...the prisoner was quite pale. She wore a black cloth jacket, which was thrown open at the top, disclosing a white knitted woollen small shawl. Her hair was neatly and carefully arranged. During the reading of the indictment she stood at the Bar, but afterwards, at the suggestion of the learned judge, a chair was handed to her, and she sat during the remainder of the day. She listened attentively to the opening speech of the Solicitor-General and subsequently scrutinised every witness before the court. Though occasionally her face wore an anxious expression, her demeanour throughout was one of 'perfect composure'.

The Solicitor General began by outlining the details of the case and describing the main characters involved. The court was told that Kate Webster had been recommended to Mrs Thomas as a general maid by a Mrs Loder and began work at Vine Cottage in January of that year. Mrs Thomas was a lively, middle-aged widow, considered a little eccentric by her neighbours although this judgement was not supported by any incidence of eccentricity.

At about six-thirty on the evening of Sunday, 2 March, she had attended church as usual at the Presbyterian Church in Richmond. On arrival, she seemed agitated, so much so that her face was flushed and at one stage her bonnet fell off. She sat, not in her usual seat at the front, near the pulpit, but at the back of the church, near the door. She left ten minutes before the end of the service and was never seen again. However, as local trades-people continued to receive orders for meat and vegetables to be delivered to 2, Vine Cottages, the alarm was not raised. Only her landlady and next door neighbour, Miss Ives, seemed to suspect that something had happened to her.

There was no doubt whatever, the Solicitor General suggested, that Mrs Thomas was murdered and that the person responsible was the prisoner in the dock, and, moreover, he would produce a witness to testify that the crime was one of premeditation.

One of the first witnesses to testify was Miss Ives's mother, who lived at 1, Vine Cottages with her daughter. She was at home that Sunday evening (while Elizabeth Ives was at church) and recalled hearing a noise 'like the fall of a heavy chair' between eight and nine o'clock. It sounded as if it came from the hallway next door.

The next morning, shortly before six o'clock, she went out to the back of the house to turn on the water tap. Looking up she noticed a light in one of the bedrooms of Mrs Thomas's house. About an hour later, she heard the sounds of washing or scrubbing coming from the scullery next door. She also heard someone poking the fire under the copper, which lay behind her own kitchen range.

At eleven o'clock that morning, she noticed various items of household linen hanging on Mrs Thomas's washing line. Asked by Mr Sleigh, for the defence, why she had not mentioned hearing any noises next door when she was questioned at the Magistrates' Court, Mrs Ives said she had been unwell at the time and was confused.

William Thomas Deane, a coal merchant, was called next. He had gone to 2, Vine Cottages, about twelve-thirty on Monday, 3 March, expecting Mrs Thomas to settle her bill. The door was opened slightly by Kate Webster; she looked distraught and answered his queries abruptly, saying that her mistress was not at home, nor did she know when she would be in. The door was slammed shut.

Questioned by Mr Poland, Emma Roberts, a friend of Mrs Thomas, said that she also called at Vine Cottage the day after the alleged murder. She received no answer but noticed lights in the hall, basement and drawing room.

She was followed into the witness box by Mary Roberts, a young woman who worked for Miss Ives. Between nine and ten on the morning of Tuesday, 4 March, she called at Vine Cottage with a message from Miss Ives, that some workmen would come round to fix the leak in the roof. Kate Webster spoke to her from a bedroom window and told her not to bother as the leak had been caused by melting snow and was now perfectly dry. Miss Roberts went on to say that, about eight o'clock that evening, she heard someone playing the piano next door and, a little later, poking the fire. Later that week, she saw Kate Webster walking arm-in-arm with a man who was dark-haired like her but slightly shorter and wearing an Ulster coat.

The landlady, Elizabeth Ives, was called next and questioned by the Solicitor General. She said she last saw Mrs Thomas planting flowers in the garden between three and four on Saturday, 1 March, the day before the alleged murder. She, too, heard the sound of the boiler being stoked early on Monday, 3 March, and saw the washing on the line before eight o'clock. She also noticed a very unpleasant smell which she thought at first was gas. Between eleven and eight o'clock that day, the house was quiet but, in the evening, the noises had started again - the sound of chopping wood, of fires being stoked and furniture being moved.

On the Tuesday evening, Miss Ives remembered hearing voices and people going into the house. The sound of someone tinkling on the piano followed, though she realised it was not Mrs Thomas, who played well. On one occasion, the landlady's gimlet eye noticed Kate leaving the house in a cab; it was late at night and she was in the company of two women, two or three men and a small child.

'During the ten days or fortnight (after the alleged murder) people were continually coming to the house at all sorts of odd hours,' announced Miss Ives, primly, 'and taking things away in cabs'.

In the evening of Wednesday, 5 March, Miss Ives - no doubt with her ear firmly pressed to the party wall - recalled hearing a filing sound coming from the kitchen next door. She seemed to think there was a man and a child in the house at the time, for she could hear a man's voice breaking into song every now and then.

By the 18th, Miss Ives realised that something was wrong and watched with alarm as the men began to load Mrs Thomas's furniture into the vans. She confirmed that when she asked about Mrs Thomas's whereabouts, Kate seemed very 'frightened' but did not take flight immediately. Miss Ives went off to find the land agent and when she got back, half an hour later, Kate was still there, standing in the road with Church and Porter and several removal men.

Young Robert Porter followed Miss Ives into the witness box, to be questioned by Harry Poland. He told the court that he was nearly sixteen and lived with his family at 10 Rose Gardens, Hammersmith. He then proceeded to relate the whole story of Kate's sudden appearance and the disposal of the black bag and the wooden box on the night of 4 March. He confirmed that he stayed that night with Kate at Richmond and that, when he went back on the following Saturday afternoon, his father was already there with a Mr Ricketts, who had a small removal van. He saw some old chairs, an india rubber plant and six flower pots being loaded into a van. These items were taken to the Porters' house in Rose Gardens but were of little worth - the family kept the plant, and the pots, he said, but broke up the chairs - the cane seats were missing - and used them as fire-wood.

On the second day of the trial, Robert Porter was recalled and cross-examined by Mr Sleigh, for the defence. He told the court how kind the prisoner had been to his young sister when she was alive - how, when Kate lived next door, she would lift the child over the wall and spent hours playing with her. In answer to further questions, he said that the first time he heard about a box being found in the Thames was 6 March but, he added:

> ...the first time I spoke about it was when I told Inspector Jones on Sunday 23 March. From the night it happened until the 23rd I never mentioned a word about the box to anybody.

The next witness was the boy's father, Henry Porter, questioned by the Solicitor General. Describing himself as a painter and decorator, he said that the prisoner always called him Harry. He confirmed his son's account of 4 March and admitted that he and

Jack Church were at Kate's house on 13th, 14th and 15th of March, 'looking over the furniture'. In addition, he said, to the chairs and plant already mentioned by his son, some linen Kate wanted to keep was brought to his house in Ricketts's van on Saturday, 15 March. She also left a basket of silver plate at Church's residence, the Rising Sun, until she went back to Ireland. Harry Porter went on to admit that Kate had given him a set of artificial teeth, set in gold, from the house in Richmond. He had sold them to Mr Nibblett, a jeweller in Hammersmith, for six shillings. He gave the money to Kate and she gave him one shilling for his trouble.[6]

Recalling the day the removal men arrived at the house in Richmond, Porter said that, after talking to Miss Ives next door, Kate had asked him to go upstairs and fetch some dresses and a fur jacket. He handed them to her and she went out of the front door - that was the last he saw of her until she was under arrest at Richmond Police Station on 30 March.

Regarding his alibi for the time of the murder, the evening of Sunday, 2 March, Porter said he was drinking in the Rising Sun until eleven o'clock - he was also there, he assured the court, the following night. In fact, he drank in Church's beer-house every night after he'd finished work, had his 'tea and a wash' - he never normally left Hammersmith at all.

Questioned about his knowledge of his son's part in disposing of the wooden box, he said that Robert had told him all about it when he heard his mother reading about The Barnes Mystery in *Lloyd's Newspaper* about 9 March, whereas Robert had said that the first time he mentioned it was 23 March, at the police station.

The next witness to be called was Harry Porter's wife, Annie. Questioned by Harry Poland, she told the court that she had looked after Kate's little boy since 12 March, until, that is, he was taken back to Ireland. At this point, Kate started to cry - which she did throughout the trial whenever her son was mentioned. Seeing this, Annie Porter immediately burst into tears as well. Still upset, she

6 A local dentist, George Henry Rudd, identified the false teeth as those he had made for Mrs Julia Thomas in February of that year, a month before she died.

said that, in return for the boy's keep, Kate had provided a generous supply of meat and vegetables and went on to describe her as a 'kind, good-natured girl'.

Having established that Mrs Porter knew about her son carrying a box for Kate Webster long before he told the police, the judge asked her why, after reading about the remains found in the river, she had said nothing. He seemed annoyed by her negative response and remonstrated with her quite mercilessly. *The Times* made a special reference to their confrontation and described Annie Porter's whole demeanour whilst giving evidence:

> The witness's behaviour was extraordinary. She laughed, cried, muttered, shook her head inexplicably, and she repeatedly spoke in so low a tone that at last the learned Judge made her come and stand beside him to give evidence. At the end of her examination he asked if she was in the habit of drinking too much and on her owning the impeachment with a titter, severely cautioned her, saying that the habit was a peculiarly disgraceful one in a mother of a family, and it was a miserable vice, which made her a terrible spectacle.

The Daily Telegraph noted that, when the judge asked the poor woman, who was standing close by, if she was 'not above taking a drop too much gin', she had laughed, causing him to snap:

> 'Do not laugh. It is a disgraceful and a melancholy thing. You stink of drink today.'

A painter and decorator, James Thurlow, who lived at 42 Rose Gardens, testified that he called at the Porters' house shortly before seven on 4 March and saw the prisoner drinking in the back parlour. He also confirmed that both Harry Porter and Jack Church were in the Rising Sun on the nights of Sunday 2 March and Monday 3 March; he knew, he told the court, because he drank there himself every night of the week.

The Porters' eldest son, twenty-two year William, was called next. He had worked at a bakery in King Street, Hammersmith, for seven years. Tuesday, 4 March, had been his birthday and he remembered meeting his father, carrying the black bag, his younger brother

Robert and Kate Webster, outside the Angel, in Hammersmith. He admitted that he went over to Richmond with Kate on the evening of Thursday, 6 March but, he insisted, he only stayed a couple of hours. He went back again with a friend early on the morning of Saturday, 15th. Jack Church was already there, but he, William, had left before the arrival of his father and Ricketts with the van.

It was with some eagerness that the crowds in the public gallery watched Jack Church enter the court on the third day of the trial - Friday, 4 July. He was questioned by the Solicitor General and said that he was at his home, the Rising Sun, all day on Sunday, 2 March. For most of the time he was serving behind the bar - they opened from one to three on Sunday lunch-times and again from six to eleven.

On the Monday evening, there was the monthly meeting of 'The Oak Slate Club', which he described as a 'sick and burial' insurance club. This was a popular way for the poor to put aside a little money by monthly instalments to cover loss of earnings through sickness and to pay their funeral expenses. Jack Church was the treasurer and he, and two stewards, held keys to the box containing the funds. A number of subscriptions were paid that evening, requiring Church's signature and there was no question whatever that he was, in fact, on the premises the whole evening.

The following day, Tuesday, 4 March, he had gone to the Vestry Hall, in Kensington, to renew his billiard and bagatelle licence, after which he went to the races at Sandown Park. He was first introduced to Kate Webster by Harry Porter, in the bar of the Rising Sun, on Sunday, 9 March. After renewing his beer and wine licence the next day, he went over to see Kate in the evening. Although her little boy was there on that occasion, they left him alone in the house while they went for a drink in the Railway Tavern in Richmond, after which Jack Church returned to Hammersmith by train.

The witness then recalled his various visits to Vine Cottage during the days that followed. Besides Church, a number of other men went to see Kate on Saturday, 15 March - William Porter, one of his friends and at least two greengrocers with their vans. They all had a good rummage through the furniture and effects looking for anything worth having. And all the while Miss Ives watched from her window - and did nothing.

Anxious to convince the court that, as far as he was concerned, his visits to Vine Cottage were not personal but strictly business, Church insisted that he did *not* buy Kate the expensive earrings already mentioned but had *lent* her the money to buy them. Asked to explain the presence of his photograph and address amongst Kate's possessions when she was arrested in Ireland, Church said that she must have stolen them from a pile of photographs that his young daughter was showing her one day in the bar of the Rising Sun.

What a sanctimonious picture Church must have made, wriggling out of his licentious liaison with Kate, pumped up with righteous indignation, with his carefully arranged, bouffant hair-style, pipe and deerstalker hat. Who can blame Kate for shouting: 'You scoundrel!' during the Magistrates' hearing.

When questioned by Mr Sleigh, for the defence, Church reacted defensively. He repeatedly refused to say what he did for a living before enlisting in the army nor would he say where he had lived as a child or even the name of the school he attended. The reason for his reticence was never made clear - he may, for instance, have been defensive about being raised in a workhouse or charitable institution - or, although he later denied it, he may have served a prison sentence whilst still in his teens.

After Jack Church had left the witness box his place was taken by his wife, Maria. They had been married for eleven years, she said, and had kept the Rising Sun for nine. Kate Webster had come there on Thursday, 13 March, she said, with a basket full of silver plate, which she asked them to keep for her. The next day she brought some tablecloths, curtains, mats and lustres for a chandelier and the day after that she presented Mrs Church with two glass vases and a carving knife and fork.

The following Monday, she came to the house and gave her a pair of boots that she said she couldn't wear because they hurt her feet. In one of Kate's subsequent statements she said that she gave Maria *two* pairs of boots - one pair, she insisted, Jack Church had bought for her.

Questioned further, Mrs Church described finding a purse in the pocket of one of the dresses brought in the van from Vine Cottage - inside were five rings, some stamps, a pencil and a small comb. She also found a diary, two pocket handkerchiefs with the name, *'J. Thomas'* embroidered on them, a pair of gloves and a letter to Mrs Menhennick. She gave all these items to her husband who, she added, never wanted them left at his house in the first place. But, said Maria Church, she took them *in lieu* of the sovereign she'd given Kate the day she took flight.

It is worth noting that, like her husband before her, Maria Church did not mention the fur jacket that Harry Porter said was taken to the Rising Sun with the dresses. She had never, she insisted, even set foot in the house at Richmond and only knew the prisoner as Mrs Thomas. She knew nothing about her husband buying Kate a pair of earrings nor had she realised he'd spent so much time alone with her, drinking brandy and smoking cigars.

Henry Weston, another greengrocer and removal man, was called to testify that he had taken two vans to Vine Cottage on 18 March. Church and the prisoner, he said, seemed to be on very familiar terms, she calling him 'Jack' and he addressing her, not as Mrs Thomas at all, but as 'Kate'.

Mrs Lucy Loder, the lady who recommended Kate Webster to Mrs Thomas, was called next. She told the court that Kate had been lodging with one of her friends, Mrs Sarah Crease, who lived about a mile and a half from Vine Cottage. Kate had done some laundering for her and she thought she would make an excellent live-in maid for Julia Thomas. Leaving her little boy with Sarah, Kate started work at Vine Cottage on 29 January.

Six days after the alleged murder, Mrs Loder called to see Julia but was told by Kate Webster that her mistress was out looking for a replacement for her as she was going to live with a *'very well to-do aunt'* in Glasgow. Mrs Loder was pleased for her as, in her opinion, Kate was *'a very obliging girl, and did her work well'*. Kate, said the witness, spoke highly of Julia Thomas, saying she was a *'very good-living woman'* and as far as she knew *'there was no animosity between her and Mrs Thomas'.*

Called as the next witness, Mrs Sarah Crease also spoke well of Kate Webster:

> 'She has always been a kind-hearted, good sort of girl so far as I know, and affectionate and grateful for kindness done to her. My husband had an illness for four months, during which time she nursed him and waited on him all day, and did all she could for him. She was then in a situation at Mr Mitchell's and came backwards and forwards simply for the purpose of being kind to my husband and bringing him things... I never heard her say or do anything unkind to anybody. She came to my house every Sunday night but one to see the child.'

But, said the witness, she always had to get back by six-thirty so her mistress could go to church. Kate had told Sarah that Mrs Thomas was a 'very nice lady, very kind and good-hearted' and she seemed 'very fond of her as a mistress.'

Later that day, Charles Menhennick also described the murder victim as an 'amiable, good-natured sort of lady, about fifty years of age and very animated in her manner'.

A total of fifty-three witnesses were called to give evidence during the trial, including William Hughes, Mrs Thomas's solicitor and Inspector John Dowdell, the officer from Scotland Yard, who had travelled to Ireland to arrest Kate Webster.

Questioned at some length, he said that Kate was 'very calm on the voyage, except when she was sick. She had a very good supper on the steamboat, and appeared an amiable, pleasant sort of woman, as far as I could judge. She gave no trouble, and came back quite quietly and calmly'.

Police Inspector John Pearman was then asked to describe his various visits to Vine Cottage. After his initial search in the company of Jack Church and Harry Porter, he made a further visit on Monday, 24 March. On that occasion, he told the court, he found 'a quantity of charred bones' and some dress buttons under the kitchen grate.

'In the coal cellar in the basement,' he said, 'I found a chopper and in the room next to the scullery I found a razor. In the area I found a nightdress which appeared to be burned. I put these things into a carpet bag and took them to the station.'

'On the 27th I went again and found a quantity of charred bones under the copper grate. The outside of the copper, the brickwork, was well whitened and clean. I took out the copper from the brickwork and about halfway down I found a fatty substance, which I scraped off and placed in a small earthen pot.'[7]

He also found traces of blood on the skirting board in the back bedroom, on a wall near the hallway and by the pantry door. Under the sink in the scullery, Pearman had found the missing handle to the wooden box in which the alleged remains of Mrs Thomas were found. He also discovered some cord identical to that used to bind the box.

Later that day, various members of the 'Oak Slate Club' - a Hammersmith bricklayer, a cabinet maker from Notting Hill, a watch and clockmaker, and a couple of labourers from Rose Gardens - were called to testify that John Church was present at the Rising Sun on the evening of 3 March, bringing to a close the fourth day of the trial.

On the fifth day of the trial, Monday, 7 July, after hearing similar testimony from yet more labourers, the court heard the evidence of Mary Durden, a straw bonnet and hat-maker from Kingston.

'I have known the accused for four years,' she said. 'I saw her on Shrove Tuesday, 25 February, at my house. She told me she was going to Birmingham to see about some property which her aunt had left her. She told me she had had a letter from her aunt telling her where to find her gold watch and her chain and her jewels; and everything the aunt had was to come to her. During the interview she told me that she was going to sell the furniture.'

Mary Durden further informed the court that Kate Webster had

7 This was probably the source of a rumour spread by Mrs Hayhoe, the landlady of the Hole in the Wall tavern, a few doors from Vine Cottage. She always maintained that shortly after the murder Kate Webster had been hawking two jars of 'best dripping' around the pubs in the area. Mrs Hayhoe was reported to have said: 'I little thought when Kate came in and I chatted with her that she had left her mistress boiling in the copper.'

laughed a lot during this conversation and seemed excited at the prospect and had spent more than an hour talking about it.

This was damning evidence indeed and the implication that Kate Webster had planned to rob - and possibly kill Mrs Thomas - as early as 25 February, less than a month after going to work for her, was not lost on the jury. However, during his cross examination, Mr Sleigh sought to establish that Mary Durden might be considered a hostile witness in that it was rumoured that there was ill-feeling between her and Kate Webster; so much so that they had been involved in a public slanging match over Mary's husband consorting with Kate in the Three Tons. Mary, of course, denied this, though it seems likely, with Kate's propensity for drink and her liking for male company, that there was some truth in the rumour.

The next witness was Dr Thomas Bond, assistant surgeon and lecturer on forensic medicine at the Westminster Hospital. He described piecing together the grisly jigsaw of boiled flesh found in the box. The body was, in fact, incomplete - the head, several ribs, a thigh and a foot were missing.

He was followed into the witness box by Dr James Adams, the local surgeon who first examined the remains by the river at Barnes. Although he had initially suggested that the body was that of a woman of about thirty, he was prepared to concede to Dr Bond's view that it was of a woman of fifty years or more and approximately five foot three in height.

John Church was further recalled as the last witness in the trial. He was questioned by Mr Sleigh who tried once more to get to the truth about the publican's life before enlisting in the army - whether, for instance, he had worked as a barman - but his answers remained non-committal. At one stage, Mr Justice Denman, clearly exasperated at the number of times Church replied with the words 'I might have been,' intervened by saying:

'Don't say that any more. Now, upon your oath, were you a barman or not?'

To which Church replied: 'I was in a public house before I entered the service.' Asked if he had ever been in prison, he said, 'Not to my knowledge.'

'Not to your knowledge?' the judge exclaimed, impatiently. 'Have you or have you not been in prison before you were arrested on this charge?'

'No', replied Church.

After this irritatingly truculent performance, the various statements made by the prisoner since her arrest were read to the court by the Solicitor General. At this juncture, Mr Warner Sleigh rose to deliver his speech on behalf of the accused. It was, he said, a puzzling and difficult case. If a murder had, indeed, been committed - and there was no proof whatever that it had - any evidence against his client was purely circumstantial; no one had seen the crime committed.

'Are you sure,' he went on, 'that the bones found are the bones of Mrs Thomas; and, if they be, are you sure that she died by violence?'

Was it not possible, he argued, that the lady had died of natural causes - a heart attack, a burst blood vessel or apoplexy? There had been witnesses, he reminded the court, to testify that, shortly before she disappeared, Mrs Thomas was showing all the signs of extreme stress, sufficient perhaps, to precipitate an attack of this sort - a flushed face, confusion and nervous agitation.

Turning now to the character and disposition of his client, Kate Webster, Sleigh pointed out that, despite the hardness of her looks, several witnesses had described her 'as kind and good-hearted a creature as ever lived'. Could they really believe that she had 'committed one of the most foul and horrible murders ever alleged to have been committed?'.

Sleigh proceeded to question the integrity of John Church, who clearly had something to hide.

'Church was such an unmitigated scoundrel,' he said, 'and the whole transaction with regard to Vine Cottage was so tainted with nefariousness, from beginning to end, that it really was not safe to act upon such testimony.'

Moreover, he suggested, it was surely naive to believe for one moment that Church and Porter did not know about the body parts found in Kate's box until Robert told the police about it on 23 March. There had been 'so much talk about the Barnes Mystery - the papers teeming with it, and all the neighbourhood being alive with the sensation'. They must have heard about it, so why didn't they say anything to the police about Kate's strange behaviour on the night of 4 March and her subsequent plans for the disposal of furniture and effects?

Finally, he reminded the jurors that they were 'the bulwarks of safety between the accused and an unjust conviction. Upon them lay the power of sending a woman to the gallows or preventing a miscarriage of justice.'

On the last day of Kate Webster's trial, Tuesday, 8 July, the Solicitor General rose to address the jurors on behalf of the Crown. He urged them to 'apply their common sense and ordinary reasoning powers to the facts before them and arrive at the conclusion which conscience dictated'.

With regard to the defence counsel's assertion that the identity of the remains in the box were not legally proved to be those of Mrs Thomas, he pointed out that Robert Porter had positively identified the box as the one he had helped the prisoner carry from Vine Cottage. Surely their common sense must tell them that, in all probability, the body inside belonged to the missing mistress of the house? And in the kitchen, despite its freshly scrubbed condition, a fatty deposit was found in the copper and traces of blood and some charred human bones were found in the fireplace - these bore *'dumb testimony'* to the fact that Julia Thomas had been murdered in that house and her body dismembered, boiled and burned in that kitchen.

He suggested that the head, which had never been found, had been disposed of separately in an attempt to prevent identification. From the evidence of Miss Ives and her mother - the 'sound of a heavy fall' on the night of Sunday, 2 March, the repeated stoking of the boiler and the putrid smell the following day, must surely coincide with the process of disposing of the body.

As to the suggestion that Mrs Thomas had died of a heart attack or something similar then why had no doctor been called and the death notified in the usual way? What need was there, if this were the case, to mutilate and dismember the body and attempt to prevent its discovery?

'These facts', said the Solicitor General, 'put together rendered the conclusion of murder having been committed absolutely irresistible' and that Kate Webster, the wretched woman in the dock, was guilty.

It was now Mr Justice Denman's turn to address the jury. He carefully summed up all the evidence heard in court for and against the prisoner, during what had been, he said, a 'long, laborious and important case'. This was made even more complicated, he added, by the prisoner having made several contradictory statements about those present at Vine Cottage when Mrs Thomas died. The jury must therefore consider 'whether it was established beyond reasonable doubt that the accused was there - whether she was alone or one of several persons who committed the murder'. He went on to say that 'if they were convinced beyond all doubt that the accused was concerned as one of several in doing the act, then she would be guilty of murder'.

Regarding the defence counsel's argument that there was no evidence to prove that the remains found in the box at Barnes were those of Julia Thomas, he said that it was not necessary to have legal proof but 'if a multitude of circumstances so combined that to hold otherwise would be contrary to common sense' then they must conclude that they were. Especially, he emphasised, as Kate Webster herself, in one of her statements, had confirmed that a murder had been committed - by Church - and had admitted to carrying the box, later found to contain human remains, from the house.

The judge then proceeded to remind the jury of all the characters involved in the case and to detail with meticulous care the evidence each had given as to the events subsequent to the death of Mrs Thomas. Some witnesses had made conflicting statements, he said, as to exact times and places, but such was the nature of memory and the jury should not interpret falsehood where none existed.

He reminded them that the prisoner had said she was in

Hammersmith with Jack Church on the evening of 3 March, yet when Emma Roberts had called at Vine Cottage in Richmond there were lights on all over the house, although no one answered her knock on the door. Furthermore, Kate Webster was certainly there at mid-day for she answered the door to Mr Deane, the coalman. It was also during that morning that Miss Ives noticed the horrible smell and heard the sound of the copper boiling.

All these facts, went on Mr Justice Denman, 'were perfectly consistent with the accused, or whoever it was in the house, being employed in getting rid of any traces of mischief, if the murder had been committed on the previous evening'.

The judge next dwelt on the part that Jack Church and Harry Porter played in the discovery of the fraud and, ultimately, in the murder. As to the prisoner's accusation that it was Church who killed Julia Thomas, if the jurors entertained 'any reasonable doubt as to whether the real fact is that Church committed the murder, and she [Kate] was a mere accessory after the fact, helping him to get rid of the body, and so forth, she would not be guilty of murder...'

Finally, he said this: 'Gentlemen, the case has been conducted most admirably by the counsel on both sides; it has been conducted impartially and fairly and mercifully by the counsel for the prosecution, and ably and efficiently by the defence. The witnesses have been examined with great elaboration and with great care. If you are satisfied beyond all reasonable doubt that the accused is guilty of this murder, you will say so. If you entertain any reasonable doubt about it, you will then acquit her and say she is not guilty.'

The jury retired at twelve minutes past five that afternoon and returned to the court shortly before half past six. As the foreman stood to deliver the verdict, the tension in the court was high. Kate Webster's life was at stake.

On hearing the word Guilty, Kate 'still showed scarcely any emotion, beyond what was expressed by a slight increase of previous pallor and a tight compression of the lips'.

Her solicitor, Mr O'Brien, was permitted to enter the dock to talk to her, and 'for about two minutes he appeared to be engaged in earnest conversation with her, not a syllable, however, being audible in court'.

When asked whether she had anything to say before being sentenced Kate, in an unusually quiet voice, replied:

> 'I am not guilty, my lord, of the murder. I have never done it, my lord. When I was taken into custody I was in a hurry, and I made a statement against Church and Porter. I am very sorry for doing so, and I want to clear them out of it. And another thing, I was led to this, my lord. The man who is guilty of all this is not in the case at all, nor never was. Therefore, I do not see why I should suffer for what other people have done. There was a child put in my hands in 1874. I had to thieve for that child, and go to prison for it. Anybody can tell it round Kingston or Richmond, too. Therefore, the father of the child is the ruin of me since 1873 up to this moment, and he is the instigation of this; he was never taken into custody. I have cherished him up to this minute, but I do not see why I should suffer for a scoundrel who has left me after what he has done.'

There was a profound silence in the court as Mr Justice Denman placed the black cap on his head.

'Prisoner at the bar,' he began, his words delivered in sombre, measured tones, 'after a very long and painful inquiry, and after a powerful advocacy on your behalf you have been found guilty upon what, even in the absence of what you have now told us, I should have ventured to say was irresistible testimony of the crime of wilful murder. You tell us now, for the first time, that you were instigated to that crime by someone who is not in custody, and whose name is not before us, and you have made some reparation at this moment by exonerating from all charge two persons, who, it was not impossible, might have been sent to the scaffold upon the statement that you made against them, coupled with circumstances which it was hard for them to explain. So far, I think, all will feel that the result of this trial is in one respect satisfactory; but though you put it to me that you ought not to suffer because another instigated you to this crime, that is a consideration which will not warrant me one moment from hesitating to pass upon you the sentence of the law. Indeed, I have no option. My duty imperatively demands it, and I must do it.

Whether your statement now be true or not, God only can tell. After so many false statements as you have made, it must not be assumed to be true as a matter of course. If it be so, it is no excuse for you, because, in point of law, you have been proved to be guilty of the crime of murder, and indeed that very statement shows the justice of the verdict of the jury. I say no more. I do not wish to hurt your feelings by saying a single unnecessary word, but it is my duty to pass upon you the sentence of the law.'

The judge thereupon passed the sentence of death.

Kate, in a firm voice that was heard throughout the courtroom, then said: 'I am not guilty, my Lord'.

Whereupon, the Clerk of Arraigns, declared; 'Prisoner at the bar, you have been convicted of the crime of murder. Have you anything to say in stay of execution of your sentence?'

'Yes, I am pregnant,' said Kate.

There were gasps from the public gallery, where a great many women had gathered throughout the trial. The judge, who admitted that such a plea had never been proposed during the whole of his court experience - under English law a pregnant woman may not hang - ordered that the prisoner be examined.[8]

A jury of matrons was selected from married women in the gallery, the previous jury having been dismissed. The prison matron, Thirza Belcher, denied that Webster was pregnant. After examining her in the jury-room, Dr Bond and the jury of matrons also declared that she was not 'quick with child'. This decision meant, of course, that the death sentence remained.

'The prisoner,' the court report went on, 'who was in a prostrate condition, was then raised by the attendants, and almost borne by them to the steps which led from the dock to the cells below.'

It was half past seven when the court finally rose. As it was a pleasantly warm evening, a huge crowd had gathered outside to

8 Charlotte Harris was sentenced to death at the Somerset Assizes in 1849 but, being pregnant at the time, her execution was postponed until after the birth of the child. More than 40,000 women petitioned Queen Victoria for mercy on Charlotte's behalf and the sentence of death was commuted to one of life imprisonment.

hear the result of the trial and to see the prisoner driven away to Wandsworth Prison to await execution. As there were no special facilities for condemned prisoners at Wandsworth at the time, Kate Webster was confined in a fairly comfortable cell and assigned, by the sympathetic intervention of the prison governor, Captain Colville, a Sister of Compassion from a convent in Hammersmith, to watch over her. She also received several visits from the prison chaplain, Rev Father McEnery.

She made two more statements, one on 10 July and the other on 17 July which were lengthy, conflicting and sanctimonious in tone. Still hoping for a last minute reprieve, she swore she knew nothing about the murder, never saw the body of Julia Thomas and blamed the father of her child, a man presumed to be Strong, although she did not divulge his name. Two of his friends, a man and a woman, were also involved, she said, but she was entirely under Strong's influence and it was he who made her incriminate Church and Porter. She also insisted that Church knew perfectly well she was not Mrs Thomas and that the furniture was not hers to sell.

Throughout the statements, she repeatedly throws herself on God's mercy 'in the last moments of her mortal existence' and forgives 'those who have been ready to condemn' her and all those people who had directed 'harsh and unkind remarks' against her. She finishes by hoping that her 'miseries, troubles, trials and awful fate' will 'serve as a warning to young girls never to be led away from the path of virtue and honesty.' The statement ended with a phrase chosen to touch the heart of the Home Secretary - 'These are the dying words of the unhappy and unfortunate - Katherine Webster.'

Although it was noted that she behaved herself remarkably well at Wandsworth, her fierce reputation as a foul-mouthed trouble-maker had preceded her from Newgate, where she had previously been confined:

> 'Kate Webster....is remembered as a defiant, brutal creature, who showed no remorse, but was subject to fits of ungovernable passion, when she broke into language the most appalling'.[9]

9 From *The Chronicles of Newgate.*

Yet the authorities at Wandsworth described her as 'remarkably submissive and docile'. This was probably due, in part at least, to the pacifying effect of the Sister of Compassion; she was also sustained by the possibility of a reprieve. She was said to be relatively cheerful until that is, on 26 July, the appeal presented to the Home Secretary on her behalf was rejected. Naturally, she was 'greatly affected'.

The time of her execution was set for nine o'clock, on Tuesday, 29 July, 1879. The barbaric and sickening practice of public hanging had been abolished in 1868 and the County Sheriff went further by depriving members of the Press access to the spectacle.

Although Kate received several visits from her spiritual adviser, Father McEnery, and was comforted by the Sister of Compassion, she was said to be 'heart broken at not seeing any of her friends.'

On the Saturday before her execution, she had hoped to see her little boy for the last time and was said to be 'inconsolable' when the visit was cancelled. Then, late on the night before she was to hang, Kate Webster made this final confession to her spiritual adviser, Father McEnery:

> I made a statement in the presence of the warders to Mr O'Brien, my solicitor, on the 10th July and a second statement in the presence of the warders on 17th July, both in reference to the Richmond murder. These statements were untrue in many ways, especially the portion of them which referred to the murder of Mrs Thomas and the man, Strong, whom I named in the last one and I am now informed by Mr O'Brien, my solicitor, that the memorial [appeal] presented on my behalf has not been successful and I will be executed at 9 o'clock on Tuesday 29 July.
>
> I see, therefore, that there is no visible hope for a respite of my sentence and I am advised by him and feel that I am bound in the sight of Almighty God to clear every one of the suspicion and especially those whose names were mentioned in my said statements before I die, which I am now happy in doing.
>
> In the first place I heartily beg God's forgiveness and mercy for numerous falsehoods I have told throughout this unfortunate case, especially because they affected the character and reputation of persons whose names are mentioned, and secondly, because of the injury they have done to myself in the sight of Almighty God, whose

mercy and forgiveness I have no doubt of having obtained.

Since I was arrested I was always in dread of the consequences of the crime and although I had all the assistance of my solicitor, who exercised every possible means, both before and after my trial, to rescue me from my untimely end, yet I had my doubts that I should escape the penalty which I must now pay by law. I was inwardly unhappy throughout but bore up under such a terrible trial with the greatest fortitude and courage I possibly could; but when I was approaching the day of my execution and fearing that nothing could be done to save me, I immediately requested the governor to send for Mr O'Brien, my solicitor, that I might open my mind and reveal all things to him immediately, without the slightest hesitation or reserve, which I now proceed to do, knowing well that I have no hope of mercy in this world.

With respect to the death of Mrs Thomas, the circumstances surrounding the murder of that lady are as follows:

I entered the lady's service in the month of January. At first I thought her a nice old lady and imagined I could be comfortable and happy with her; but I found her very trying. She used to do many things to annoy me. When I had finished my work in the rooms she used to go over it and point out places where she said I did not clean, thus showing evidence of a nasty spirit towards me. This sort of conduct made me have an ill-feeling towards her but I had no intention of killing her, at least, not then. One day I had an altercation with her and we mutually arranged I should leave her service and she made an entrance to that effect in her memorandum book.

On the Sunday evening, 2nd March last, Mrs Thomas and I were alone in the house. We had some argument at which she and myself were enraged and she became very agitated and left the house to go to church in that state, leaving me at home. Upon her return from church, before her usual hour, she came in and went upstairs. I went up after her and we had an argument which ripened into a quarrel and in the height of my anger and rage I threw her from the top of the stairs to the ground floor. She had a heavy fall. I felt that she was seriously injured and I became agitated at what had occurred, lost all control of myself and, to prevent her screaming or getting me into trouble, I caught her by the throat and in the struggle she was choked. I threw her on the floor.

I then became entirely lost and without any control over myself and looking on what had happened and the fear of being discovered, I determined to do away with the body as best I could. I chopped the head from the body with the assistance of a razor which I used to cut through the flesh afterwards. I also used the meat saw and the carving knife to cut the body up with. I prepared the copper with water to boil the body to prevent identity; as soon as I had succeeded in cutting it up I placed it in the copper and boiled it.

I opened the stomach with the carving knife and burned up as much of the parts as I could. During the whole of this time there was nobody in the house but myself. When I looked upon the scene before me and saw the blood around my feet, the horror and dread I felt was inconceivable. I was bewildered, acted as if I was mad and did everything I possibly could to conceal the occurrence, keep it quiet, and everything regular, fearing the neighbours might suspect something had happened. I was greatly overcome, both from the horrible sight before me and the smell and I failed several times in my strength and determination, but was helped by the devil in this vile purpose. I remained in the house all night endeavouring to clear up the place and clean away traces of the murder.

I burned one part of the body after chopping it up and boiled the other. I think I boiled one of the feet. I emptied the copper, throwing the water away after having washed and cleaned the outside. I then put parts of the body into the little wooden box which was produced in court and tied it up with cord and determined to deposit it in the Thames, which was afterwards done with the help of young Porter.

I remember the coalman, Mr Deane, coming to the house and knocking at the door. I was greatly frightened but in dread of creating suspicion I opened the door to answer him and spoke to him as he stated in his evidence...

I put the head of Mrs Thomas into the black bag, and being weary and afraid to stay in the house, I carried it to the Porters and had some tea there. I placed the bag with the head in it under the tea table and afterwards took it away from the house and disposed of it in the way and in the place I have described to my solicitor, Mr O'Brien.

The deposition of this black bag gave me great uneasiness as I feared it might be discovered....and when I heard a black bag had been found I was greatly troubled.[10] I pretended to Mr O'Brien that the bag contained nothing of the kind. The foot found in the dunghill

10 Three black canvas bags similar to Kate Webster's were found in the Thames during the investigation.

at Kingston was placed there by me, for when I came to realise the true state of things and the great danger I stood in, I resolved to do everything in my power to keep everything secret and prevent [it] being discovered.

When I placed the box in the river and disposed of the head and other parts of the body as best I could... ...it was suggested to my mind to sell all that there was in the house and go away; and with that view I went and saw Porter and introduced the sale of the things to him. I gave the chairs to Porter as a gift and also kept ordering things for the house from trades people in order to evade suspicion...

At the time of the murder I took possession of Mrs Thomas's gold watch and chain and also of all the money in the house, which was only seven or eight pounds.... I threw the dresses and bonnet of Mrs Thomas into the van which was brought to fetch the furniture and they were taken to Church's....I determined to proceed to Ireland at once to avoid being discovered but was not surprised at being arrested.

I did not murder Mrs Thomas from any premeditation. I was enraged and in a passion and I cannot now recollect why I did it; something seemed to seize me at the time. I threw her downstairs in the heat of passion and strong impulse... I never had a hatred towards anybody in my lifetime, certainly not as such as would have induced me to do them bodily injury and I cannot account for the awful feelings that came over me from the time Mrs Thomas came home from church until the murder was completed...

I have now relieved my mind by making a full and sincere confession that myself, without help or assistance of any person whatever, committed the murder. I have accounted for it and described it in this statement to the best of my power and recollection. I heartily exonerate every one from having any hand or part in it.

When I got into trouble in Liverpool it was owing in a great measure to poverty and evil associations which led me step by step into badness. When I got over that trouble I formed an intimate acquaintance with one who should have protected me and, being led away by evil associates and bad companions, I became, as it were, forlorn and forsook everything that might have kept me in the path of rectitude and prevented my unhappy end.

I was afraid to make known the real state of things to my solicitor lest he might have abandoned my case and taken no interest in it. I therefore concealed the truth from him until I sent for him and he

> told me of the reply to the memorial sent up for me. I then fully and candidly confessed to him the facts, in order that everything might be cleared up and that I alone should be blamed. I am perfectly resigned to my fate and am full of confidence in a happy eternity. If I had a choice I would almost sooner die than return to a life of misery, deception and wickedness. I die with great fortitude and confidence in my faith and in our blessed God, whom I beseech to have mercy on my soul.

Having made her confession, Kate told Father McEnery that she 'felt relieved having unburdened her conscience', and that she 'would sleep more calmly' on her last night on earth. According to *The Penny Illustrated Paper*, she went to bed soon after ten o'clock and slept 'fairly well'.

On the day of her execution, she rose at about five o'clock in the morning and spoke to the Governor, Captain Colville, thanking him for his kindness to her. At 7.30am Father McEnery arrived, followed by the prison surgeon. As required by law, the public hangman, William Marwood, had slept on the premises the night before the execution, and had made the final adjustments to the scaffold and rope, arriving at the correct correlation between the weight and the drop to ensure that death was caused by the instantaneous fracture of the neck, not slow strangulation.

At a quarter to nine the prison bell began to toll. A few minutes later, her arms pinioned, Kate Webster was led down a flight of steps to the scaffold, accompanied by several officials, the Prison Governor and Father McEnery, who was reading the Catholic burial service. Once positioned on the scaffold, a white hood was placed over her head and a strap around her legs, not, as some might imagine, to ensure that her modesty was not compromised as she crashed through the trap-doors, but to prevent her kicking out.

As the chaplain read the words, 'Jesus, Good Shepherd, come', Kate said, in a loud voice, 'Lord, have mercy upon me.'

The bolt was drawn. It was all over.

At three minutes past nine, a black flag was hoisted on the flagstaff to signal that Kate Webster was dead. The sight of it was greeted by a few cheers from the large, but fairly quiet, crowd that had gathered outside the prison.

This comment in *The Penny Illustrated Paper* was typical of many at the time:

> The public must feel greatly relieved at the world being rid of so atrocious a criminal - a criminal who scrupled not to endeavour to incriminate innocent men to shield herself from the consequences of a monstrous crime.

That Kate Webster's crime was one of the most callous ever recorded cannot be denied. But what of Church and Porter - what a reprehensible pair they turned out to be. Especially Jack Church, who was anything but an 'honest' broker; he was a slimy character with a dubious past and clearly had something to hide. How, one wonders, had he amassed a sum of £500 without any evident source of income besides the hand-to-mouth running of the Rising Sun beer-house?

At the sale of Mrs Thomas's remaining furniture and effects, held at Vine Cottage the day after Kate's execution, Church, said to be in a jocular mood, was the main purchaser, buying a number of items including the gold watch and the carving knife Kate had used to dismember her victim's body. These trophies were, no doubt, subsequently displayed to great effect in the bar of the Rising Sun, by its decidedly obnoxious landlord.

Unlike Jack Church, Harry Porter and his family were all hard workers - except, of course, poor Annie Porter, described by the judge in his summing-up as a miserable drunkard - but the way they, and all their friends, had swarmed over the contents of Vine Cottage, like the proverbial maggots over a rotting corpse, was despicable. They were quite prepared to take anything they could lay their hands on, either for nothing or going cheap - and not one of them questioned Kate's legal entitlement to the bounty. They knew her background perfectly well; they knew she was a liar and a thief and had, in all probability, come by the house and its contents, the jewels, the dresses and the fancy bonnets, by some foul means or other. Big-hearted, boozy Kate, good for a laugh and free with her affections, playing the lady bountiful with poor Mrs Thomas's worldly goods.

Mrs Loder certainly did her friend Julia no favours when she recommended Kate Webster as a live-in maid. If it was another of Mrs Thomas's attempts to 'tame the savage' it went tragically wrong. Poor Julia, with her veneer of gentility, a fussy ex-school mistress, highly-strung, pernickety in her ways, forever finding fault - and Kate, quick-tempered, devious, slap-happy and deeply resentful. Who can tell what made her snap and completely lose control? Quite suddenly, that Sunday evening, all the envy, hatred, resentment and insecurity, culminated in a terrible surge of violence. To commit such a savage act, Kate must, herself, have been a woman deeply brutalised by the circumstances of her life. As a result of her long periods of imprisonment, she was naturally resentful of authority and, forever fighting to survive, she harboured a deep-seated envy of the good fortune of others. The closeting together of these two women was destined to end in disaster. The situation had become so tense that Mrs Thomas had given Kate notice to leave on 28 February but was persuaded to let her stay until Sunday, 2 March. As this was her half-day, Kate went out drinking and was late returning to the house to help prepare her mistress for church that evening. A heated argument ensued and Mrs Thomas arrived at church late and extremely agitated.

Kate Webster was, without doubt, a rough and ready young woman, a born hustler, yet she doggedly supported her son against all the odds. She could have so easily abandoned him to the workhouse, sold him to one of the baby-farmers prolific at the time, or simply given him away, as an unnecessary encumbrance, a drain on her erratic and ill-gotten resources. With her need to keep one step ahead of the police, he was nothing but a millstone around her neck. But she chose to keep him, and even when she knew her crime would soon be discovered and her arrest imminent, she did not abandon him and escape - instead, she took him back to the safety of her family in Ireland.

As for her associates, there was little honour amongst this

particular band of thieves. Not one of these fair-weather friends, not even one of her family, or the women who had spoken of her kindness, bothered to bring her little boy to Wandsworth so that Kate could see him for the last time.

And what of the child's father, her former accomplice - the man Kate called Strong? Was he, perhaps, despite her last minute denial, involved in the murder, or at least, in disposing of parts of the body? He was seen in her company on 27 February, three days before the murder. Was he, perhaps, the dark-haired man in the Ulster coat seen walking arm-in-arm with Kate Webster soon after the murder? And did she protect his identity for so long, not only because he was her young son's father, but because he was also the one man Kate really loved and did not use?

The denouement of this case is quite extraordinary. In October, 2010, whilst workmen were excavating part of the garden belonging to the naturalist and broadcaster, Sir David Attenborough, in Park Road, Richmond, a skull was unearthed. It was suggested that this may have been the missing head of Mrs Julia Thomas as the location was close to Mrs Thomas's house and extended to the derelict site of The Hole in the Wall public house frequented by Kate Webster and her drinking cronies.

The skull was removed by Richmond Police and subjected to carbon dating tests at the University of Edinburgh and these results, along with historical researches, were presented as evidence at the inquest. On Tuesday, 5 July, 2011, the West London Coroner, Alison Thompson, formally identified the skull as that of Julia Thomas and recorded a verdict of unlawful killing - the cause of death being asphyxiation and head injury.

In her confession, written on the night before her execution, Kate said that she 'placed the box in the river (containing body parts) and disposed of the head and other parts of the body as best I could'. She does not actually say that she threw the black bag containing Julia Thomas's head into the Thames at Hammersmith Bridge. Yet there was no way she would have had time to walk from Hammersmith to Richmond, bury the head and rejoin her friends in the pub twenty minutes later as indicated in their witness statements.

Kate told her friends that she had arranged to meet someone in Barnes that night and hand over the black bag. Did she meet that person near Hammersmith Bridge and hand over the black bag? Who was this unknown accomplice - the mysterious Mr Strong, perhaps?

Did he then carry the bag to Park Road, in Richmond, and bury it behind The Hole in the Wall where it remained for some hundred and thirty years?

Jane Cannon Cox

A Companion Most Cruel

Before Jane Cannon Cox became Florence Bravo's companion at The Priory, in Balham, she had led a hard, humdrum sort of existence. Previous writers on this famous case, a truly Victorian *cause célèbre,* have always accepted the version of her background which she had invented for herself in later life - that her maiden name was Jane Édouard and that she was born in the East Indies in 1837, of a French father. She was, in fact, born Jane Edwards, in Liverpool about 1827, of middle class English stock. Her father, John, was a merchant and her mother, Martha, ran an Elementary School in the Wirrall in which Jane and her two sisters became pupil teachers. She subsequently left to seek work as a governess and her first post was teaching the children of a curate in Nottinghamshire, after which she spent a year with a rector's family in Kent.

In 1858, Jane married twenty-one year old Philip Cox, a civil engineer; but she lied to the registrar, giving herself the same age as her bridegroom when, in fact, she was thirty-one. Two years later, their first son, Leslie, was born, and the following year, Philip Cox, who was employed by the East India Company, took his family to live in the St Ann's district of Jamaica, where their second son, Henry, was born. Jane Cox subsequently gave birth to twins, both of whom died in infancy, and a third son, Charles.

Jane was desperate when, in 1867, her husband died and with three young children to support she decided to return to England to seek re-employment as a governess. She tried to establish a Dame School in Woodbridge, Suffolk, but without success. From then on her life became a perpetual struggle and, in order to survive, she took various teaching jobs, living with her three young children in a succession of rented rooms.

Intent on improving her circumstances, she went to London to find Mr Joseph Bravo, a wealthy merchant, who lived with his wife, Mary, and step-son Charles, in Lancaster Road, Notting Hill. Mr Bravo had known Jane Cox's husband in the West Indies and was sorry to hear of his widow's predicament. He advised her to use the little savings she had left to purchase a house he knew to be vacant in Lancaster Road. With an outlay of £200, he assured her, she could buy the house and rent out rooms - in this way she would never be destitute.

Jane Cox took his advice and also accepted a loan of £60 to enrol her two elder boys as boarders at St Anne's, a school for 'children of distressed gentlefolk' in Streatham. So generous had Joseph Bravo been to Jane, with both advice and money, one might suppose she was grateful. Later events, however, were to suggest otherwise.

In 1871, Mrs Cox was employed as a daily governess to the children of Mr Henry Brooks and his wife, in Streatham. It was here that she met Florence Ricardo, an attractive auburn-haired young woman of twenty-six. She was the daughter of Robert Campbell, the High Sheriff of Berkshire. The family was both wealthy and well-connected and Florence had enjoyed a privileged childhood in the family home, Buscot Park, one of the largest and most elegant eighteenth century houses in the county.

In 1864, at the time of her marriage, Florence was a charming, but wilful young woman of nineteen; her bridegroom, twenty-one year old Grenadier Guardsman, Alexander Ricardo, was even more wealthy and well-connected.[11] They made an attractive couple and, with inherited wealth behind them, it seemed that their future happiness was assured. Sadly, after the death of his mother a few years later, Alexander's drinking increased to such an extent that before long he had squandered much of his fortune and destroyed his health. He became morose and violent and regularly suffered

11 Alexander Louis Ricardo, only son of John Lewis Ricardo, MP for Stoke-on-Trent, and the Rt. Hon. Catherine, née Duff, sister to the fifth Earl of Fife.

from distressing attacks of delirium tremens.

The effect of his drinking on Florence was equally devastating. Always highly strung and prone to collapse she became so nervously depleted that, in 1870, her mother suggested she travel to Malvern to consult Dr James Gully,[12] an old family friend.

Dr Gully was, at sixty-two, a highly cultured and charming man, a renowned and respected homeopathic practitioner and one of the foremost pioneers of hydropathy in the country. Many thousands of patients, including society's rich, fashionable and famous, flocked to his hydropathic centre at Malvern, in the Worcestershire hills. His patience and sensitivity were balm indeed to Florence's shattered nerves and before long, despite the thirty-six year difference in their ages, their relationship flourished, developing into a passionate affair.

Not surprisingly, this caused a tremendous scandal in Malvern, not only with the doctor's family and friends but also with Florence's parents. Her father, in particular, was enraged by the affair and threatened to disinherit Florence unless she returned to her husband. With Gully's backing, Florence resisted both her husband's entreaties and her father's wrath. Determined to break free, she flounced out of Buscot Park and headed for Brooklands, in Streatham, the home of her solicitor, Henry Brooks.

It was during her stay at Brooklands that Florence met Mrs Jane Cox. At the time, her affair with Gully was at its height and she frequently entertained him on his trips to London. There was no way, therefore, that Mrs Cox could have doubted the nature of their relationship. The couple were far from discreet; in fact, Mrs Brooks eventually had to ask Florence to leave, after one of her lady visitors had seen her and the elderly doctor kissing on the sofa. Such a blatant affair was shocking enough - made worse by the fact that

12 Dr James Manby Gully, born in Jamaica in 1808: son of a rich coffee planter. Educated in Paris and Edinburgh. Established a Hydropathic Centre at Malvern in 1842. A charismatic personality revered by Victorian society who listed among his patients such famous names as Tennyson, Dickens, George Eliot and Florence Nightingale.

both parties were married.[13] But fortunately for Florence, death was soon to release her for Alexander died of alcoholism in Cologne a few months later, leaving her free to continue her affair with a relatively clear conscience and a fortune of £40,000 at her disposal.[14]

When she left Brooklands she rented a house called Stokefield, in Streatham, and set about establishing an independent household. The following December, Dr Gully shocked everyone in Malvern by retiring early and taking a house a few doors from his young mistress. His coachman, Griffiths, had already been sent from Malvern to drive Florence's carriages, and convention was further flouted when the lovers spent six weeks together in Italy. It soon became clear in the months that followed that Florence's reputation had been so damaged by her affair with Dr Gully that she was ostracised by London society and became the subject of malicious gossip amongst her neighbours. Florence was naturally gregarious and hated her isolation. She particularly missed the support of her mother, Anne, who, probably on instructions from her bombastic husband, refused to have anything to do with her. Now that she had made the break and determined to lead an independent life in the face of such abject disapproval, she needed someone to act as her housekeeper and companion - someone who would be discreet, unobtrusive, sympathetic and grateful - someone like the inscrutable little governess at Brooklands - yes, she thought Mrs Cox would be ideal.

In the summer of 1872, when Jane Cox was offered the job as Florence's companion, she accepted gladly and borrowed a further £81 from Mr Joseph Bravo to place her youngest son in St Anne's. Her relief must have been tremendous; at last she had fallen on her feet, for Florence was a warm-hearted, generous woman, allowing her a salary of £80 a year, whereas most companions were lucky to get £30 and a kitchen maid might expect a mere £12 a year for her labours. And the only price she was asked to pay for living in relative

13 Dr Gully's wife was seventeen years his senior and had been living in a nursing home for a number of years.

14 More like two million pounds in today's currency.

luxury was to accept without reservation her mistress's affair with the charming and sophisticated Dr Gully. This proved no hardship at all for she had, in fact, already met the doctor in Jamaica and admired him tremendously.

The following year, Dr Gully took Florence to the German hydropathic spa at Kissingen so that she could undergo a number of rigorous and unpalatable water-cure treatments. Mrs Cox, by now well-entrenched in Florence's favour, was left in charge of the household at Stokefield. She wrote several letters to her mistress - mainly telling tales on the other servants - and the letters she received in reply addressed her as *'my dearest Mrs Cox'* and signed *'with kindest love'*. But on her return, Florence found that she was pregnant and it was the scandalous aftermath of the German holiday that was to cement the friendship between the two women and make Florence view Jane Cox, for a while at least, as indispensable.

To avoid the scandal, Dr Gully performed an abortion on Florence after which she became seriously ill. In the circumstances, Gully was reluctant to engage a nurse so the care of Florence fell to Mrs Cox. She performed her duties with professional excellence and, furthermore, she was the essence of discretion, making sure that no one else in the house ever suspected the true nature of Florence's illness. During the course of this worrying and tricky episode the relationship between the two women underwent a significant change. So strong was their mutual dependence that they became close friends, no longer merely mistress and servant, and began to call each other by their first names.

The effect of their new intimacy was, of course, inevitable - it replaced Florence's dependence on Dr Gully and weakened his influence. He lost control of her, she no longer needed him and, still sickened by the effects of the abortion, she refused to sleep with him. After all, she always had 'Janey' to comfort her, pander to her needs and sit quietly by her bedside every night to watch over her until she finally drifted off to sleep. Only then would the dedicated companion, exhausted from a day of ceaseless service, climb the stairs to her own room in the servants' quarters.

In March, 1874, Florence and her entourage moved to The Priory at Balham. Built in 1806, it was a charming example of the 'Strawberry Hill' pseudo-Gothic style, set in ten acres of private land near Tooting Common. Besides the paddocks, orchards, stable block and large kitchen plot there were formal shrubberies and an abundance of flower beds. Fruits of every description were cultivated, including pears, grapes, melons, strawberries and figs. Exquisite ornamental ducks and white fantail doves roamed freely amongst the fruit trees and rose-walks. In addition to the ground staff, Florence also employed George Griffiths, the coachman, Frederick Rowe, the butler, the cook and two maids, Mary Ann Keeber and Elizabeth Evans. The inside of The Priory was expensively furnished, festooned with silken draperies and lavishly dotted with little pieces of Dresden and Sèvres. The conservatory was filled with rare ferns and a fine Broadwood piano graced the drawing room.

By now high up in the pecking order, Mrs Cox, instead of having to share with the other servants, was given a comfortable room to herself on the second floor. In addition, her wages went up to £100 a year and she was even allowed to have her three sons spend the school holidays at The Priory. There was no doubt about it, Mrs Cox was living in clover and still further good fortune lay ahead. An ailing aunt by marriage, living in Jamaica, wrote to say that in her will Mrs Cox's eldest son, Leslie, could expect to inherit her house, land and other property.

As for Florence and Dr Gully, their relationship, whilst still affectionate, had cooled. They travelled to Italy in the autumn of that year - with Mrs Cox in tow, putting pay to any idea the doctor may have had about rekindling the affair. In fact, the two women dumped him in Paris and returned to England alone.

It was in December 1874 that Mrs Cox inadvertently brought about the fateful meeting that would not only end in death but also destroy her relationship with her mistress for ever. Florence had decided to go shopping in the West End and Mrs Cox had promised to take her three sons on a traditional pre-Christmas visit to Mr Joseph Bravo and his family, who were now living in style at 2 Palace Green, Kensington. Florence insisted on giving Mrs Cox and the boys a lift in her carriage and promised to collect them on her way back to Balham.

When she called for them later that afternoon she was invited into the house by Mr and Mrs Bravo. While she was there, Charles Bravo entered the room and the two were introduced. It would seem that the attraction between them, however, was not immediate for they did not meet again until ten months later - and then by chance.

In the early autumn of 1875, whilst Dr Gully was travelling abroad, Florence and Mrs Cox decided to take a holiday in Brighton. It was here, on the promenade, that Charles and Florence met for the second time. The young barrister was clearly impressed with the gay young widow - she had taken to dying her hair a deeper shade of red and using make-up or 'face paints' - and persuaded her to receive him at her lodgings the following day.

Charles was a handsome young barrister of thirty, educated at Oxford, sophisticated, cynical and with a somewhat rakish manner. He was born Charles Delauney Turner, in 1845, probably in Jamaica. Little is known of his natural father, except that he died young and his death certificate gave his name as Augustus Charles Turner, gentleman. His widow, Mary, née Hougham, was left with three young children - Charles, Alice, a deaf-mute and Ellen, a mentally defective child who was placed in a convent. Despite this unfortunate burden, Mary married again, this time to Mr Joseph Bravo, who proved to be an excellent step-father, so much so that, at twenty-one, Charles chose to take his surname as his own.

Although at the time of his meeting with Florence, Charles was only earning about £200 a year from his legal work, he was expected to inherit his father's considerable wealth. It seems likely, therefore, having been accustomed to money, that he was attracted to Florence's other assets rather than for financial reasons. As for Florence, she readily accepted the attentions of the young barrister after spending four years on the arm of her elderly lover.

Suspecting that Charles might be sufficiently smitten to eventually propose marriage, she decided to get rid of Gully as soon as possible. She wrote asking him to visit her in Brighton but lacked the courage to tell him of her decision. She merely said that whilst their association continued she could not be reconciled with her parents - the fact that her mother was ill, she said, made their estrangement more distressing. She could not bring herself, however, to mention her meeting with Charles Bravo.

In truth, the affair with Charles was well under way. He had already confessed a four year liaison with a woman in Maidenhead and Florence had mentioned her affection for Dr Gully, whom she described as 'an old family friend'. When he learned the doctor's age, he had no difficulty in believing her when she assured him that the relationship was an innocent one. However, when Dr Gully received a letter from Florence ending the affair he was devastated and arrived in Brighton hoping for a reconciliation. An emotional scene ensued and Gully, unable to dissuade Florence from marrying Charles, returned to London a very bitter man.

Mrs Cox shared his displeasure at the prospect of the marriage though she was far too canny to show it. Nor was Charles's mother pleased - after all, in her eyes, Florence's affair with Dr Gully had irrevocably sullied her reputation and made her a totally unacceptable choice as a wife for her only son. Throughout all the ensuing family arguments, Mrs Cox remained diplomatic and calm, first placating one party and then the other, without giving any indication of her own feelings. News of the forthcoming marriage came as a great relief to Florence's parents, however, and a timely reconciliation took place. Not only did they forgive their errant daughter for her past indiscretions, they warmly welcomed Charles into the family.

The marriage between Charles Bravo and Florence Ricardo took place on 7 December, 1875, at All Saints Church, Kensington. Although they seemed very fond of each other, their life together proved far from idyllic. Florence was already drinking heavily, matched by Mrs Cox, and Charles showed signs of being overcautious with money. As Florence had become used to running her own financial affairs, she objected to any retrenchments he suggested and they frequently quarrelled over money. If they got rid of Mrs Cox and two of the horses, Charles argued, they could save at least three hundred pounds a year. But Florence strongly objected and refused to give up either. Mrs Cox, although now relegated to a back seat since the marriage, was still very important to Florence, especially as she had suffered two miscarriages in quick succession. 'Janey' was an absolute godsend when she was feeling unwell. She also relied on her to ward off the amorous attentions of Charles when she was indisposed. She did this most effectively by asking Mrs Cox to share her bed. Charles's feelings towards the companion can therefore be imagined yet despite this impasse, he continued to treat her with courtesy and kindness.

As for Mrs Cox, she remained civil and was cunning enough to appear to sympathise with Charles whenever Florence complained about his behaviour. She was, however, only too aware of her precarious position. To complicate matters, her aunt, Margaret, in Jamaica, was urging her to go over to settle a potentially lucrative inheritance promised to her son, Leslie. It would be foolish to delay, yet Mrs Cox knew that, once she left The Priory, her absence would provide Charles with the perfect opportunity to get rid of her - he would simply refuse to take her back. It seems, however, that she decided, at least for the time being, to do nothing.

On 7 April, shortly after Florence's second miscarriage, Mrs Cox met Dr Gully by chance - for the third time, apparently, at Balham Railway Station. As old friends they soon fell into conversation; she told him about her possible trip to the West Indies (asking him for a remedy for Jamaica fever) and that Florence's condition was causing her to suffer from sleeplessness and backache. Gully thought laurel water might help her sleep; he would leave a small bottle at Mrs Cox's house in Lancaster Road.

The following Monday, Mrs Cox went to her house and collected Dr Gully's bottle of laurel water as arranged. On her return to The Priory, however, Florence said that, as she was sleeping better, she did not need it, so Mrs Cox took the bottle and put it away in the medicine chest in her room.

Florence continued to improve and during the early part of April Charles was at home a good deal, strolling about the grounds reciting Shakespeare. He was in fine form and he and Florence seemed to share a wry humour illustrated in this letter he wrote to his mother on 14 April:

> My fowls lay as if they were Turks and their eggs the money due on coupons, and my spirits are nothing like they would be if the sun was visible. Florence is better, but very cross. I went to the library and brought her six volumes of books; three she had read, and three contain the uninspired preachings of an idiot. She has finished a pair of slippers for me in a rage, and is slanging me for not being able to tell a good book, as you tell good music, by the look...
>
> I rode the cobs the day before yesterday, and feel very much as if the muscles in my legs are ossifying. I have difficulty in dragging on my shooting-boots, which I am obliged 'par ordre superieur' to wear in addition to a red flannel garment which is a cross between a kilt and a sporran and a pair of bathing drawers, and has as many strings as a harp...

There was a carefree atmosphere at The Priory that Easter with no apparent hint of the disaster to come. Charles had a great time playing tennis with first Rowe, the butler, and then Osman, the gardener. His uncle, James Orr, and his wife, Peggy, came to visit and Charles, *'proud as a king'*, showed them around the estate. There were rides across the common in the carriage and fun and games with Mrs Cox's two younger boys who were spending the holiday with them.

In letters to her mother, Florence said she hoped to spend a couple of weeks convalescing in Worthing but assured her that she was already feeling so much better. It was so lovely at The Priory, she said, and the garden, filled with flowers, was a delight. As for Charles, except for a sudden and unexplained bout of vomiting on his way to Palace Green early in March (when Florence had been visiting her parents at Buscot) the country life seemed to suit him and she had never seen him look so well.

On 18 April, Mrs Cox, armed with a small flask of sherry in her reticule, set off by train to Worthing to rent a house for Florence's convalescence. Back at The Priory, Charles and Florence, despite her weakness and the sudden change in the weather - there was heavy rain and sleet - prepared to drive into town. Florence wished to do some shopping and Charles had arranged to meet his uncle, James Orr, for lunch. Leaving Charles at the Turkish Baths in Jermyn Street, Florence went to the Haymarket Stores and purchased some tobacco and hair-wash for Charles, after which she ordered Parton, the coachman, to drive her back to Balham.

When Charles returned to The Priory at four thirty, Florence, having taken some champagne with her lunch, was resting on the sofa in the morning room. They talked briefly and Florence gave him his tobacco and shampoo. Shortly afterwards, Charles came downstairs in his riding clothes. George Younger, the groom, advised him against riding the cobs as they were both very skittish, having been in harness the day before. Ignoring his advice, Charles rode out of the stable yard on Cremorne, declaring that he would be back to exercise the other pony as well before dinner.

On his return an hour and a half later, Charles looked pale and shaken; he told the groom that the animal had bolted with him.

'He galloped so hard,' he said, 'my hat blew off.'

He was also annoyed that he'd had to pay a lad a shilling to retrieve his hat from the grass.

As soon as Florence saw the state Charles was in, she asked Rowe, the butler, to arrange a warm bath and help him upstairs.

When he had finished his bath he told the maid, Mary Ann Keeber, to leave the water in the tub as he would use it again the next day.[15]

Mrs Cox returned to The Priory at twenty-past seven to find Florence dressing for dinner; she had begged Charles to let her join him and Mrs Cox that evening for the first time since her illness. He agreed, but made her promise to go straight to bed as soon as

15 Charles told the maid to leave the bath water for the morning as they had been having trouble with the pipes at The Priory.

she had eaten. Having just got back from her trip to Worthing, Mrs Cox didn't have time to change but simply washed her hands before joining the others in the dining room.

The atmosphere during the meal was tense and Charles, out of sorts after his fall, was in no mood for chatter. He refused to discuss the holiday in Worthing or look at the photograph of the house Mrs Cox had rented. To make matters worse, a letter arrived from his stockbroker informing him that he had lost £20. He was even more annoyed to find that his step-father (the letter had gone to Palace Green by mistake) had enclosed a somewhat 'shirty letter' warning him about the pitfalls of speculation.

Throughout the meal, Florence and Mrs Cox drank freely, consuming two bottles of sherry between them. This, according to the butler, was their usual consumption, although Charles was more moderate, taking no more than three or four glasses of burgundy. After dinner, the three retired to the morning room but the atmosphere remained tense.

Shortly before nine o'clock, Florence went to bed, with Mrs Cox in attendance. Charles, already disgruntled and suffering from neuralgia and aching limbs, was not pleased at being relegated to the spare room once more. As the two women reached the staircase, Florence asked Mrs Cox to bring her a little Marsala and water from the dining room. Having poured the wine, the companion took it up to Florence's dressing-room where she found her mistress already in her nightclothes.

Just before nine-thirty, the maid, not waiting to be sent for, carried two cans of hot water upstairs, one for Florence, the other for Mrs Cox. Florence answered her knock on the door and, giving the girl a small tumbler, asked her to go down and fetch some more wine. Leaving Mrs Cox's can of hot water on the landing, Mary Ann went back downstairs to fetch the Marsala. As she carried the filled tumbler out of the dining room, Charles came from the morning room. She stood aside to let him precede her. He did so without speaking and, as he climbed the stairs ahead of her, he turned around twice to look at her, but said nothing.

Charles went first to Florence's dressing room and, as the maid could hear him upbraiding his wife for drinking too much, she took the wine to the bedroom. As she heard Charles cross the landing to the spare room, she came out of the bedroom and met Florence and Mrs Cox coming from the dressing room. After telling her mistress where she had left the wine, she went into the dressing room to put away Florence's clothes.

When this was done, Mary Ann returned to the bedroom where she saw that Florence was already in bed, apparently, asleep. Mrs Cox, still in her outdoor clothes, was sitting in her usual position on a small stool between the bed and the door. She asked the maid if she had seen to her mistress's night tray and, satisfied that all was in order, told her to take Mrs Bravo's two little dogs downstairs for the night. When only one of the dogs could be found in the bedroom Mrs Cox suggested that the other might be upstairs in her room. Mary Ann closed the bedroom door behind her and went out onto the landing. Standing at the foot of the stairs, she called to the dog.

A moment later, the door of the spare room was flung open and Charles appeared in the doorway in his nightshirt.

"Florence! Florence!" he screamed. "Hot water! Hot water!"

With these words, he staggered back into the room.

Shocked, Mary Ann turned and rushed back into her mistress's room where she told Mrs Cox that the master had been taken ill. Mrs Cox hurried to the spare room to find Charles standing near the open casement; as she moved towards him he was violently sick out of the window, the vomit landing on the leaded roof of the window below. Then, very loudly, he shouted once more for hot water.

From that moment, Mrs Cox took complete charge. She told Mary Ann to run downstairs to fetch some water. When she got back, Charles was propped up on the floor near the window, unconscious, with Mrs Cox rubbing his chest. She sent the maid downstairs again, this time to fetch some mustard. When she returned, Mrs Cox told her to mix it with water in a bowl and between them they managed to lift Charles's legs into the bowl - but he suddenly kicked out and then lay rigid.

The companion then told the maid to mix some mustard and water in a tumbler but the girl was unsure how to do it. Impatiently, Mrs Cox took it from her and mixed it herself, using her finger. Raising Charles's head, she tried to pour some of the solution into his mouth. He was insensible, however, with his jaws locked and, as he was unable to swallow, most of the mixture spilled down the front of his nightshirt.

Mrs Cox then sent Mary Ann downstairs again to make some strong coffee, which in the pre-electric era must have taken several minutes. When she returned, they managed to get a little down his throat, but he was immediately sick into a basin. After being sent to wash the basin and bring it back, Mary Ann was sent off again, this time up to Mrs Cox's room to fetch some camphor from her medicine chest. While the maid was gone Mrs Cox hurried downstairs to the pantry where she shouted to Rowe to rouse the groom and send him to fetch Dr Harrison, the family physician in Streatham. Returning to Charles, she began to massage his feet.

Mary Ann, unable to find the camphor in Mrs Cox's room, took it upon herself to awaken her mistress and tell her what had happened. Florence jumped out of bed immediately and dashed into the spare room while Mary Ann went off to continue her search for the camphor.

As soon as Florence saw Charles, she burst into tears. On learning that Mrs Cox had sent for Dr Harrison, she became agitated and demanded to know why a local doctor had not been summoned. Then, still in her nightclothes, she ran downstairs, calling for Rowe. He said later that, although he could hear the commotion in the spare room, he had remained downstairs for the sake of decency as the housemaid had said that Mrs Bravo was 'in her nightclothes'.

'She was crying as she came,' he later recalled, 'and she was crying out to me to fetch someone quickly. 'I don't care who it is,' she said, 'get someone from Balham!' She screamed it at me.'

As the butler ran off to fetch Dr Moore, who lived nearby, Florence, Mrs Cox and Mary Ann Keeber - having sent for the other maid to help - managed to lift Charles from the floor and into a chair. That done, Florence and Mrs Cox changed his soiled nightshirt and waited. The companion ordered the maid to empty the bath-tub in readiness for the doctor's arrival.

It was gone ten o'clock when Dr Moore arrived. Having heard Mrs Cox's account of what had happened, he examined Charles and, fearing heart failure, had his patient placed on the bed and then administered an enema of brandy. He then applied a mustard poultice to his chest using water from the bottle by Charles's bed.

When Dr Harrison arrived from Streatham about half an hour later, Mrs Cox was waiting in the hall to meet him.

'Dr Harrison,' she said, 'I am sure he has taken chloroform.'

Hurrying to the spare room, the doctor examined Charles but failed to detect any smell of chloroform. Suspecting that a large vessel near the heart had given way, the two doctors decided to inject brandy as a stimulant. Although they were doubtful of his recovery, they advised Florence to seek another opinion.

She insisted on contacting Charles's cousin, Mr Royes Bell, immediately; he was a surgeon and had known Charles all his life. An urgent summons was delivered to his Harley Street home by carriage. When Florence learned that the hired horses and not the cobs, which were much faster, had been used she became angry and upset.

Exasperated, she returned to the sickroom and lay beside Charles, who was still unconscious, and, in an effort to waken him, she began to whisper endearments in his ear. However, exhausted by her recent illness, her anxiety and the effects of too much sherry, she fell asleep, her arms still entwined around his neck. Dr Harrison, afraid that she might interfere with his patient's breathing, made her sit in a chair by the bedside. Mrs Cox, who had remained calm throughout the drama, sat quietly on the other side of the bed as their vigil began.

About two-thirty in the morning, Royes Bell arrived with a colleague, Dr Johnson, to find that Charles had just suffered a painful attack of vomiting and had passed a bloody mucus from the bowel. With this, he regained consciousness and recognised his cousin and the other doctors and, even though he was in agonising abdominal pain, he asked Florence to kiss him.

At times, the pain was so severe Charles would cry out, 'Oh, Christ have mercy upon me!'

By now convinced that Charles was the victim of a powerful poison, Dr Johnson administered a morphia suppository whilst Royes Bell tried to find out what he had taken. He begged him to say but Charles kept repeating:

'I have taken nothing. I rubbed my gums with laudanum for neuralgia and may have swallowed some.'

When told that laudanum could not possibly be the cause of such terrible symptoms, he said, wearily:

'If it isn't laudanum I don't know what it is.'

The doctors had noted bottles of chloroform, laudanum and Condy's Fluid [an antiseptic in common use] - also a packet of Epsom Salts and some camphor liniment which Royes Bell had prescribed for Charles's rheumatism. Charles suffered a second bout of vomiting and bowel evacuation, both bloodied, which confirmed the doctors' view that he was suffering from an irritant, not a narcotic, poison and was, therefore, most unlikely to recover.

Shortly before three o'clock in the morning, the butler entered the sickroom to say that Mrs Cox wished to speak to Royes Bell. The companion was waiting in the dressing room and, after hearing what she had to say, Bell quickly went to fetch Dr Johnson and Dr Harrison. All three then hastened to the dressing room and Mrs Cox repeated her statement. She told them that when she had gone to Mr Bravo soon after he collapsed he had said to her:

'I've taken poison. Don't tell Florence.'

Hearing this, Dr Harrison angrily asked her why she had not told him so before. She replied that she *had* told him when he arrived at the house.

'You did nothing of the kind!' retorted Harrison.

Mrs Cox, however, would not be swayed and insisted that she had told him some four hours before.

The doctors returned to the sickroom but when they told Charles what Mrs Cox had said, he denied it, saying again that he had only rubbed some laudanum on his gums. Still mystified as to the specific poison involved, the doctors decided at this late stage to take samples of vomit and excreta for analysis.

At five-thirty in the morning, the doctors left The Priory but Royes Bell remained at his cousin's bedside. The two men were very close and although Bell told Charles quite frankly that he was unlikely to recover, at no time did he confess to taking poison or suggest that anyone had given it to him.

As the first light of that Wednesday morning warmed the walls of The Priory, the gravity of Charles's condition seemed more harshly revealed. Florence sent a telegram summoning Charles's parents and another informing her mother of the tragedy. In preparation for the arrival of Charles's parents, the maid was instructed to tidy the sickroom. As she entered the room, Charles, with Florence and Royes standing close by, asked her how she was.

'Very well, sir, thank you,' Mary Ann replied. 'How are you feeling?'

'Not much better, Mary Ann,' Charles replied. 'We shan't have our trip to Worthing now.'

Mary Ann expressed the hope that they would, but Charles said, 'No, my next trip will be to Streatham cemetery.'

At this, Mary Ann burst into tears. Charles then looked up at Florence, saying: 'When you bury me, make no fuss and have no feathers...' to which Florence replied that she would do as he wished, and then she, too, began to cry. Then Charles turned to Royes and said with great weariness:

'Oh, Royes, I'm dying. Shall I linger long in such pain?'

A little later, Charles sent Mrs Cox for writing materials and dictated a simple will, leaving all he possessed to his wife. Charles Bravo's suffering continued throughout that day and he bore it with great courage. About three o'clock in the afternoon, the doctors returned to The Priory but there was little they could do. Questioning Charles yet again as to whether he had taken poison, he replied, impatiently:

'If I knew what I was suffering from, why the devil should I send for you?'

Soon after four o'clock, his parents arrived and were greatly shocked at the sight of their desperately-ill son. All antagonism between Florence and Mrs Bravo was temporarily forgotten and the whole household, servants included, waited with a mounting feeling of helplessness. Whereas Joseph Bravo gravely prepared his son for death, Florence, refusing to give up hope, sent Mrs Cox scurrying off to Dr Gully's house with an urgent plea for him to prescribe something for Charles. She returned with a homeopathic remedy which Dr Johnson allowed her to give, though he was sceptical of its benefit. He left The Priory soon after but returned with Henry Smith, who was a surgeon related to Mrs Joseph Bravo. Sadly, he could do no more than all the other doctors.

Still determined to save her husband's life, Florence sent for one of her father's associates, Sir William Gull, a man recognised as the finest diagnostician of the day.[16] She felt that, if anyone could determine the cause of Charles's condition, he could. Mrs Cox was sent off to Sir William's residence in Mayfair and he arrived at The Priory by six-thirty that evening. At the age of sixty, Sir William was still a powerful and authoritative figure; it was said that he was kind-hearted and benevolent, yet at times he could be brutally honest. After a brief examination of Charles's pulse and abdomen, he said:

'This isn't disease. You are poisoned. Pray tell me how you came by it.'

'Laudanum,' came the weary reply. 'I took it myself.'

'You've taken more than laudanum,' observed Sir William, to which Dr Johnson added:

'If you die without telling us more than we know at present someone may be accused or suspected of having poisoned you.'

'I am aware of that,' Charles said, 'but I can tell you nothing more.'

Sir William asked him yet again to reveal the name of the poison so that an antidote might be found, though he feared it would be too late to save his life. Charles responded by closing his eyes and

16 Sir William Gull: highly regarded by the medical profession. In 1871, a grateful Queen Victoria awarded him a baronetcy for his successful treatment of the Prince of Wales when he was gravely ill with typhoid.

turning away.

At this point, Mrs Cox decided to mention the vomit on the leads and Sir William ordered a footman to climb out and scoop up a sample using a silver spoon to avoid contamination. This done, the doctors gathered in the dressing room to discuss the case. Sir William was of the opinion that Charles had swallowed arsenic, not realising that samples of vomit and excreta had already been tested for arsenic with negative results.

During the course of their discussion, Sir William was summoned to the sickroom where Charles said:

'Sir William, I wish to tell you now that I've told you the truth and nothing but the truth.'

In reply, Sir William repeated his conviction that laudanum was not the cause of his illness and told him bluntly that he could not live much longer.

'I know that,' said Charles. 'I know that I'm going to appear before my Maker. I can't tell you anything more. I took nothing but laudanum to rub on my lower jaw for toothache - like this ...' With these words, he lifted his hand and feebly touched his mouth with his fingers. In excruciating pain and weary beyond endurance, he then asked whether there was any hope for him.

'Looking at your condition, Mr Bravo,' Sir William replied, 'it wouldn't be right to give you any hope.' Then, feeling the pulse of the stricken man, he added, bluntly: 'There's very little life left in you. In fact, you're half dead now.'

Refusing a visit from the local rector, Charles slowly and falteringly recited the Lord's Prayer while his family and friends knelt by the bedside, their heads bowed. When they had finished praying, only Florence, Mrs Bravo, Royes Bell and his wife, Anna Maria, remained. Sharing the night's vigil and taking short rests in turn, the four watched helplessly as Charles bore the agony of his last hours.

As for Mrs Cox, she had remained in the background, running errands, organising the household, carrying on with her usual efficiency. Not one person recalled her crying in a house overcome with sadness and where everyone else had succumbed to tears.

At four-thirty in the morning of Friday, 21 April, the Bravos' old servant, Amelia Bushell, was sent to Mrs Cox's room to fetch Florence as it was clear that Charles was close to death. She found Florence asleep with Mrs Cox sitting on the bed beside her.[17]

They went downstairs together and found Charles unconscious, watched over by his mother and Royes Bell. Not long after five o'clock, Florence, weeping pitifully, woke Mary Ann, and asked her to make some tea. Shortly afterwards, the maid was coming upstairs with the tea tray when she was met by Mrs Cox who told her that Florence wished to speak to her in the dressing room. When the maid entered the room, Florence said to her:

'Mary Ann, Mr Bravo is dead.'

'Oh, madam, when did he die?' the maid cried, very upset.

'A few minutes ago.'

Charles had died at five-thirty that morning. His last words had been to his mother; before finally losing consciousness, he had turned to her and whispered, 'Ah, Granny...'

It was a ghastly end to a young life and too pitiful to dwell upon but for the mystery that surrounded it - a mystery which made it no ordinary death but one which guaranteed Charles Bravo a degree of immortality that, with his love of life, he would have enjoyed tremendously.

As Charles's parents were completely grief-stricken - his mother never fully recovered from her bereavement - it was left to Royes Bell to inform the coroner for East Surrey of his cousin's death. As none of the doctors would issue a death certificate, an inquest was necessary. With the agreement of the bereaved family, Bell enlisted Dr Joseph Payne of St Thomas's Hospital to perform a post-mortem the following day. Various organs and the vomit collected from the leads were sent to Mr Theophilus Redwood, Professor of Chemistry to the Pharmaceutical Society of Great Britain, for analysis.

It was arranged that the inquest would be held at The Priory on the following Tuesday. Inquests (and post-mortems) were commonly

17 Florence had given her bedroom to Charles's mother so she could remain close to her dying son.

held in the homes of the deceased and the coroner, Mr William Carter, probably assumed, or had been led to believe, that he was dealing with a case of suicide and thus hoped to shield the dead man's widow and family from the strain of a more public inquiry.

The inquest jury was selected from local tradesmen, seventeen in number, a saddler, a couple of gardeners, a groom and several shopkeepers. The enquiry was held in the dining room on Tuesday, 25 April, but Florence did not attend - she remained in her room upstairs. One person who did attend was John Reid, one of Charles's friends and a fellow barrister - and it was to prove most fortunate that he was there for he took notes during the proceedings, without which only the barest outline of the evidence would have been recorded.

As soon as the inquiry had been opened, the jurors were conducted to a room upstairs to view the mortal remains of Charles Bravo as he lay in a coffin lined with white satin. His hands had been laid across his chest and white lilies placed between his fingers. The room was peaceful and filled with flowers, carefully arranged by Mrs Cox and the two maids.

Various family members were asked to give an account of Charles's illness and each emphasised that he was the least likely person to commit suicide. Mrs Cox said that he lived on 'good and affectionate' terms with his wife and she could not imagine why he should kill himself - she added, however, that Charles had told her soon after his collapse that he had taken poison.

The inquest was adjourned until Friday, 28 April at which time it was hoped that Professor Redwood would provide the results of his post-mortem analysis. When the inquiry re-opened, John Reid was joined by two of Charles's other friends who were equally puzzled by the death and wholly dismissive of the suicide theory.

When the maid, Mary Ann Keeber, was called to give evidence, she described the scene in the spare-room on the night Mr Bravo collapsed but said he did not use the word 'poison' in her hearing nor did Mrs Cox, at any time, mention that possibility. Mr Harrison rose to insist that Mrs Cox definitely did not tell him about any poison - she only mentioned that she thought he might have taken chloroform.

Dr Joseph Payne confirmed that during the post-mortem examination of Mr Bravo's body there were no signs of any disease that would account for his death. He was followed by Professor Redwood who testified that he had found ten grains of antimony in the vomit found on the leads - this was a lethal metallic poison, probably ingested in the form of tartar emetic, a white powder which would dissolve easily in water and would be virtually tasteless.

Evidence was then given about the food consumed at dinner on the night of Charles's collapse and it was noted that no one else in the household had been affected in any way. At this point, the coroner seemed anxious to terminate the inquiry but attention was drawn to the fact that the important question of Charles's state of mind prior to his death had not been addressed. Rather reluctantly he allowed Charles's friend, Frederick MacCalmont, to tell the jury that, when he met Charles in Piccadilly on the day he became ill, he had been 'in his usual health and spirits' and, in his opinion, he was the last person on earth likely to kill himself.

This said, Mr Carter had just begun to sum up once more when Dr Johnson rose to protest that he had not been called to give evidence. Much to his surprise and embarrassment, the coroner dismissed his offer, saying that the jury did not require any further medical evidence. Anxious to bring the proceedings to a close, Carter asked the jury to consider its verdict.

Though Joseph Bravo had his suspicions of foul play, Florence's father hoped for a verdict of suicide, which, though extremely unpleasant, was at least straightforward and uncontroversial. Yet clearly the jurors did not accept this theory, supported by Mrs Cox's statement about the poison; they rejected the idea of suicide in favour of an ambiguous and open verdict, one that satisfied neither faction:

> 'We find that the deceased died from the effects of poison, antimony - but we have not sufficient evidence to show under which circumstances it came into his body.'

If there had been a gulf between the Campbells and the Bravos before the jury's verdict, it was now wider than ever. Sadly, the one person who might have united them and helped smooth the edges of their discontent with his hearty bonhomie was Charles - and he was to be buried the next day.

On the morning of Saturday, 29 April, the day of Charles's funeral, the atmosphere was tense and fraught with suspicion. At the start of the funeral, his friend Carlyle Willoughby refused to enter The Priory, electing instead to wait at the front door. Whilst standing there he saw Florence, unaware of his presence, carrying a wreath of white blossoms through the hall. It was not customary for women to attend funerals at this time so Florence was not among the mourners who followed the coffin to the cemetery. Remaining at home, she watched from an upstairs window as the procession carrying Charles's body on an open horse-drawn hearse, fringed with violet trappings, left the gates of The Priory on its way to Norwood (now West Norwood) Cemetery.

As the body was buried on the higher slopes of the tree-lined cemetery, Charles's family and friends were far from tranquil in their thoughts. Joseph Bravo was so troubled, in fact, that, as soon as the ceremony was over, he voiced his growing disquiet to his physician brother-in-law, Henry Smith. He felt sure that his son had been poisoned and remarked that there were 'poisons in every room' of The Priory.[18] He had already hurled this comment at Robert Campbell in retaliation for a remark made by the latter to the effect that antimony was used in the stables at Joseph Bravo's house at Palace Green - a remark which insinuated that Charles had killed himself with poison belonging to his stepfather.

Joseph Bravo took Henry Smith's advice and hired the services of

18 This remark referred to the dozens of homeopathic remedies that the police found in the medicine chests belonging to both Florence Bravo and Jane Cox.

a rising young lawyer, George Lewis,[19] who immediately contacted Chief Inspector Clarke, at Scotland Yard. Charles's friend, Carlyle Willoughby, also informed the police that there were 'several circumstances which were worrying him' about Charles Bravo's death.

Mrs Cox did not attend the funeral; she spent the day in Brighton, arranging the rental of a house in Brunswick Terrace, close to one taken by the Campbells, so that Florence might recuperate after the traumatic events of the previous week.

On 3 May, Florence, Mrs Cox and other members of the staff travelled to Brighton. Soon after her arrival the Campbell family held a conference during which they discussed the theory of Charles's suicide, no doubt finding comfort in Sir William Gull's avowed opinion that Charles Bravo had taken his own life.

However, if the change of scene and support of her family brought Florence any sense of peace, it did not last long for she soon learned of Joseph Bravo's visit to Scotland Yard. She wrote her father-in-law an angry letter, berating him for his actions, and reminding him that Charles had left everything he possessed to her. She was slightly placated when she received a letter from Royes Bell in which he suggested the possibility that Charles was being blackmailed by his ex-mistress. But Florence was clutching at straws. At no time was there any evidence that the woman was demanding money or anything else from Charles.[20] But Florence, having learned that Joseph Bravo and others were suspicious, was desperate to push the theory of suicide. The open verdict had, of course, allowed an assumption of murder, which came as a terrible shock to everyone.

More frightening still, on 8 May, Chief Inspector George Clarke travelled to Brighton to interview her and members of her household. He also had the 'Sale of Poison' registers checked in

19 George Lewis, an imposing, monocled interrogator. He was involved in many of the great nineteenth century trials and was said to know 'more than any man about the scandalous secrets of Victorian society'.

20 Charles had a child called Katie by the woman in Maidenhead; he also borrowed £500 from her sister and, after her death, it was left to Joseph Bravo to settle the debt.

every chemist shop in Worthing - just in case Mrs Cox had popped in for some antimony during her visit on the day Charles Bravo died. In the meantime, the rumblings of disquiet over Charles's death, and the inadequacy of the inquest, continued from his friends and colleagues, growing in volume to such a degree that eventually there was a veritable avalanche of press coverage.

The article that nudged the first stone appeared in the weekly newspaper, *The World*, dated 10 May, under the title 'A Tragedy?' From then there were countless letters to the press voicing opinions and offering suggestions as to the identity of the poisoner and *The Daily Telegraph* devoted several columns each day to 'The Death of Charles Bravo'. Day after day, the press continued to devote space to 'The Balham Mystery'[21] and, such was the growing strength of opinion from both professional and lay people alike, that it seemed inevitable that eventually an attempt would be made to instigate a second and more stringent inquiry to determine the real cause of the death.

On 15 May, Chief Inspector Clarke interviewed Florence once more - this time at the police station in Brighton where he requested and received permission to make a search of The Priory and its grounds. This development was ominous for it was now abundantly clear that the police suspected murder. Florence, distressed and feeling besieged by the publicity and unrest, was persuaded by her father to take the initiative in the drama - she instructed her solicitor to insert an announcement in the press. It appeared in a dozen newspapers on Tuesday, 16 May, and offered £500 to 'any one who will prove the sale of the said antimony or tartar emetic in such a manner as will throw satisfactory light on the mode by which Mr Bravo came by his death'.

That same day, it was announced that the Home Secretary was considering all the evidence in the case with a view to opening a fresh inquiry. This spawned a further flood of letters and articles in the press and the principal participants also received numerous,

21 *The Balham Mystery*: a contemporary illustrated pamphlet issued in seven weekly parts, costing one penny each.

and in some instances, bizarre, letters from the public.

The police also had quite a collection. One writer suggested that *'the woman calling herself Mrs Cox and companion to Mrs Bravo should be subjected to a medical examination and the real sex ascertained'.* The writer added, *'It may be, and the idea is quite feasible, that she is a male in female disguise, for obvious reasons.'*

Mrs Cox received a number of letters, many of which she found intimidating. One was accompanied by a drawing of her hanging from a gibbet. Another letter informed Chief Inspector Clarke that Florence had been seen driving with Dr Gully in Brighton on the day after Charles's funeral, despite the fact that she was in Balham that day. Via local gossip, the police soon learned of Florence's affair with Dr Gully and his name had become fully integrated in all the gossip and speculation surrounding the case. Clearly, there were a great many questions still unanswered.

A letter from an anonymous barrister appeared in *The Daily Telegraph*, rejecting the idea of suicide and accident, leaving one possibility only - murder.

'Now in the first place,' he wrote, *'a large dose of tartar emetic is not the kind of thing that goes straying about a house casually. Ladies paint their eyebrows with antimony and I believe they dye their hair with it, but it is by a very unusual mischance indeed that a poisonous dose of the wife's hair dye should find its way into her husband's soup! The hypothesis of accident is as absurd as that of suicide.*

'....a man does not commit suicide,' the article continued, *'with thirty grains of tartar emetic [a particularly painful death]. Similarly, thirty grains of tartar emetic do not go straying about at random in an ordinary and well-regulated household.'*

Meanwhile, in Brighton, Mrs Cox was getting worried. It was clear that the jury, by reaching an open verdict, had not believed her statement about Charles having taken poison. Unable to contain her disquiet any longer, she wrote to Dr Harrison saying that *'the reports and comments in the papers make me most unhappy. I do wish you would try to remember what I said to you about the poison'.*

Dr Harrison's reply, however, was far from reassuring:

> 'I am willing to do my best to relieve your mind, but you did not use the word poison to me, nor did you tell me that he had told you he had taken it; but you did tell me that he had taken chloroform....'

Disturbing, too, was the news that Mr A K Stephenson, Solicitor to the Treasury, had taken charge of the case and had received the results of the search of The Priory and its grounds. In the meantime, extensive enquiries continued and more than thirty individuals were interviewed - doctors, maids, grooms and chemists. The two persons most closely connected with the death, however, Florence and Mrs Cox, had not been asked to give statements - with the obvious implication that they were the prime suspects.

Taking her father's advice once more, Florence and the companion travelled to London on 1 June, where both women made voluntary statements to Mr Stephenson. Their portrayal of Charles Bravo differed greatly from the congenial, devil-may-care sort of chap depicted in the press and by his friends. In Florence's statement, she detailed her marriage to Alexander Ricardo and then went on to say that, although her affair with Dr Gully had been quite innocent and she had not seen him since her marriage, Charles was insanely jealous and constantly referred to the past. She emphasised her husband's ill-humour on the night he collapsed, suggesting that the trouble with the horse and the loss of the money on the Stock Exchange might have been sufficient to induce the idea of suicide.

Mrs Cox's statement, however, went further. She started by admitting that, in an attempt to protect Florence's reputation, she had not told the whole truth at the inquest. She said that whereas she had originally said that Charles's words to her were, *'I have taken poison. Don't tell Florence'*, he had actually said he had taken poison *'for Dr Gully'*.

Having said this, Mrs Cox, in a perfect example of her duplicity, added that her mistress's relationship with the doctor was, 'though imprudent, I conscientiously believed, entirely of an innocent nature'. She, too, described Charles as a passionately jealous man and whenever he and his wife quarrelled, the obsequious companion said, she 'always tried to make the peace between them'.

She also detailed a number of occasions when the couple had fought, saying that Charles had called Florence 'a selfish pig' and said he despised himself for ever marrying her. Casting herself as the kindly mediator, she said that during one such argument, it was only her intervention that prevented him from leaving the house for good. She depicted Charles as a mean, arrogant and cruel man, a martinet subject to unreasonable temper tantrums.

'He often said how he hated Dr Gully and wished him dead,' Mrs Cox confided. 'These sudden passions seemed to overtake him, because at other times he was quite pleasant. He was jealous of Dr Gully, though he knew everything before marriage.'

The image of Charles Bravo conjured up by Mrs Cox was clearly designed to persuade the authorities that the relationship between the Bravos was a turbulent one and Charles, a volatile and irrational man obsessed with his wife's past, might well, whilst in the throes of jealousy, decide to end his suffering by suicide. The picture both women had sought to conjure, however, was in complete contrast to that portrayed by the servants and family and friends who regularly visited The Priory. They also failed to realise that the very same marital strife of which they spoke provided equal support for a theory of murder.

The two statements, the evidence concerning the unsatisfactory inquest and the results of the exhaustive police investigation, were then submitted to the Home Office. Under growing pressure from, not only the Bravo family, but virtually the whole British press, the verdict of the inquest held at The Priory was eventually quashed and a new inquiry ordered.

In the meantime, there was a dramatic change in Florence Bravo's household. Soon after she returned to Brighton after making her Treasury statement, she became very ill, the local doctor referring to it as a 'brain fever' caused by hysteria and delayed shock. She was also drinking heavily and, for reasons never revealed, the unthinkable happened - she sacked Mrs Cox. The ingratiating companion had somehow fallen from favour and was unceremoniously banished. The friendship between the two women, which had been so intimate, had now been severed. After hurrying to The Priory to collect her belongings, Mrs Cox went to Birmingham, where she took lodgings in Villa Road, Handsworth.

Some hint of a possible cause for the sudden rift may be gleaned from a letter Mrs Cox subsequently wrote to Dr Harrison, in which she said that 'Mrs C.Bravo has told me several times that she thought had a stomach pump been used, Mr C Bravo's life might have been saved. I told her you told me afterwards it was impossible to use...'

The underlying anxiety in this letter is plain. Clearly, she hoped the doctor could absolve her from any blame. Did Florence somehow suspect that the emergency treatment given by Mrs Cox when Charles collapsed was, to say the least, ineffectual? Or was the cause of their rift the fact that the companion had been callous enough to introduce the name of Dr Gully in her statement, with all the shameful repercussions she knew it would cause?

Florence only saw Mrs Cox once more - at a contingency meeting of the Campbell family in London on 7 July to discuss the forthcoming inquest. Mrs Cox travelled from Birmingham to be there; also present was Frederick Rowe, the butler at The Priory. Afterwards, he was said to have told Mr Willis, proprietor of The Bedford Hotel, that 'the old woman has got herself into a good deal of trouble from not telling the truth'.

Whereas the first inquest into Charles Bravo's death was virtually a private affair, programmed to record a convenient verdict of suicide, the second inquiry was held with extensive publicity. The press coverage was immense. Nearly every newspaper in the land reported the protracted proceedings verbatim and *ad nauseam*; no detail was too dull or irrelevant for a public enthralled by the whole affair - especially, of course, when Florence was questioned mercilessly on the subject of her shocking liaison with Dr Gully.

The coroner, having had his knuckles soundly rapped by the law lords for his mishandling of the first inquest, was anxious to suppress nothing that may have been even slightly relevant, to the extent that it resembled, not simply an inquest to ascertain the cause of death, but a full-blown and sensational trial of all the characters involved.

The Crown was represented by Mr John Gorst, QC, and Mr Harry Poland, assisted by the Attorney General, Sir John Holker.[22] Conscious that his daughter was, however obliquely, under suspicion, Robert Campbell had wisely hired Sir Henry James, QC, one-time Solicitor-General and Attorney General, at a phenomenal fee of 100 guineas a day. He also enlisted the services of Mr Murphy, QC, on behalf of Mrs Cox at a cost of a further 50 guineas a day.

Acting for Mr Joseph Bravo was the monocled Mr George Lewis, a ruthless examiner who received a fee of £1000 for his services. In addition to the lucrative rewards on offer, his participation in the case served as the springboard for a highly successful legal career. Finally, now that his name was before the authorities, Dr Gully took the wise precaution of instructing Mr Sergeant Parry to watch the proceedings on his behalf.

The venue for the inquest was the billiards room above The Bedford Hotel, in Balham, a short distance from The Priory. Huge crowds gathered early on the morning of 11 July - fashionable society ladies and their escorts alongside the locals who came to gawp at the central characters in the sensational drama in their midst - all of them eager to watch the arrival of the legal dignitaries before scrambling to find a place along the public benches. The fight for seats caused a great deal of pushing and shoving and although a considerable number gained access, many more were turned away. At one stage, it was feared that the floor would give way and a surveyor was brought in to estimate the effect of the extra load.

In complete contrast to the first inquest, the second inquiry was to run for twenty-three days, during which a great many witnesses were called to give evidence. In the main, they reiterated details of

22 John Gorst, Harry Poland and George Lewis subsequently received knighthoods.

the tragedy already familiar to those who had scrutinised their daily newspapers - but there were one or two surprises and, towards the end of the proceedings, when it was the turn of Florence Bravo, Mrs Cox and Dr Gully to give evidence, the public, gripped by an insatiable fascination for the case, was rewarded with some startling revelations.

During the examination of those who had been close to Charles Bravo, it was evident that he had been a lively and intelligent young man. According to Joseph Bravo, he was always full of fun and showed no tendency to self-destruction - on the contrary, the court was told, he considered suicide to be an act of cowardice and had often debated the point with his stepfather. Nor did he have any financial worries, knowing that he could always turn to his family for money. He was invariably in good health and spirits - except for that bout of sickness early in March - and had been until the day he was poisoned.

A fellow barrister, John Atkinson, who had known Charles since their Oxford days, had this to say:

> 'I noticed that he always drank a very large drink of cold water. In fact, I have never seen him go to bed without doing so. He very often took it from the water bottle in his room and almost invariably without using a tumbler.'

Describing Charles's character, he said: 'He was the last man on earth to commit suicide. He was better acquainted than any other barrister I know with medicine and medical jurisprudence. He was a very clear-headed man with a great deal of common sense and very little sentiment. No feeling for any woman would make him take a painful and uncertain poison, the effects of which he was thoroughly acquainted with. I also know he was in no money difficulty.'

Royes Bell described him as a truthful man - rather outspoken in fact - and certainly not the sort to keep quiet if he thought he had been poisoned. Furthermore, insisted Bell, as he and Charles had been such close friends for twenty-five years, had he suspected anyone of poisoning him, he would have denounced them without the slightest hesitation.

'During the three days I was with him before his death,' Royes Bell assured the court, 'there was nothing in his conduct, demeanour or language which could induce me to believe that he had committed suicide.'

He was also quite adamant that Charles and Florence were happily married, saying: 'When she came in early in the morning [during his illness] he kissed her and used some French expressions. He appeared pleased to see her and commissioned me to ask his mother 'to be kind to Florence'.'

When questioned about life at The Priory, the young maid-servant, Mary Ann Keeber, who had been very fond of her master, also felt that Mr and Mrs Bravo had lived 'very happily together'. Despite living as she did, in such close proximity to the couple, she had never seen any sign of jealousy or heard Charles berating the name of Dr Gully. The maid told the court that when Charles Bravo was taken ill her mistress was 'very much distressed.'

The butler, Frederick Rowe also said that he never heard the Bravos quarrel.

'I saw a great deal of Mr and Mrs Bravo and they appeared to live very happily together,' he said.

When Charles collapsed in the spare room, Mrs Bravo was in a terrible state. The housemaid had told him that she was running about in her nightclothes so, for decency's sake, he had remained at the foot of the stairs. When she ran downstairs to summon help, she was shouting very loudly;

'She was running screaming along the passage with the housemaid,' he said.

Mr Carlyle Willoughby, who had known Charles for several years, was also of the opinion that the marriage had been a happy one. Charles, he said, was very open about such things and spoke freely to him about the marriage. Willoughby had been so convinced that Charles was the 'most unlikely person to commit suicide' that he felt compelled to contact the police.

Great sympathy was felt for Mrs Campbell, Florence's mother, as she gave evidence, telling the court that her daughter had 'cried very much, appearing to be stunned' after Charles had died. The doctors who attended him also testified to Florence's evident distress. Dr Moore said that she was 'very much grieved' and, despite being in great pain, Charles had treated her with spontaneous affection.

'I saw no trace of temper between them,' the doctor continued, 'and from the time he recovered consciousness to the time I left, I saw nothing but affectionate intercourse between them.'

Dr Harrison also referred to Florence's anguish, and, disagreeing with Joseph Bravo, who said she did not seem very concerned, he saw 'no sign of feigning on her part' saying that 'her grief seemed quite genuine'. He also testified once more that Mrs Cox did not tell him that Charles had said he had taken poison. If she persisted in saying otherwise, he suggested, using a polite euphemism, she was 'mistaken'.

The fact that Mrs Cox had not mentioned poison until four hours later, when Charles had regained consciousness, had particularly annoyed Royes Bell, who had said to her:

'It's no good sending for doctors if you don't tell them what is the matter!'

Questioned further on the subject of Mrs Cox, he said that he knew for a fact that Charles had always treated her kindly.

When Joseph Bravo was asked to specify the exact nature of Mrs Cox's position at The Priory, he said:

'Mrs Cox was Florence's companion. She had a salary and she had a seat at his table...one way or another my son estimated the probable cost to him would be £300 or £400 a year. I agreed with him that it was not a wise thing to tax his establishment with that charge. I suggested that she should go to Jamaica but she declined to go.'

Frederick Rowe described Mrs Cox's function at The Priory was 'getting anything Mrs Bravo wished for. She used to be always in attendance on Mrs Bravo and going out shopping in the carriage. She was always with Mrs Bravo.'

Even when Charles and Florence went to bed, which was usually about nine-thirty, Mrs Cox would often remain in her mistress's dressing room, sorting and mending her clothes.

Mary Ann Keeber also spoke of Mrs Cox's devoted attendance on Florence Bravo. It was her habit, she said, to sit by her bedside during her miscarriages, watching over her until she was asleep. On the night Mr Bravo collapsed, Mary Ann had run to Mrs Bravo's bedroom where she found her mistress asleep and Mrs Cox, still dressed in the outdoor clothes she had worn to Worthing, sitting motionless on a small stool between the bed and the door. The door of the bedroom was little more than four feet from the landing where Charles Bravo had screamed for hot water. There was an outer, green baize door to the bedroom but the maid could not remember whether she had closed both doors before going to fetch the little dog from Mrs Cox's room. Despite the close proximity to the landing, however, Mrs Cox appeared not to have heard a thing.

Several days of the inquiry were given over to a meticulous examination of the medical witnesses during which they gave detailed accounts of their unsuccessful treatment of Charles Bravo. Dr Payne explained the post-mortem findings, confirming that Charles Bravo was not suffering from any disease at the time of his death. Royes Bell, who attended the post-mortem with the other doctors in the case, expressed his surprise that the intestines were not excessively inflamed. If the poison that caused Charles Bravo's death had been the first dose he had received he would have expected to see far more extensive inflammation.

Unquestionably, it was a lethal dose of antimony, possibly as much as 40 grains that had been the cause of death. Ten grains were found in the vomit gathered from the leads, the rest had passed into the stomach and from there it had entered the bloodstream, pervaded the whole system, and finally caused a protracted and agonising death. Because of its emetic effect, death by antimonial poisoning was fairly uncommon. If taken with food it would usually be ejected almost immediately, thus preventing it from passing into the system. [Small doses were sometimes used to curb excessive drinking and some writers on the case have suggested that Charles was dosing

Florence in this way and poisoned himself by accident].[23]

After giving a thorough account of his analysis of vomit and organs Professor Redwood also gave the court a resume of the nature and properties of antimony or tartar emetic. In the form of a white powder, he said, it was easily dissolved in water, more so, if the water was warm. In its dilute form, it would be completely tasteless and would not even cause a burning sensation in the throat. Several members of the jury were persuaded to take a small solution of tartar emetic into their mouths for a few minutes without suffering any ill effects. The professor went on to discount the theory that Charles took the poison in either the food or the wine at dinner. Had it been in his burgundy (the ladies were drinking sherry) he would, being something of a wine connoisseur, have noticed the turgid reaction in his glass.

As for the food, the whole household partook of the same food without being harmed - besides which, he said, had this been the vehicle for the poison, Charles would have vomited violently within minutes, even before he reached the morning room. It seemed more than likely, went on Professor Redwood, that the poison was in the water bottle (a glass carafe with a tumbler on top which Charles always kept by his bedside and which Mary Ann filled with fresh water each night). It was Charles's *'inveterate habit'* to dispense with the tumbler and quaff the whole draft in one go. Drunk in this way, he would have been quite unaware that the water contained a lethal solution of tartar emetic - as much as forty grains, enough to kill a horse.

But how did the killer obtain the tartar emetic? During the police enquiries every 'Sale of Poison' register in every chemist shop for miles around (including shops in Worthing and Brighton) had been meticulously checked. Not one had recorded selling tartar emetic to anyone remotely connected with the tragedy. Could it be that the poison that killed Charles Bravo was already at hand in The Priory?

23 A Mr Ponsford Raymond claimed to have sold Charles Bravo six packets of his 'miraculous' Heymen's Remedy through the post. Containing a small amount of antimony it was sold as a cure for alcoholism.

Next to be called to the witness box was the groom, George Griffiths (now married to Florence's maid, Fanny Plascot) formerly in charge of the stables at The Priory until, that is, he was sacked by Charles Bravo for reckless driving. He freely admitted that he had bought antimony for Dr Gully when he worked for him in Malvern. Acting on a recommendation in *The Pocket Farrier,* he always used it on his horses when they suffered from worm infestation - it was also good for maintaining their glossy coats. A proof of sale, dated June 1869, bearing the names of both Dr Gully and Griffiths, was produced in court, though the groom, being somewhat inarticulate and possessing a very poor memory, proved a most unsatisfactory witness.[24]

Under further examination, however, it was eventually established that, unknown to Florence Bravo, when he came London to work for her, he continued to use antimony - and in the form of tartar emetic, a white powder, not the black or liver antimony usually used in stables. Although he had brought with him from Malvern the antimony he had purchased for Dr Gully - enough for 200 treatments - he admitted that he had bought even more from a couple of chemist shops in Balham. He could not account for all the antimony he'd bought as the horses were rarely ill but swore that he had thrown away all the antimony in his possession when he left The Priory on 3 January, more than three months before Charles Bravo's death.

With the knowledge of Dr Gully's use of tartar emetic still fresh in their minds, the eager spectators packed into The Bedford Hotel on Thursday, 27 July, to hear the evidence of the enigmatic companion, Jane Cox. Despite the stifling summer heat in the crowded courtroom, she arrived dressed entirely in black and wearing a rather pert, feathered hat. Although appearing outwardly composed during her gruelling interrogation she frequently stroked the surface of the table with her gloved hand making tense, compulsive movements.

Throughout her testimony, she still insisted that she *had* mentioned poison to Dr Harrison - but without mentioning the words *'for Dr*

24 It was rumoured at the time that Dr Gully may also have used antimony at his clinic to procure abortions for his society clients.

Gully'. She had thought it best, she said, not to say anything to the local doctor for fear of the scandal. She admitted that she had not mentioned the vomit on the leads to any of the doctors treating Charles - until, that is, some four hours later, after Sir William Gull had confirmed that Charles Bravo was dying and there was no hope of recovery. She was questioned aggressively by George Lewis on this point and he also demanded to know why, if she *had* already told Dr Harrison about poison, she felt it necessary to tell Royes Bell the same thing several hours later. She was unable to give a satisfactory explanation for this.

Questioned at length about her meetings with Dr Gully and the bottle of laurel water he prescribed for Florence Bravo, it transpired that the small, fluted bottle had a white leather top and a red label marked 'Poison'. Gully had left it at her house in Lancaster Road with a note telling her not to worry about the word '*poison'* as it was not strong. As Florence had not needed it after all, Mrs Cox said she had put it away in her bedroom and had later (at the suggestion of Florence and her mother) thrown the contents away. She had kept the bottle, however, which she filled it with vinegar and kept on her dressing table. Asked point blank by Lewis whether she had tampered with the contents of the bottle, the companion answered firmly that she had not.

When she returned to The Priory, she said, after her trip to Worthing on the evening Charles Bravo was poisoned, it was about twenty minutes past seven. She had looked briefly into the morning room and seen Charles sitting with his head on his knees, looking drawn and out-of-sorts. She had gone straight up to her room but, as there was no time to change, she merely washed her hands before joining the others for dinner.

When asked why, knowing that Charles had taken poison, she had told the maid to throw away the vomit in the bowl instead of keeping it for the doctors to examine, she said 'so he would have a clean basin when he wanted it'. Her credibility was further stretched when she insisted that both Florence and Charles wanted her to stay on at The Priory and repeated much of her Treasury statement in which she represented herself as a saintly and indispensable asset to the household. Yet, she told the court, in answer to some vigorous questioning by George Lewis, she did not know of Charles's 'inveterate habit' of taking a huge quaff of water before retiring and, as far as she knew, nobody touched or emptied the water bottle that night. To this, she added disdainfully, that it was the housemaid's job to attend to water bottles, not hers.

Much to their annoyance, the crowds of women who had gathered outside The Bedford Hotel on the morning of Tuesday, 1 August, were turned away as the coroner had ordered that *'no ladies or children'* were to be admitted. The men were delighted, of course, as they raced up the stairs to grab a seat, for it was clear that more scurrilous revelations were expected when the interrogation of Mrs Cox was resumed.

The companion was questioned at great length about the relationship between Florence Bravo and Dr Gully but maintained a sanctimonious and non-committal stance. Pursing her lips and lowering her eyes behind her gold-rimmed spectacles, she continually stroked the table and refused to admit that she had known that her mistress and the doctor were lovers. With her false modesty and sanctimonious posturing, she made an infuriating witness. She was, however, highly efficient at 'stone walling' and her evasive remarks taxed George Lewis to the limit. Finally losing his temper he demanded:

'Did you know that Dr Gully was Mrs Ricardo's lover? You were there. You lived with her for four years. You must have had a shrewd idea. I ask you now, having had all the experience you have had, did you not know, sooner or later, that Dr Gully was Mrs Ricardo's lover?'

After a long pause, the companion said: 'Yes, I think I did.' She denied, however, that an abortion was ever performed by Gully insisting that Florence was suffering from a 'sort of stomach tumour', which he removed. Finally, Mrs Cox was asked why, if Charles Bravo had asked her not to tell Florence he had taken poison, the first person he called for when he was taken ill was his wife?

Mrs Cox thought for a moment and then said, 'It never struck me.'

This simple reply concluded Mrs Cox's testimony, leaving her free to go, making way for her former mistress whose interrogation was scheduled for the following day.

It was not until the afternoon of the next day, Thursday, 3 August, that Florence Bravo, dubbed by the press 'the beautiful young widow of Balham', made her entrance on the arm of her brother.[25] She was heavily veiled and in deep mourning and her hand trembled as she took the oath. Once seated, she lifted the veil and sighed deeply. Her face was pale but composed and one reporter noted that the colour of her hair had changed from deep auburn to 'canary yellow'.

During her evidence on the first day, she said that 'criminal intimacy' between Dr James Gully and herself had happened only once - when they went to the hydropathic centre at Kissingen in 1872. The following day, however, she admitted this was not the only occasion they had made love although she had misled Charles into thinking it was. She also admitted lying in her Treasury statement (although she was not then under oath) because her mother, who must have been devastated by these revelations in court, had not known the true nature of the relationship until two or three days before. Several times during her evidence, Florence began to weep pitifully and the proceedings had to be adjourned until she had composed herself.

Asked whether Charles had been a difficult man to live with, she said she did not wish to say 'anything against him' and again began to cry. Questioned further regarding her husband's temperament, she admitted that he had struck her once but that he had 'burst into tears immediately he had done it.'

'He was only like a child,' she said. 'He was excessively sorry for it afterwards.'

With regard to their alleged disputes over money, she put the blame firmly on his mother. She was forever interfering with the running of their household and urging him to make retrenchments

25 Despite tremendous pressure from the Campbell family and society in general, Florence's brother William and his wife, Augusta, continued to support Florence throughout her life.

but when they were left to themselves they never argued about money. She went on to describe the Easter weekend before the tragedy - his parents were on holiday and they were left in peace to enjoy an idyllic interlude entertaining some of their friends. She went on to say that she had been 'utterly exhausted' the night Charles collapsed and had fallen asleep the moment she got into bed. She had not heard her husband's cries for help. She wished she had, she said, as she would have gone to him at once. By the time she was told he had been taken ill, he was already unconscious and being attended to by Mrs Cox.

Asked when she knew for certain that Charles had been poisoned, she said:

'When Sir William Gull came. I should not have sent for him if I had known he had taken poison. He would have been of no use.'[26]

When she had heard the doctors use the word poison, she had assumed they had meant a dangerous dose of chloroform or laudanum, not an irritant poison. As to treating her horses, she said that she 'totally disapproved of horses taking medicine' and was not aware that Griffiths was using antimony on them.

Concerning Dr Gully's little bottle of laurel water, which George Lewis obviously thought suspicious, Florence said that she did not ask Mrs Cox to get it for her, nor had she ever touched or tampered with it for any reason whatsoever. In fact, she said,

'Mrs Cox took the bottle away immediately. I never had it in my possession.'

After Charles had died and following Mr Joseph Bravo's vindictive remarks about Florence's homeopathic remedies being dangerous 'poisons', her mother had asked Mrs Cox to hand it over so that she could throw it away. But Mrs Cox resisted any attempt to retrieve the bottle, and had refused to hand it over, saying that she would destroy the contents herself.

26 Sir William Gull was 'the first opinion in London' as far as diagnosing disease was concerned. Cases where poison was involved were not his particular forte.

On Tuesday, 8 August[27] Florence took her seat opposite the imperious figure of George Lewis and braced herself for his cross-examination. She denied, as Mrs Cox had done, any knowledge of Charles's habit of drinking a large quantity of water before he went to sleep. But she did admit that he had 'found fault' with her alcoholic consumption for he 'had a horror of ladies taking too much wine'.

Passages were then read from some of Charles's love letters during which Florence bent her head and wept. Despite her distress, George Lewis was quite merciless and proceeded to prove (by means of an incriminating letter to her maid) that she had lied when she said that her affair with Dr Gully did not commence while she was still married to Alexander Ricardo. Adjusting his monocle, he glared menacingly across the table at her. He seemed impervious to her tears and the humiliation he was subjecting her to, surrounded as she was in that sweltering heat by eager spectators, some of whom were only too happy to witness her shame. At one point, she retaliated angrily and demanded to know how all these questions related to her husband's death.

'Mr Lewis,' she cried, 'I have been sufficiently pained and humiliated, and I appeal to the coroner and the jury, who are gentlemen and Britons, to protect me!'

But she was not without her supporters for this outburst was followed by loud applause and Florence burst into tears.

'I am willing to tell you anything to help you find out how Mr Charles Bravo met his death,' she said, 'but with Dr Gully you have nothing to do, and I refuse to answer any further questions. It seems to be impossible that a woman can love a man without doing what is wrong with him, according to you.'

When she had recovered her composure, Florence insisted that she did not know of Mrs Cox's meetings with Dr Gully nor had she even heard of laurel water.

Questioned a little later by Mr Gorst, representing the Crown,

27 It was decided that Florence Bravo would not be called to give evidence on the Bank Holiday Monday to avoid the gawping crowds, many of whom regularly gathered outside The Priory to stare ghoulishly at its walls. A special guard was put on it during the holiday weekend.

Florence said that her affection for Dr Gully had not diminished in any way. As she said this, she broke into unrestrained sobbing once more. She said that they had parted with 'a very painful interview', adding that she did 'not wish to remember the contents of the angry letter' he had sent to her.

She became angry again when questioned about intimate details of her marriage to Charles and when asked how she felt about her ex-companion, Mrs Cox, she became extremely agitated and paused for a considerable time before answering. Then, with dignity, she replied:

'I think she might have spared me a great many of these painful inquiries that have been made.'

This epitaph to the close friendship that had once existed between the two women ended Florence Bravo's evidence and she left the room on the arm of her brother.

Her examination had been long and turbulent and her complex emotional state was painfully obvious. She had cried pathetically over her husband's memory and yet had vigorously defended her ex-lover. On the other hand, she had dismissed Jane Cox, with whom she had lived on the most intimate terms, with cold indifference.

The following day, the jostling crowds inside and outside The Bedford Hotel were rewarded with the appearance of the last witness to be called - Dr James Manby Gully.

At sixty-six, still a sophisticated and distinguished figure, he entered the courtroom smiling, exuding an air of extreme self-confidence. He was questioned fully on the little bottle of laurel water he prescribed for Florence and naturally denied that he had put any tartar emetic into it. When George Lewis questioned him about his affair with Florence, many of his replies were sardonic, flippant even, and he gave no indication whatever that he regretted the scandalous affair. Although he admitted to being upset when Florence broke off their relationship, he swore that he knew nothing of her life at The Priory after she had married Charles Bravo - nor, he insisted, did he bear any grudge against the latter.

Dr Gully, who had remained composed even slightly bemused

whilst giving evidence, was the last witness to be called in what had been a long and painful inquiry. At last it was over, but for the three persons most involved - Florence Bravo, Jane Cox and Dr Gully - there was a further agonising wait of two days while the jury considered its verdict, which was as follows:

> We find that Mr Charles Delauney Turner (Bravo) did not commit suicide, that he did not meet his death by misadventure, but that he was wilfully murdered by the administration of tartar emetic, but there is not sufficient evidence to fix the guilt upon any person or persons.

In other words, the killer was still free.

Sadly, the aftermath of Charles Bravo's death was equally tragic for his widow. Although Dr Gully was subsequently penalised for his part in the scandal, in that he was refused membership of a number of clubs and academic societies and had his name struck off the Medical Register, he remained in Balham, cared for by his family and the butler, until he died in March 1883.

As for Florence, her life was ruined. She had been shamed beyond measure by the public exposure of her immorality and she sought comfort and oblivion in alcohol. She had been ostracised before her marriage to Charles but after his death society's rejection of her was complete and irrevocable.

Calling herself Mrs Turner, she rented a secluded house in Southsea and locked herself away. Eighteen months later, on 17 September, 1878, she died, having literally drunk herself to death at the age of thirty-three.

So many questions remain unanswered in this most baffling of all the great Victorian murder cases. Why, for instance, did Florence suddenly sack Mrs Cox? Did she suspect - or realise - that her faithful servant 'Janey' had killed her 'dearest Charlie'?

If so, why didn't she tell the police - or did she, perhaps, know or suspect that Dr Gully, of whom she was still fond, was also involved in some way? Did she maintain her silence to protect him, at the same time hating the sight of Mrs Cox whom she suspected of actually pouring the poison into Charles's water bottle? Unless, of course, her own guilt ensured her silence. Had she been guilty, however, one must suppose that the companion was also involved - and, if that were the case, the two women would undoubtedly have remained together as partners in crime, bound for ever by their complicity in the Bravo murder.

Although some writers on the case, and there have been many, have been convinced that Florence murdered her husband, it seems more likely that Jane Cox was the killer.[28] Like all the other servants in this book, she attacked when she was cornered, finding herself compelled to face a situation that was out of her control. She knew perfectly well that Charles had no intention of keeping her job open when she went to the West Indies to sort out her business affairs. She was in a cleft stick. If she didn't go, her sons' inheritance would be lost - yet, if she did go she would lose her lucrative job. Either way, it was only a matter of time before Charles, urged by his parents to economise, would have dispensed with her services. Now that Florence was married she was, after all, despite her inflated idea of her own importance, superfluous in the household. Gone were the days when, shunned by society, Florence had depended on her for company and support against the gossips. Once Florence married Charles, Mrs Cox was redundant, a costly and unnecessary indulgence.

Jane Cox, however, had no intention of being pushed aside. After all, the future prosperity of her sons was thrown into jeopardy when Florence married Charles - and there is no creature more dangerous under threat than a tiger with her cubs. And so it was with Jane Cox. She had to act.

As she saw it, only Charles Bravo stood in her way, someone who had led a privileged life and had never known the hardships she had endured. And, moreover, it was clear that Mrs Cox was emotionally

28 This theory is fully expounded in the author's book on the case: *Murder at The Priory: The Mysterious Poisoning of Charles Bravo*, co-author, Bernard Taylor.

attached to Florence, devoted to her, in fact, and now Charles had come between them. Not only that, he was the cause of her mistress's suffering – two miscarriages, one after the other – how Janey must have hated him!

She was, however, an extremely clever opportunist, and a two-faced woman if ever there was one, and had become accustomed to the luxurious lifestyle. She enjoyed an extremely generous salary and lived as part of the family in the beautiful surroundings of The Priory. When running errands for Florence, she had become used to being driven in a fine carriage, enjoyed good food and a plentiful supply of wine at every meal, her own room and licence to have her children 'home' from their private schools for the holidays.

After her years of penny-pinching as a poorly-paid governess, worrying about the welfare of her children and living in rented rooms, Mrs Cox was in clover from the moment she went to live with Florence - and she was reluctant to give it all up.

She must have planned the murder of Charles Bravo with consummate care. Having secured the tartar emetic from the stables while George Griffiths was in residence, she mixed the lethal solution with warm water in a small bottle - possibly using Dr Gully's laurel water bottle, complete with a red label marked POISON. This done, she locked it in her medicine chest and waited, biding her time.

Once she had spoken to Joseph Bravo about her dilemma, and he had told her frankly that her days at The Priory were numbered, she knew it was time to act. With murder very much on her mind, she had returned from her trip to Worthing and, on looking into the morning room she had seen Charles looking ill and out-of-sorts. He was in pain from the fall from the horse and suffering from neuralgia - now was her chance.

Hurrying upstairs to her room, she probably checked that the bottle of poison was still in her medicine chest and then simply washed her hands as there was no time to change for dinner. She knew that, while they were downstairs, the maid would be up to check the rooms, sort out Florence's night-tray and fill Charles's water bottle before going down to the kitchen to have her supper with the other servants. After that, no one in the house would touch the water bottle - except Charles.

Mrs Cox must have been relieved to note that her master's temper did not improve during the meal. He was clearly depressed, in pain and in no mood for small talk. When she tried to show him a picture of the house she had rented, he made some dismissive, and tragically prophetic remark, to the effect that he would not be going to Worthing. At this point, the butler noticed that Mrs Cox looked up sharply and stared at Charles over her gold-rimmed glasses. With murder foremost on her mind, had she wondered, for that split second, whether Charles had somehow guessed her thoughts?

As Florence was so tired, the two women went upstairs shortly after nine that evening. As soon as they reached the dressing room, Florence asked Mrs Cox to fetch some more wine. Was it then, while Florence was undressing, still weak, unsteady and befuddled by the bottle of sherry she had consumed, that Mrs Cox hurried up to her room, took the bottle containing the deadly solution and scuttled into the spare room where she knew Charles would be sleeping that night?

She was so intent on her task that she did not notice that one of Florence's little dogs had followed her up to her room and, on leaving, she had closed the door on it. She gave herself away when she told Mary Ann Keeber that the dog was probably up there. It could only have followed her up from the dressing room, where it had been with Florence and the other dog after dinner, proving that she went up to her room - but what for, if not the poison? The wine was downstairs in the dining room.

Quickly pouring some of the water from Charles's bottle into the bath-tub, she replaced it with the tartar emetic solution. Satisfied that there was no discernible difference in the appearance of the water, she replaced the tumbler, slipped the empty laurel water bottle in her pocket and hurried downstairs to fetch the wine from the dining room. By the time she got back, Florence was already undressed and her hair plaited for the night.

Florence, exhausted and inebriated, had fallen asleep immediately she crawled into bed. Mrs Cox, her brain in a turmoil at what she had just done and knowing what was about to happen, stayed where she was. Why else did she stay when Florence was already asleep? And with her old maid's modesty, knowing the house would soon be filled with doctors - and she certainly wouldn't allow the likes of Rowe, the butler, to see her in her nightclothes - she remained in her outdoor clothes, the ones she had worn since seven o'clock that morning. And so it was that she remained motionless on the stool by her mistress's bed, waiting - waiting for the piercing cry from Charles that she knew would surely come.

It seems likely that she had already tried to kill him in early March but she hadn't given him enough and only managed to make him very sick. She was determined to kill him outright the second time and would have succeeded if he hadn't thrown off some of the poison when he vomited so violently.

A detailed study of Mrs Cox's actions from the moment she found Charles collapsed by the window of the spare room, does much to illustrate her guilt. It appeared that she did everything in her power to aid his recovery when, in fact, the *opposite* was true. She did everything she could to allow the poison time to enter her victim's blood-stream and thereby cause his death.

She immediately sent the maid away on a number of errands, leaving her alone with her victim - even sending her to look for camphor when it was already in the room. While the maid was away, Mrs Cox emptied any poisoned water that remained in the water bottle into the bath-tub and, quickly fetching the jug of water from the landing, she rinsed it thoroughly and refilled it with fresh water. By the time Dr Harrison drank from it in the early hours of the morning it was perfectly harmless. Clearly, someone had refilled it with fresh water and it certainly wasn't the maid. There was no risk of discovery as Charles lay slumped on the floor, unconscious.

When the maid came back, Mrs Cox told her to empty the bath-tub in readiness for the arrival of the doctor and then busied herself by rubbing Charles's chest. Having seen Charles being sick out of the window just before he collapsed, and knowing that a great deal of antimony would be found in the vomited matter, she had no intention of mentioning it to anyone, least of all the doctors. She had also told the maid to throw away the second lot of vomit in the bowl, for the last thing she wanted was for the poison to be identified and an antidote given.

Of course, with such a massive dose of antimony, she had expected Charles to die outright but when this failed, she kept her head. She only told Sir William Gull about the vomit still on the leads *after* he had pronounced that Charles was dying. Likewise, she only came up with her evil allegation that Charles said he had taken poison when she knew he could not recover sufficiently to contradict her and, lest murder be suspected, it would possibly provide proof of suicidal intent.

It is difficult to imagine how, on the day of Charles Bravo's funeral, this cold and devious woman had the gall to fill the room with flowers and help the maids arrange the white lilies between the fingers of her victim. Whilst everyone involved that night spoke of Florence's anguish, not one witness recalled seeing Mrs Cox shed any tears for Charles Bravo.

One can but speculate whether Dr Gully played any part in her treachery? Despite the evidence he gave at the inquest, surely he must have resented the handsome young barrister who had usurped him? We cannot know whether, in fact, the little bottle he gave Mrs Cox contained tartar emetic, not laurel water. He would, of course, have known that tartar emetic in Charles's water bottle would prove an ideal murder weapon, provided, of course, it was given time to invade the system. Had he primed Mrs Cox with the best method of killing his rival? We shall never know.

It was certainly likely that Mrs Cox, if she mixed it herself, did use that particular bottle as a vehicle for the poison, merely because she was so reticent about it, refusing to hand it over after Charles's death - not because it was full of poison but because, of course, it was *empty* - proving that, as Florence had not used it, it had been used for something else. Had it still been filled with Dr Gully's harmless laurel water, she could have handed it over without any qualms whatever. And sometime during that dreadful night, did the devious companion slip up to her room (Dr Moore said that no one took any notice of Mrs Cox) thoroughly wash out the little bottle, fill it with vinegar, and keep it as a grim trophy, a chilling reminder of her triumph.

Yet, had she hoped that, by killing Charles, the future for herself and her boys would be secure and she and Florence would live happily together once more, it all went badly wrong. She gained nothing and lost everything she held dear in this country - her job, her home and her credibility. She was lucky not to lose her life.

In his extensively researched book, *Death At The Priory,* James Ruddick confirms that Mrs Cox was, at the time of the murder, in line to inherit three estates from her aunt, Margaret, in Jamaica – *Content, Endeavour* and *Carlton* – amounting to some thousand acres. Within months of Charles Bravo's death she had travelled to the West Indies to take charge of these properties, valued at approximately £6,800 - a fortune at the time.

Anyone who has studied this case must ask why, in the circumstances, would Mrs Cox have resorted to poisoning Charles Bravo to ensure her lucrative position as Florence Bravo's companion? Clearly, Mrs Cox knew of her expected inheritance as early as 1874 but she seemed reluctant to travel to Jamaica to consolidate the legacy. Undecided on the best course of action, she sought the advice of Joseph Bravo and he advised her to go without delay. But she was still unsure perhaps knowing that if she did Charles Bravo would definitely not reinstate her on her return. The key to her reluctance must have been two-fold – firstly, her loyalty to Florence of whom she had grown very fond. Could she leave her mistress in ill-health and in a stormy, even abusive marriage? More importantly, perhaps, her three young sons had settled well in their school: would she really want to uproot them and transport them to live on a remote pimento plantation in the West Indies before their prestigious English education was complete?

In addition, whilst working for Florence, Jane Cox had become accustomed to a life of ease, luxury even – was she prepared to give this up to live on a plantation thousands of miles from the country of her birth? The three properties – she inherited them in 1879 when her aunt Margaret died - would indeed ensure her sons' future solvency but the timing was all wrong. She needed to stay in England at least until her sons had reached maturity.

Henry and John Leslie Cox did, in fact, eventually settle in Jamaica where they farmed the vast family estates in the St Ann's district. The grand house, *Content*, on a pimento plantation, was the family home, whereas tea was grown on the *Carlton* plantation and coffee and tobacco was produced on the *Endeavour* estate. John Leslie married a Jamaican woman and some of their Creole descendants still live on the island.

We may never know who poured the lethal dose of antimony into Charles Bravo's water bottle that night. Clearly, both Florence and Mrs Cox knew what happened and closed ranks. If, as James Ruddick and others have suggested, it was Florence who poisoned her husband surely she would have kept Jane Cox with her when she went to live in Brighton, as her confidante-accomplice and trusted friend. The crime would have irrevocably cemented their allegiance. Yet, whatever Jane Cox had done so shocked and angered Florence that immediately after the humiliating inquest at Balham she dispensed with Mrs Cox, never spoke to her again, and literally drank herself to death. George Lewis, for one, was convinced Jane Cox was guilty of the murder of Charles Bravo.

Soon after the inquest, she went to the West Indies and it was assumed by previous writers that she remained there for the rest of her life. She did, in fact, return to England at some stage and it was rumoured that, at one time, she was working in a bank in Brighton. She died in 1917, in the village of Lee, in the borough of Lewisham, and is buried in an unmarked grave in Hither Green Cemetery. She was in her ninetieth year and, with her sanctimonious, self-centred callousness, she may even have died with a clear conscience.

Christine and Léa Papin

Maids of Horror

The case of the Papin sisters is one of the most shocking in the history of crime - strange, terrible, grotesque and, it seems, even to the murderers themselves, somehow inexplicable.

The year was 1933 and the setting for the crime was Le Mans, a small, provincial town in Western France, some 120 miles from Paris. On the evening of 2 February, Monsieur René Lancelin, an attorney, and his family, had planned to dine with friends. It had been decided that, rather than go home first, he would go directly to the friends' house that evening and there meet his wife, Marie, and their twenty-seven year old daughter, Geneviève.

By the time he got there, however, they had not arrived for the dinner engagement and, after waiting for some time, Monsieur Lancelin began to worry. He tried to contact them by telephone but received no answer. Seriously worried by now, he excused himself from the dinner party and hurried to his house, a somewhat sombre building with an expressionless facade, flat-fronted and shuttered, on the rue Bruyère.

To his surprise, he found the front door locked - from the inside. Stranger still, although there was a light in the upstairs room occupied by the two maids, twenty-eight year old Christine Papin and her twenty-one year old sister, Léa, the rest of the house was in darkness. He knocked several times on the front door and called out but there was no answer. Not a sound came from inside the house.

Monsieur Lancelin, filled now with a sense of foreboding, rang the local police. When two officers arrived, they broke into the house and, using a torch, accompanied Monsieur Lancelin through the rooms on the ground floor. There was no sign of Madame Lancelin or her daughter. Nor was there any noise; the house was ominously quiet - quiet as a grave.

Climbing the stairs to the first floor, Monsieur Lancelin's worst fears were soon realised. Confronting him in the beam of the torch was a truly appalling sight - it was the stuff of nightmares. The words of one of the police officers will best describe the scene:

'The corpses of Madame and Mademoiselle Lancelin were lying stretched out on the floor and were frightfully mutilated. Mademoiselle Lancelin's corpse was lying face downward, head bare, coat pulled up and with her knickers down, revealing deep wounds in the buttocks and multiple cuts in the calves. Madame Lancelin's body was lying on its back. The eyes had disappeared, she seemed no longer to have a mouth and all the teeth had been knocked out.'

'The walls and doors were covered with splashes of blood to a height of more than seven feet. On the floor we found fragments of bone and teeth, one eye, hair pins, a handbag, a key ring, an untied parcel, numerous bits of white, decorated porcelain and a coat button.'

A search of the immediate area produced a blood-stained kitchen knife, a badly-battered pewter pot and a bloodied hammer. Groceries, including a joint of meat, were found scattered on the landing and an eyeball lay on one of the stairs. One can barely imagine the feelings of Monsieur Lancelin as he followed the policemen up the next flight of stairs to the second floor. It was here that the two maids shared a room. From under the door there was the faint glow of a candle but not a sound came from inside. Unable to get a response to knocking on the door, a locksmith was called to break into the room. There, naked and huddled together in one of the beds, were the two servant-girls, Christine and Léa Papin. Christine, the elder of the two, immediately confessed to the killings. Her statement, part of which is quoted below, was taken down after her arrest and given in evidence at her subsequent trial:

'When Madame came back to the house, I informed her that the iron was broken again and that I had not been able to iron. She wanted to jump on me. My sister and I and our two mistresses were on the first-floor landing. When I saw that Madame Lancelin was going to jump on me, I leaped at her face and scratched out her eyes with my fingers. No, I made a mistake when I said that I leaped on Madame Lancelin. It was Mademoiselle Lancelin that I leaped on and it was her eyes that I scratched out.'

'Meanwhile, my sister, Léa, had jumped on Madame Lancelin and scratched her eyes out in the same way. After we had done this, they lay and crouched down on the spot. I then rushed down to the kitchen to fetch a hammer and a knife. With these two instruments, my sister and I fell upon our two mistresses. We struck at the head with the knife, hacked at the bodies and legs, and also struck with a pewter pot which was standing on a little table on the landing.'

'We exchanged one instrument for another several times. By that I mean that I would pass the hammer over to my sister so that she could hit with it while she handed me the knife, and we did the same with the pewter pot. The victims began to cry out but I don't remember that they said anything.'

'When we had done the job, I went to bolt the front door, and I also shut the vestibule door. I shut these doors because I wanted the police to find out our crime before our master. My sister and I then went and washed our hands in the kitchen because they were covered with blood.'

'We then went to our room, took off all our clothes, which were stained with blood, put on a dressing-gown, shut the door of our room with a key and lay down on the same bed. That's where you found us when you broke the door down.'

'I have no regrets or, rather, I can't tell you whether I have any or not. I'd rather have had the skin of my mistresses than they should have had mine or my sister's. I did not plan my crime and I didn't feel hatred towards them, but I don't put up with the sort of gesture that Madame Lancelin was making at me that evening.'

Léa, the younger of the Papin sisters, also made a statement which gave a similar account of the murder:

'Like my sister,' she said, 'I affirm that we had not planned to kill our mistresses. The idea came suddenly when we heard Madame Lancelin scolding us. I don't have any more regrets for the criminal act we have committed than my sister does. Like her, I would rather have had my mistresses' skins than their having ours.'

Incredibly, such terrible violence was triggered by an object as innocuous as the iron mentioned in Christine's statement. Léa had broken it sometime in January and on 1 February, the day before the murder, when Madame Lancelin came to pay the girls she withheld five francs from Léa's wages to pay for the repair of the iron.

The following day, while their mistress was out of the house, the sisters used the iron again and somehow or other managed to break it for the second time, fusing all the lights in the house. Accustomed to being scolded for the most petty trifles and fined for any breakages, the sisters were understandably apprehensive about Madame's reaction when she came back to find the ironing still not done and the house in darkness. Yet could this relatively trivial domestic occurrence have really been the precursor to an outburst of such violent savagery?

It was evident when examined by the magistrates after their arrest that, contrary to speculation, the sisters did not hate their employers. Léa did admit, however, that Madame Lancelin could sometimes be harsh.

'Life with the Lancelins was hard,' she said. 'We never went out. Madame was haughty and distant. She only spoke to us when she wanted to scold us. She was always spying on us behind our backs and counting the lumps of sugar that remained in the basin. When the housework was done in the morning Madame Lancelin would put on white gloves and run her fingers over the furniture to see if the dusting had been done carefully and whether any speck of dust remained. If we had the misfortune to break the slightest thing, she at once took it out of our wages. It couldn't go on. It had to come to an end. We were too unhappy.'

In the course of the police investigations, statements made by

Monsieur Lancelin and others familiar with the Lancelin household, left no doubt that, compared to many other girls in service, their position in the rue Bruyère was perfectly acceptable. Their wages were quite adequate for their needs; more so, in fact, for in the seven years they had worked for the Lancelin family, they had managed to save twenty-four thousand francs. Besides being given the same food as their employers - which was not a common practice - they also enjoyed the luxury of electric lighting and heating in their bedroom.

Despite the girls' comments about being unhappy with their situation, they had never made any attempt to leave and seek employment elsewhere. Questioned at length, Léa's resentment of Madame Lancelin's pettiness became clear, whereas Christine felt that her mistress was quite right to be strict with them. In fact, she said that, in her position as maid, she expected to be reprimanded and, if necessary, punished.

Of course, such a bizarre and sensational murder was a gift for the French press and speculation was fuelled by reports of remarks attributed to Christine on her arrest;

'I'm not mad,' she had said. 'I know what I've done. We've been servants long enough. We've showed them our power.'

Was this, then, a simple breakdown of the master-servant relationship, worthy of note merely because of the violence involved and the fact that it ended in the death of two women? Or was it more complex than that? The hint of a sexual element in some of the wounds inflicted on the two women suggested that this might be so.

Dubbed the *'diabolical sisters'* the press soon began referring to the girls as *'the monsters of Le Mans'* or the *'lambs who had become wolves'* and hinted at the *'indescribable'* nature of the wounds inflicted on their victims. It was also suggested that Christine and Léa had a lesbian relationship; perhaps the fact that they had been found naked together in bed, added some credence to this speculation. This was further fuelled by their strange behaviour after their arrest. They were taken to the local police station and, in the weeks that followed, they were questioned at length by a number of officials and medical men including the public prosecutor, the examining magistrate, the police and several psychiatrists.

Although they were repeatedly asked why, when Madame Lancelin and her daughter returned to the house about five o'clock that afternoon, they didn't go first to the kitchen to off-load the groceries - why did they go straight up the stairs? Had they been, it was suggested, creeping upstairs to spy on the two maids in the bedroom on the second floor? But surely, the two women would have first rid themselves of their packages, the better to creep quietly up the stairs?

Both Christine and Léa remained silent when asked to suggest a reason - but they did admit that Madame Lancelin and her daughter had come back unexpectedly. It was their original intention, they said, to go straight to their friends' house where they would meet Monsieur Lancelin for dinner.

But the sisters were adamant about one thing - they accepted joint responsibility for the murders and insisted that they had both participated equally in the killings - and, although it was Christine who had run down to the kitchen to fetch the knife, both had used it in the attack. Likewise, they had both used the pewter pot, knife and hammer alternately during the slaughter and both women had dug out the eyes of their victims with their fingers.

Investigations into the early life of these extraordinary women revealed a background of neglect and deprivation, in a family that today would be defined as acutely dysfunctional. Born in 1905, Christine was brought up by an aunt until the age of seven at which time she was placed in the Convent of the Good Shepherd in Le Mans. Her elder sister, Emilia, of whom she was very fond, was already there and eventually became a nun. Christine seemed fairly settled during this time and was a well-behaved pupil, with an especial aptitude for embroidery.

In the meantime, her mother, Clémence Derée, also in service, had left her drunken husband, Gustave. Unfortunately, as is so often the case, having thus far abdicated responsibility for her daughter, she decided, when Christine reached the age of fifteen (and therefore able to earn a wage) to remove her from the convent. Despite her protests, the mother put her to work as a maid, little realising the damaging effect of separating her from her sister, Emilia, who had become essential to her, both as a substitute mother and a childhood companion.

Christine stayed in her first job for three years but was eventually made to leave by her mother, who considered her wages too low. She found a number of other positions, always urging the girl to earn more money - some of which, she, of course, took for herself. She did the same with young Léa in 1927, finding her a job with the Lancelins where Christine was already employed; it was here that their solidarity and inter-dependence grew to sustain them in their arid and lonely existence.

As for Léa, she had also been farmed out at an early age, living with an uncle before being deposited in an orphanage. She remained in the institution until she was thirteen and was considered to be, though not very bright, a good, reliable worker - just the sort of girl to fit easily into domestic service. Only once did she kick against the petty restrictions of institutional life by making a threatening remark to the Sister Superior. She, too, must have felt tremendous relief to be free of the orphanage, especially when she joined Christine at the Lancelins; they formed an intense and emotional bond, strengthened by the paucity of their childhood attachments, and insulating them from the harsh realities of life outside the cocoon of intimacy they had made for themselves.

Little wonder that they excluded the world that had offered them so little comfort and no joy whatsoever. There was none of the 'below stairs' camaraderie for them - no days off spent on carefree jaunts in the park or trips to the Music Hall with the other girls in service in the town. They never so much as spoke to any of their neighbours' servants and only to their employers when they were spoken to.

After three years closeted together, their resentment of their mother surfaced at last. She said later that they would pretend not to recognise her in the street and would refuse to answer when she spoke to them. When questioned by psychiatrists and examining magistrates after her arrest, Christine complained that her mother constantly interfered in their lives, nagged and manipulated them and even commandeered their wages - sometimes putting it in savings accounts for them or, more often than not, keeping the money for herself.

Two years later, their mother was still trying to dominate their lives. At the time, Léa was still a minor but Christine, furious at her meddling, challenged their mother's right to influence her and to take her earnings. She took Léa to the council offices at the Town Hall and, in the interview that ensued, the Papin sisters were highly agitated, incoherent and spoke of 'being persecuted'.

As the girls' mother was considered locally to be a hardworking, respectable woman, anxious to watch over her girls and safeguard their money, the officials were at a loss to know how to intervene. They found the girls' irate behaviour and near-hysterical agitation disturbing and even suggested to Monsieur Lancelin that he break up the pair by getting rid of one of them - advice he no doubt fervently wished he had acted upon. Maids, after all, must remain passive, servile and easily managed. Expressions of independence such as these were quite unacceptable in the servant classes and threatened to undermine the status quo.

As well as the gruesome details of the killing itself, the supposed sexual aspect of the sisters' relationship became a subject of great interest to the public and the press coverage was as prolific as it was speculative. It was said that Christine reacted violently, not to her arrest or prolonged examination, but to her separation from her sister, Léa. Put in a cell by herself, she seemed to lose control, all defiance gone, crying pathetically and howling as though in great torment. According to Raymond Rudorff's excellent account of the case,[29] Christine called out continually for her sister, 'like a lover separated from his adored mistress'.

One of the prison warders described Christine rolling on the floor of her cell, 'screaming obscene words as though tormented by sexual desire' and she was supposed to have said to another prisoner:

29 *The Case of the Papin Sisters* by Raymond Rudorff.

'At one time, I must have been Léa's husband.'

Christine often talked of reincarnation and professed a belief that Marie and Geneviève Lancelin were no longer dead but reincarnated. Her whole demeanour whilst awaiting trial was bizarre. It was said that she would crawl around her cell on all fours, licking the walls and howling. She also made threatening gestures to a warder who displeased her, as though she was going to scratch her eyes out and when it seemed that she might tear out her own eyes, she was put in a straightjacket for her own protection.

Perhaps hoping to blackmail the authorities into letting her see Léa, she refused to eat and had to be force-fed. A fellow prisoner described her begging, over and over again, to be allowed to see her beloved sister and another swore that Christine had confessed that she, alone, had killed both Madame and Mademoiselle Lancelin.

After the preliminary investigations had been completed and the statements transcribed, the two sisters were finally reunited. Witnesses to the scene told of Christine hugging her sister so hard they had to be forced apart. It was also revealed that, whilst sitting on the bed in her cell, Christine had tried to pull her sister's blouse off, saying:

'Say yes to me, Léa! Say yes to me!'

She had also lifted up her skirt, displaying her thighs to her sister in a suggestive manner and then tried to kiss Léa on the mouth. She became distraught and violent when her sister was eventually returned to her own cell. Throughout the disturbing and emotional reunion, Léa remained completely passive.

The director of the local lunatic asylum and two other doctors had been appointed to examine the sisters to determine whether they were fit to stand trial. Their report concluded that 'no equivocal explanation can be given for the affection uniting the two sisters, nor is there any question of an attachment of a sexual nature'.

As far as they could ascertain, Christine had become a mother substitute for Léa, who was an immature personality and very much influenced by her sister. Whether or not Christine's erratic and distressing behaviour was genuine, triggered by delayed shock after the killing and the traumatic separation from Léa, the doctors decided that she was perfectly sane. Both Christine and Léa were quite able, they concluded, to answer questions coherently, to recall incidences, especially the crime itself, with clarity. Christine, in fact, seemed quite happy to describe the whole scene of the murder many times and in great detail, though Léa showed more reluctance when questioned about the actual killing.

The two sisters were deemed, therefore, to be, in the eyes of the law, sane and perfectly normal, in that they knew what they were doing when they killed their mistresses and, moreover, that what they were doing was wrong - and fully expected to be severely punished for what they had done.

According to the doctors' report:

> Christine and Léa are in no way depraved. They are not suffering from any mental illness and are in no way labouring under the burden of a defective heredity. From an intellectual, affective and emotive point of view they are completely normal.

The medical examination did reveal, however, that both girls had stopped menstruating after the murder and both were virgins.

The Papin sisters were brought to trial at the autumn Assize Court at the Palais de Justice in Le Mans, on 29 September 1933. In the eight months between their arrest and trial the press continued to pontificate, suggest and question every aspect of the crime and its perpetrators were still described as the 'eye-gougers of Le Mans' or the 'enraged lambs'.

Yet a subtle hint of sympathy for the two supposedly down-trodden maids of servitude, the pathetic under-dogs in an unfair social system, had begun to creep into certain reports. Crowds clamoured to see the maids arrive at the court-house and the lucky few were allowed to watch the proceedings from the public gallery.

The two prisoners made an odd pair. Flanked by prison guards, they stood impassively, eyes downcast, without a flicker of emotion crossing their faces, as the charge against them was read. They came across as completely insular, immune from the everyday world - not like other young women, they were indifferent, withdrawn, almost like another species compared to the court officials and the people who had come to see them. It was as though the intense scrutiny of the spectators might somehow enable them to comprehend the motive behind their terrible crime - even to understand it.

The trial only lasted for thirteen hours, for, despite its notoriety it was, in fact, a straightforward case. Though having confessed to the crime both women had pleaded Not Guilty on the grounds of insanity. According to the newspaper reporters, Christine, looking haggard and older than her twenty-eight years, kept her eyes downcast the whole time, never once looking up to face her accusers - although occasionally a faint, secret smile played on her lips.

Léa, smaller and more frail, was the epitome of defensiveness, her hands jammed into the pockets of her overcoat, which was buttoned to the neck. She looked up but rarely, preferring to stare at the floor, lost in thought and seemingly oblivious of the court drama in which she and her sister were the centre. When required to answer questions, her voice was barely audible.

The presiding judge clearly found the motive for the sisters' crime impossible to fathom, but made every effort to elicit some response from them.

'What did you have against the Lancelin family?' he asked, his tone patient and almost fatherly. 'There has been mention of social hatred, that of the employee against the employer. But this was not the case, since you suffered from no feeling of inferiority. As you rightly said, 'a servant's profession is as good as any other'. You had no preconceived ideas against your employer in his quality as employer. Nor had your mind been inflamed by certain reading matter...'

His remark referred to the mounting propaganda issued by the underground press - yet the two inscrutable sisters, dressed like old maids, standing mute and passive before him, were the absolute antithesis of Left Wing sympathisers and rioting anarchists. Seeking some other explanation for the explosion of violence that led to the killing, the judge ventured to ask them about their unusually close relationship. Why, he asked, did they never go out and mix with other young people in the town? And why was it they didn't have boy-friends, preferring to shut themselves away in their room on Sundays when they had time off? And could they explain why, when they were discovered after the murder, they were both naked and occupying the same bed? Asked specifically if their relationship was a lesbian one, it was Christine who answered:

'There was nothing else between us,' she said.

Having learned nothing further from this interrogation, the court heard, once again, the whole series of events leading to the murder. Christine insisted that there was no argument between her and Madame Lancelin shortly before the murder yet she went on to say that her mistress had grabbed her arm to make her go downstairs - this would surely indicate that some sort of altercation had begun.

'She didn't say anything to me,' Christine went on. 'It was I who attacked her. I knocked her out with the pewter pot.'

She then confirmed that, hearing their mistress cry out, Léa had come running down the stairs. Asked what she had said to her sister, Christine announced to a hushed court:

'I told Léa to tear her eyes out.'

The judge then turned his attention to Léa and, in the course of her questioning, she was asked whether she had been fond of her employers.

'We served them, that was all,' she said. 'We never talked to them.'

She confirmed that Christine, having knocked Madame Lancelin to the floor, had told her to tear her eyes out.

Asked how she did this, she replied, in a dull monotone:

'With my fingers.'

Then she used the knife Christine had fetched from the kitchen to slash the body of Mademoiselle Lancelin, after her sister had gouged out her eyes. The post-mortem examination revealed that the young woman was already dead. Léa, however, insisted that Geneviève Lancelin was still alive when she stabbed her. Asked to explain why she had behaved with such incomprehensible savagery towards two persons she did not even hate, Léa said nothing.

The court was then asked to witness the pewter pot, knives and hammer used by the sisters. The pot, which had been standing on a small table on the first landing, was badly-dented, indicating the tremendous force used by the killers. A forensic doctor called to give evidence told the court that he had never, in the whole of his career, seen bodies with such sickening mutilations. As he gave detailed evidence of these violations, there was complete uproar in the court with cries of 'Death to them!'. The judge was only able to resume the proceedings after threatening to clear the court if order was not restored.

Dr Schwarzimmer, and two other psychiatrists, were called for the prosecution and stated that neither Christine nor Léa were mentally ill. In their opinion, sheer anger, not pathological disease, was the cause of their sudden attack. The prosecution counsel then referred to several Parisian newspapers which, in his view, attempted to sway public opinion in favour of the Papin sisters - even going so far as to insinuate that the Lancelins were not the respectable middle-class family they appeared to be. The vicious attack, he insisted, was entirely unprovoked and was the result of repressed feelings of hatred and desire for revenge which made them give way to 'their most savage instincts'.

Someone who completely rejected this view was Dr Logre, an experienced and well-respected psychiatrist, who appeared for the defence. He reminded the jury of Christine's curious and far from 'normal' behaviour whilst in custody and the sadistic nature of the mutilation of the bodies. As for the peculiarly intense bond between the sisters, he felt that Christine was the more dominant of the two and went on to refer to the almost robot-like compliance of Léa. Taking into account the crime itself, the unorthodox relationship that existed between the women and their strangely withdrawn behaviour, the doctor urged the court to allow time for further analysis. His request was rejected.

In the closing speech for the prosecution, the murder was described as 'the most horrible, and the most abominable ever recorded in the annals of justice'. The jurors were urged to totally reject the plea of insanity - Christine and Léa Papin, the prosecutor insisted, were completely sane and must be held responsible for the orgy of violence that resulted in the death of Madame and Mademoiselle Lancelin. He concluded by saying this:

> 'The Papin girls are bad-tempered but not mad. Mad dogs bite as a result of a morbid craving; snarling dogs, which can sometimes show affection, bite at random. The Papin girls are not mad dogs but simply snarling, bad-tempered dogs!'

Naturally, Dr Logre sought to counter this emotive tirade by refusing to admit that the sisters were responsible for their actions - further analysis, he insisted, at a much deeper level, would be needed to reach such a conclusion. The jury must also take into account the suggestion that the sisters' father had sexually abused Emilia, with whom Christine had spent her childhood in the convent. There was the possibility, was there not, that the two sisters in the dock, may well have suffered in the same way? This was rejected by the prosecution on the grounds that such a supposition could not be proved and the court refused to sanction any further investigation into the complex psychology of either of the women.

The jury returned its verdict in less than two hours, finding both Christine and Léa guilty as charged. Christine was sentenced to death but Léa, in whose case the jury found extenuating circumstances, was given ten years' imprisonment with hard labour. On hearing her sentence, Christine's knees buckled for a moment and she had to be supported by her lawyer. Neither sentence was contested although Christine's was subsequently commuted to life imprisonment. Part of her sentence was hard labour but she reacted truculently, and, after years of passive servitude, refused to work. Her mental instability, first manifest after her arrest, increased and she was finally transferred to the psychiatric hospital at Rennes, where she died four years later, in 1937.

As for Léa, she did not rebel against her sentence, performed routine tasks without question, and was finally released in 1942. Assuming a new name, she was employed as a nanny in Nantes and managed to live in quiet anonymity, her neighbours being completely unaware of her true identity. She was located by an investigative film maker, Claude Ventura, whose documentary, *In Search of the Papin Sisters*, was released in November, 2000. Frustratingly, however, having found Léa Papin, aged 88, he discovered that she had recently suffered a stroke and was unable to either speak or write: she died the following year.

Another film about the case was also screened that year, *Les Blessures Assassines*, directed by Jean-Pierre Denis and, previously, a film by Claude Chabrol, *La Cérémonie*. A number of writers have also produced works on the case - Jean-Paul Sartre, Simone de Beauvoir and Jean Genet's play, *Les Bonnes*, was based on the lives of the extraordinary Papin sisters. Details and analysis of the various articles, books and films that feature the Papin case can be found in *The Papin Sisters* by Rachel Edwards and Keith Reader.

The case of the Papin sisters was 'one of the most awesome recorded occurrences of motiveless ferocity'; one that had 'shocked France, baffled psychiatrists and has yet to be satisfactorily explained'. Even the murderers themselves seemed unable to fathom the source of their own savagery. Sudden, blind rage and loss of control, though reprehensible can, nevertheless, be understood - what is more difficult to understand is how two individuals might share the same uncontrollable impulse to kill, simultaneously.

Despite looking alike and, to some extent, thinking alike, the sisters were not even twins and there were more than seven years between them. Could it be that once Christine, seeing Madame Lancelin's hand raised to hit her, had retaliated by knocking her to the ground, shattering in that instant the fragile master/slave balance. Seeing the woman who for years had been in authority over them, had berated them and belittled them, lying there, momentarily helpless and, for once, at their mercy, their suppressed feelings of resentment and anger were allowed free rein. Like predatory animals, once Christine, the stronger and more experienced of the two women, had immobilised the prey, Léa, who in this instance represented the rest of the pack, joined in the slaughter - the joint responsibility for the slaughter somehow lessening the guilt and abhorrence.

It seems likely that Christine and Léa had, since their early years of abuse and rejection, harboured the most bitter feelings of hatred towards their mother. Yet, having been fostered by the nuns in the convent and the women in the orphanage, both girls only felt safe in an environment of females. Even after they left the institutions, their lives were governed by their mistresses - every minute of their day was dictated by them - their very food and clothing provided by them. They were still, in effect, confined to their institutions; their lives were not their own. Fortified by their isolation and the intimacy that grew between them whilst living in rue Bruyère, the seeds of rebellion grew from this well of resentment. Yet, although they were clearly unhappy in their situation, they seemed unable to move of their own volition - they were still, in effect, institutionalised infants. This, in itself, must have added to their suppressed fury.

When Christine challenged Mrs Papin's right to dominate Léa she was attempting to adjust the natural order - manoeuvring herself into the position of dominance, assuming the role of protector. Every time Madame Lancelin rebuked the girls, it was their mother finding fault and when she took five francs from Léa for the broken iron she became, again, their mother taking their hard-earned money.

One can only guess what happened shortly after five o'clock that cold, winter evening in the rue Bruyère. Coming home to find the house in darkness, all the lights fused, Madame Lancelin, vexed at the inconvenience, must have seen the 'faint glow' in the window of the maids' bedroom. Clearly suspicious of their relationship and already accustomed to spying on them, did Madame and her daughter decide to investigate? And, not wishing to warn the girls of their unexpected return by moving about in the darkened kitchen, did they creep up the stairs, still carrying their groceries, intent on listening at the door?

Did they ever reach the maids' room on the second floor? Or were they met on the pitch-black landing by the sisters? And did an argument between Christine and Madame Lancelin ensue? In one of her statements, Christine said that her mistress caught hold of her arm, pinching it as she attempted to frog-march her down the stairs. Was it then that Madame Lancelin became, in the maid's deranged mind, Madame Papin (and all the other women in authority) and the rage boiling inside her exploded? And did one of the women raise her hand to hit Léa for breaking the iron? With her fierce love of her sister, Christine would undoubtedly have sprung to her defence, shielding her from any blows. And did Madame Lancelin, in the heat of the moment, threaten to separate the sisters once and for all by sacking Léa? Was it this final threat that sparked the scuffle on the landing?

Once Madame Lancelin had fallen to the floor, the sudden loss of her dignity and dominion over them, the unaccustomed and disorientating darkness, anger and fear causing their hearts to race, and the physical intervention of Geneviève, all culminated in a sudden and almost surreal conflict that ended in death. At last the Papin sisters were in control. At last, they were able to give full vent to all the feelings of hostility they had suppressed since childhood - able, at last, to revenge themselves on the trauma of their early years - and kill their mother. No one would ever separate them again, or bully them, or find fault with them and take away their money.

In their warped and desperate minds, did they, perhaps, steeped in religious dogma, somehow feel that 'an eye for an eye' was justified? Was that why they, literally, gouged out their victims' eyes? But why did they not include Monsieur Lancelin in their revenge? Why had they subconsciously forgiven their father who had either abandoned or brutalised them but not their mother? Not only did they leave him out of the massacre - they could easily have overpowered him on his return to the house - but even protected him from the horror of discovering the killings by locking all the doors. It is possible, of course, that they harboured a secret crush on René Lancelin, thus sparing his life and engendering the sexually oriented mutilations to his wife and daughter. If this was the case, their savagery may have been an appalling manifestation of the commonplace utterance of the jealous female: 'I'll scratch her eyes out!

There are so many inconsistencies in this extraordinary case that can never be fully explained. Why, for instance, after the killings, didn't the maids try to escape? It was almost as if they felt entirely justified in the killing and accepted the need to be punished. Christine, whilst in prison awaiting trial, had said:

'I shall be punished - my head cut off, even. Tant pis!'

Perhaps the most extraordinary aspect of all was that, after the trial, Christine never once asked about Léa, the sister whom she had supposedly loved to distraction and, perhaps, even killed to protect. Or was it that the mirror image of herself was by now so severely distorted that it had ceased to exist because she could no longer see it?

Charles Houghton

The Butler Of Burghill

The scene of this unusual crime was the village of Burghill, some six miles north west of Hereford. In 1926, the occupants of Burghill Court, undoubtedly the most imposing country house in the area, were the Woodhouse sisters; both spinsters, Miss Elinor Drinkwater Woodhouse, was sixty-five years old and known as Miss Ella and Miss Martha Gordon Woodhouse, who was fifty-seven and known as Miss May. Both women were wealthy and, like their mother before them, imperious and dictatorial, belonging to the old 'born to rule' section of English society.

Their father, John George Gordon Woodhouse, a prosperous wine merchant, had bought Burghill House, as it was then called, in 1875, and, following the Victorian vogue for pseudo-royal pretensions, changed the name to Burghill Court. The family, mindful of their position in society, soon became involved in the affairs of the village and subscribed to a number of local causes - in particular, the fund-raising efforts to pay for the restoration of the ancient parish church.

When Mrs Woodhouse, senior, died in 1923, Burghill Court was left, not to her two spinster daughters, but to their brother, Mr Gordon Woodhouse, but, as he already owned an estate in Yorkshire, he allowed his sisters to remain in the house. Miss Ella and Miss May were, moreover, well-provided for and able to maintain a very comfortable lifestyle. They employed a coachman, Mr John Towne, who lived with his wife, Fanny, in the Estate Offices, and several men to work on the estate. In addition, they had five live-in domestic servants - a cook, Mrs Mary Ann Smith, a housekeeper, two maids and a butler, Charles Houghton.

In Edwardian society, retaining the services of an indoor man-servant had been considered highly prestigious, the majority of houses making do with cheaper female labour - a cook and one or two maids-of-all-work. Charles Houghton, at forty-five, was a relic of that era - the gentleman's gentleman. He had been with the Woodhouse family for twenty-one years, starting as a footman and working his way up to the prized position of butler. And it certainly was an excellent position. He was trusted, well-liked and lived in beautiful surroundings; added to which, as his duties were fairly light, he was able to spend most mornings shooting on the three hundred acre estate, for all the world like a country gentleman. For this, he borrowed a 12-bore shot gun from one of his employers' cousins, Mr Ernest William Jackson, a schoolmaster from Brighton, who was a frequent visitor to Burghill Court. After an afternoon's sport, the butler would always return the gun to its usual place - propped up behind the door of the pantry.

The length of Charles Houghton's employment with the Woodhouse family would suggest that, at one time, at least, he must have possessed all the attributes of a good butler - honesty and discretion - and moreover, if he was a little fond of the bottle, the ability to hold his drink and at least maintain the appearance of sobriety. One cannot help feeling, however, that once he had started to drink to excess, the two maiden ladies, albeit shrouded in a mist of lavender water and *sal volatile*, would have been able to detect the smell of liquor on a servant's breath at twenty paces.

Yet, despite his bouts of inebriation, he was a kindly and courteous man. This is certainly how Mr Towne's granddaughter remembers him. At the age of seven, being rather pale and thin, she was sent from her home in London to stay with the coachman and his wife at Burghill. She remembers the butler as a friendly and amusing companion; so, too, does another lady, related to the Woodhouse family, who often stayed at the Court as a child. As she recalls, the servants were obliged to join the sisters for morning prayers in the echoing grand hall - an ordeal for any five year old, one would imagine, having to keep still and quiet for ages while the old ladies called upon the Almighty. She has a touching memory of standing close to Charles Houghton throughout this procedure, and, to keep her amused, he would surreptitiously drop raisins into her raised palm.

By the summer of 1926, the Woodhouse sisters were well aware that Houghton was drinking heavily with his friends in the village and it worried them greatly. He was often missing when required to serve at table or open the front door to visitors; they may have given him a few discreet warnings about his behaviour but when, on 31 August, he served dinner whilst plainly drunk, it was the last straw. The sisters felt that, not only was he setting a bad example to the other employees, drunken behaviour was totally unacceptable in an all-female household. They decided, reluctantly, to dispense with his services, although there was some talk of transferring him to their brother's estate in Yorkshire.

Distressed at having to do this and possibly in need of a little moral support, they waited until Monday, 6 September, when their brother, Gordon, and cousin, Ernest Jackson, and his wife, were staying at the Court. In fact, there seems to have been something of a family gathering that weekend, probably connected with Gordon's decision to sell the house to his sisters for a reputed £60,000. As a result of their discussions, Ella and May had arranged to go into Hereford to see their solicitor and sign the documents necessary for the transferral of the deeds. In the circumstances, it must have seemed the most opportune moment to also dismiss Houghton and arrange his transfer to Yorkshire.

So it was that on Sunday afternoon Houghton was sent for and told by Miss Ella that, although she did not harbour any anger or ill-feeling towards him, his drinking propensity was such that she and her sister had decided to get rid of him. Houghton made no attempt to deny that he had been drunk during dinner the week before but said that, as the cook had not given him enough to eat, he had sustained himself with liquor. But the ladies dismissed this feeble excuse, refused to reconsider their decision and gave him twenty-four hours' notice.

Understandably, this came as a great shock and Houghton protested at being given so little time to get out after twenty-one years' service. He was offered a transfer to Yorkshire but rejected the idea of being suddenly uprooted and transplanted, like a piece of furniture, to an estate where he knew no one. After some discussion, it was agreed to let him stay until the end of the week; he was also to be given a month's wages *in lieu* of notice.

Houghton went up to his room, absolutely devastated by what had happened. He knew perfectly well that few households in the area could afford a butler, and, considering his age and drink problem, he knew he was unlikely to find employment elsewhere. After all, he had lived at Burghill Court all his adult life and had some good friends in the village - it was his home, not just his place of work. Little wonder that Houghton took his dismissal so badly and refused to come down to serve dinner that evening. The cook, realising how upset he was, felt sorry for him and took some bread and milk up to his room.

The following morning, Charles Houghton seemed to have accepted his dismissal. He came down, had his breakfast in the servants' hall and, at 8.45 am, attended morning prayers with the rest of the household. His behaviour seemed perfectly normal. The day's routine proceeded as usual; he served breakfast to the Woodhouse sisters without making any reference to his sacking and everyone thought he was taking it very well indeed in the circumstances.

Soon after 9.30 am, Houghton appeared in the kitchen with some coffee in a silver pot for Mary Smith, the cook. She said later that he seemed 'just the same as always'. Mary asked him when Miss Ella would be coming to discuss the day's arrangements and the butler said she'd be 'round in a minute' and then left the room.

A few minutes later, at 9.45 am, Miss Ella came into the kitchen and spent about ten minutes talking to the cook. Then, as she went back through the kitchen door into the passage she was shot at point blank range. A second shot followed almost immediately, accompanied by dreadful screams. Instinctively, the cook opened the kitchen door to see what had happened and heard someone running up the back stairs towards the butler's bedroom.

At the same moment, she saw the body of Miss Ella slumped in the passage close to the kitchen door, with a gunshot wound to her neck. Further along the passage, near the back stair lobby, she saw Miss May 'unconscious and bleeding profusely'. At the same time, the housemaid, Beatrice Cotterell, had heard the two shots from the top of the back stairs and, thinking Houghton had shot himself, she ran to his room but found the door locked.

Another maid, on her way up the stairs to find the housekeeper, saw Ernest Jackson come out of the smoke room. He was to say later that he had heard the first shot and thought it was a tray crashing to the floor - but, recognising the second shot, he opened his door just in time to see Charles Houghton disappear into his bedroom. Jackson hurried downstairs and, seeing Miss Ella's body in the passage, he ran out of the front door to summon help. He found the coachman, John Towne, in the stable, preparing the pony and trap ready to drive the sisters into Hereford as planned. Towne hurried into the house and found Miss May's body in the lobby. She, too, had been shot at close range and was barely alive. While the coachman cradled Miss May in his arms until she died, Jackson went in search of the weapon. He found his 12-bore shot gun in its usual place behind the pantry door; inside were two spent cartridges.

The police and a doctor were called and arrived about 10.20 am. Dr Vincent Shaw confirmed that both Miss Ella and Miss May were dead. Ernest Jackson spoke briefly to Superintendent Albert Weaver[30] and gave him the shot gun. Weaver, who had known Charles Houghton for some time, went straight upstairs to his room but found it locked. He called out for Houghton to open the door but at first the butler refused. After repeated requests, he opened the door a little but when he saw Weaver he quickly locked it again. The policeman ordered him again to open up and, when Houghton

30 In 1922, when he was Deputy Chief Constable of Herefordshire, he assisted Chief Inspector Crutchett of New Scotland Yard in the arrest of Major Herbert Armstrong at Hay.

did so, he managed to grab his wrist. It was then that he noticed that the butler was bleeding from several lacerations on his neck. Whether stricken by remorse or in a bid to hasten his own certain death, Houghton had attempted to cut his own throat.

Superintendent Weaver took him down to the storeroom and held on to him while Dr Shaw attended to the wounds. There were seven in number but they appeared fairly superficial.

At this point, Charles Houghton said to Weaver: 'Oh, dear! This is a bad job, Super.'

The policeman agreed, to which the butler replied: 'It is passion.'

Before leaving the house Weaver searched Houghton and found two unfired cartridges; he then took him straight to Hereford County Police Station, his neck swathed in bandages. When charged with the murder of the Misses Woodhouse, he said: 'I do not wish to say anything.'

When asked if he wished to attend the inquest into the ladies' death, he declined, saying: 'I do not wish to attend. I cannot do any good.'

A week later, Charles Houghton was brought from Gloucester Prison to attend the committal proceedings at the Magistrates' Court in Hereford. A crowd, mainly consisting of women, had already gathered outside the court. The two Woodhouse sisters were well-known in the area for their support of many worthy causes and it was not surprising that the public gallery was filled with spectators curious to see the man accused of their murder. Houghton was given the chance of having a solicitor defend him but, having no money, he declined. He appeared before the Bench in a light raincoat over the same navy blue suit he had been wearing on the day of his arrest and his neck was still bandaged.

Mr G R Paling outlined the case on behalf of the Director of Public Prosecutions and called Ernest Jackson, the cook, Mary Smith and the maid, Beatrice Cotterell, as witnesses. Superintendent Weaver told of Houghton's arrest and the finding of the shot gun and the two spent cartridges. Dr Shaw testified that both Miss Ella and Miss May had been shot at close range and confirmed that, whereas Miss Ella had died instantly, Miss May had remained alive but unconscious for several minutes.

When formally charged with the murders and asked if he had anything to say Houghton replied: 'No, sir.'

When asked what means he had to pay for a counsel to defend him, he said: 'Not a great deal, sir.'

When it was ascertained that he had less than seven pounds to his name, he was granted a certificate [legal aid] to pay for his defence. According to a report in *The Hereford Times,* Houghton 'remained in Court some time after the general public had left and chatted for several minutes with Commander Drinkwater, a cousin of the deceased ladies. The accused also had a conversation with his brother, his step-brother and friends and also the cook and Miss Cotterell. He appeared in good spirits and smiled occasionally. He was later taken to the County Police Station through a side exit and returned to Gloucester [gaol] late in the afternoon.'

More than a thousand mourners attended the funeral of Ella and May Woodhouse. It was described in the local press as a 'simple and beautiful' occasion when 'every resident in the district, from the oldest to the youngest, and from the richest to the poorest, seemed to be present'. The gardeners and outdoor staff conveyed the two coffins, which were laid out on wheeled biers, from the house to the church of St Mary The Virgin. A superb passage of purple prose appeared in *The Hereford Times* to describe the scene for its readers:

> Slowly and sadly the procession wends its way from the scene of the tragedy through the avenue of overhanging boughs, footed by a bed of beautiful flowers and then along the long drive by the side of which the tall trees rustled a mournful adieu and out on to the main road lined with sorrowing cottagers.
>
> Behind the biers walked Mr J G Woodhouse, the sole surviving immediate relative, with other private mourners and in turn came members of the household staff, each dressed in deep mourning and carrying a huge wreath of lovely flowers. At the rear of the funeral

> cortege was the deceased ladies' favourite pony drawing a carriage full of floral tributes and a motor car similarly laden.
>
> A midsummerlike sun shone as the procession steadily climbed the hill of mourning to the church, the silence being now and again broken by the tolling of the bell and the sobbing of women and children among the spectators who lined the route. Then through the shade of the friendly yew trees it passed into the mellow light of the church wherein are tablets perpetuating the noble lives of the deceaseds' parents and visible signs of their own love and generosity.
>
> The service ended with the 'ethereal, pulsating and finally triumphant strains of the *Dead March*'. The Woodhouse sisters' graves - the bricked sides white-washed and surmounted with a wide black border - were decorated with brightly coloured dahlias, their favourite flowers. Close by were their parents' graves and in another lay the weary bones of an old retainer, Ellen George, who had served the Woodhouse family for thirty-six years.
>
> After the three officiating clergy and chief mourners - among them the staff and pupils of two local schools and representatives of various charitable associations - had gone back to the church the villagers filed past the grave casting loving and sorrowing eyes on where their 'ladies bountiful' slept. Most pathetic of all was the way in which the oldest of the employees lingered by the graveside, weeping unrestrainedly because of the sadness within them. From the church floated the solemn strains of the organ, heavy with grief but expressing in music 'thought which lay too deep for tears'. When the sun went down the ladies were left alone with the flowers that so fittingly symbolised the beauty and saintliness of their lives.

Two months later, equally vast crowds had gathered outside The Shire Hall, Hereford, on the morning of Friday, 7 November, for the trial of Charles Houghton. He was brought from Gloucester Prison by train, as Major Armstrong had been four years before. According to a reporter on *The Hereford Times*, Houghton was *'neatly dressed in a navy blue suit and looking well'.*

The case came before Mr Justice Rigby Swift with Mr Ronald Powell for the Prosecution and Mr A J Long for the Defence - instructed by the Hereford solicitor, Mr F Craze. Charged first with the murder of Miss Elinor Woodhouse and then with that of Miss May Woodhouse,

Houghton replied firmly and in a clear voice: Not Guilty.

Outlining the background of the case for the jury, Mr Powell said that 'by reason of their social position and the length of time they [the Woodhouse sisters] had been in the neighbourhood, they were well-known to all in the district and were looked upon with great respect and affection by all who knew them'.

He went on the describe Charles Houghton's place in the household at Burghill Court as a 'very comfortable billet', one which he had every reason to expect to enjoy for the rest of his working life. During the previous summer, said Mr Powell, the prisoner had become 'intemperate in his habits' and, as he was the only man living in a household of women, the Misses Woodhouse had felt it best that he should go. He went on to describe to the jury the events that followed the butler's dismissal and the tragic shooting the following day.

This done, he called Ernest Jackson as a witness who testified that, as far as he could tell, the relationship between the Woodhouse sisters and their staff had always been 'of the happiest character'. They were treated well, he said, and lived comfortably and, in the circumstances, he did not doubt for one moment that the prisoner was greatly upset by his dismissal.

Next in the witness box was the cook, Mrs Mary Ann Smith[31] who admitted that she had noticed that Houghton had been drinking heavily throughout the summer. Questioned by Mr Long, for the Defence, Mrs Smith confirmed that the butler had previously been a 'hardworking, faithful servant'. She testified that he valued his position at Burghill Court very highly and was extremely distressed at being sacked. He was also annoyed at the way he'd been treated and told Mary that it was a disgrace that he had been given such short notice. He also said that he felt that the only solution was to 'end it himself'.

31 According to Mrs Smith's grandson, Fred Bond, Mary was so traumatised by the murders that she suffered badly with her nerves thereafter and for a while after the tragedy experienced some paralysis down the left side of her body. In the circumstances she was allowed to sit whilst giving her evidence.

Miss Beatrice Cotterell, the second housemaid, then told the court her version of the events on the day of the shooting. She was followed into the witness box by Dr Vincent Shaw who, when questioned by the defence, admitted that, although Charles Houghton was on his panel of patients, he had never treated him. Nor did he realise, as now suggested by the Defence, that he suffered from epilepsy. He confirmed that a person with epilepsy might go for years between attacks and appear to be in excellent health. Although he conceded that it was, in theory, possible that Houghton had shot the two ladies as a result of an epileptic seizure, he thought it unlikely as, when he examined him about half an hour later, he seemed perfectly normal.

This evidence was endorsed by Superintendent Weaver who said that he knew Charles Houghton well and had never known him have an attack of epilepsy. When he saw him shortly after the murders, he seemed 'remarkably cool under the circumstances'.

Charles Houghton's sister, Mrs Sarah Worrall, was called next for the Defence. She confirmed that her brother, who had lived at home until the age of fourteen, had suffered childhood convulsions on three occasions - he had, she said, 'lain on his bed, clenched his hands, foamed at the mouth and gone black in the face'.

A specialist on epilepsy, Dr C Francis, was called and explained to the court that he had examined Charles Houghton earlier that day and found 'his intellect dull and he seemed to take a very casual interest in the examination'. He also found that the prisoner's right ear drum had been ruptured causing a 'chronic suppurative inflammation'.

Closely questioned by Dr Francis, Houghton admitted to having received a blow to the head 'some time ago'. Examination of his knee and wrist reflexes, along with other features, made the doctor consider the possibility of the presence of 'some cerebral irritation'. He went further, saying that he thought it quite possible that Houghton's childhood convulsions were epileptic in origin and, moreover, the shock and worry of his sudden dismissal, might well have brought on an epileptic attack. As to the possibility that Houghton, if he were in the throes of an attack, being able to carry out the murders, the doctor said that 'it is well-known that an epileptic may do something in an organised manner although he has no knowledge of it himself.'

It may be interesting to note here that epilepsy has been similarly used as a defence in a number of murder cases. Lee Harvey Oswald, the alleged killer of President John F Kennedy, in 1963, was himself shot by Jack Ruby. At Ruby's subsequent trial, he pleaded Not Guilty on the grounds that he was undergoing a psychomotor epileptic seizure at the time of the shooting. According to a number of expert witnesses, sufferers of this disorder are prone to uncontrollable and explosive behaviour if emotionally upset. Their consciousness becomes impaired and aggressive acts may be committed automatically. Other experts, however, did not agree that this was the case when Ruby shot Oswald. He was found guilty and sentenced to death but died in custody in 1967.

A survey conducted by specialists at the Maudsley Hospital in 1953, however, found that, of the 105 murderers screened, 18 showed symptoms of epilepsy, some thirty times greater than the incidence of the disorder among the general population.

The last witness to be called was Dr Bell, the medical officer at Gloucester Prison, who said that whilst in custody Charles Houghton had 'showed no signs of insanity or epilepsy or mental disease'.

The case against Charles Houghton, though circumstantial, in that no one had actually seen him fire the gun at the two ladies, was a most convincing one. Yet it still remained for the Prosecution to persuade the jury that Houghton, according to M'Naghten Law,[32] knew what he was doing when he aimed the gun and pulled the trigger and, moreover, that he knew that what he was doing was wrong.

Since the M'Naghten case, the law has stipulated that a person cannot be convicted if proved insane - if, that is, when the crime

32 M'Naghten was a young artisan with a persecution complex. He was convinced he was being spied upon by Sir Robert Peel. In 1843 he shot Peel's Private Secretary by mistake. As a result of his trial and the verdict of insanity the M'Naghten Law was introduced to safeguard those who kill whilst suffering from mental disease.

was committed, that person, firstly, did not know what he or she was doing and secondly, was incapable of distinguishing right from wrong - then that person must be deemed not responsible for their actions.

The jurors at Charles Houghton's trial were clearly convinced that he was perfectly sane at the time of the murders, knew what he was doing and knew that it was wrong, and dismissed the Defence proposition that he was suffering from an epileptic seizure at the time. They brought in a verdict of Guilty on both counts and Mr Justice Rigby Swift sentenced Houghton to death.

Mr Craze, Houghton's solicitor, in the ten days allowed after conviction, put up a gallant fight on his client's behalf. He submitted various documents relating to evidence that Charles Houghton suffered a number of epileptic attacks whilst serving as a soldier in the First World War. These were lodged with the Court of Criminal Appeal and in consequence of this the arrangements for Houghton's execution at Gloucester Prison on 23 November were suspended until the outcome of the appeal.

A week later, however, after consultation with the Home Secretary, who decided he was unable to intervene, the appeal failed. Charles Houghton's execution was set for eight o'clock on the morning of 4 December, 1926. But whereas on the morning of Major Armstrong's execution four years earlier, a crowd of more than two thousand had gathered outside the prison gates since dawn, there was little interest in Charles Houghton. A reporter noted that 'half an hour before the execution there was hardly a soul to be seen in the dim greyness of the cold morning. From time to time, business people on their way to work, paused to glance at the customary notice posted on the prison door overnight prior to an execution.'

The State Executioner, Thomas Pierrepoint[33] and his assistant had, in accordance with the regulations, arrived the day before to spend

33 Thomas Pierrepoint, official executioner for thirty-six years. Brother of Henry Pierrepoint, also an executioner, who retired in 1917. His son, Albert, also became a hangman in 1931: he retired in 1956 and in his autobiography proclaimed his opposition to capital punishment regarding it not only as barbaric but also ineffective as a deterrent. He died in 1992.

Illustrated Police News, 3rd May 1879

Mrs Julia Thomas, the victim
Illustrated Police News, 12th April 1879

Kate Webster denounces John Church
Illustrated Police News, 10th May 1879

Mr Justice Denman
Illustrated Police News, 17th May 1879

Effigy of Kate Webster at Madame Tussauds

Sketches from the Illustrated Police News relating to the Richmond murder
Top: 26th April 1879; Middle: 12th July 1879

An emotional illustration of Kate Webster's son visiting his mother in Wandsworth jail from the Illustrated Police News, 19th July 1879. In reality, not one of her fair-weather friends or even one of her family bothered to bring him so that Kate could see him for the last time

Jane Cannon Cox

Florence Bravo

Charles Bravo

The Priory, Balham
from The Illustrated London News, 5th August 1876

Rue Bruyère,
scene of the murders

Above: The Papin sisters prior to their arrest
Below: In custody

Above: Charles Houghton (centre and inset) and other members of staff at Burghill Court. Photograph taken in the grounds circa four years before the murder of Ella and May Woodhouse

Below: Burghill Court

Left and above: Louisa Merrfield and husband Albert 'Pop' Merrifield

Below: Louisa gives a cheery wave on her way to court

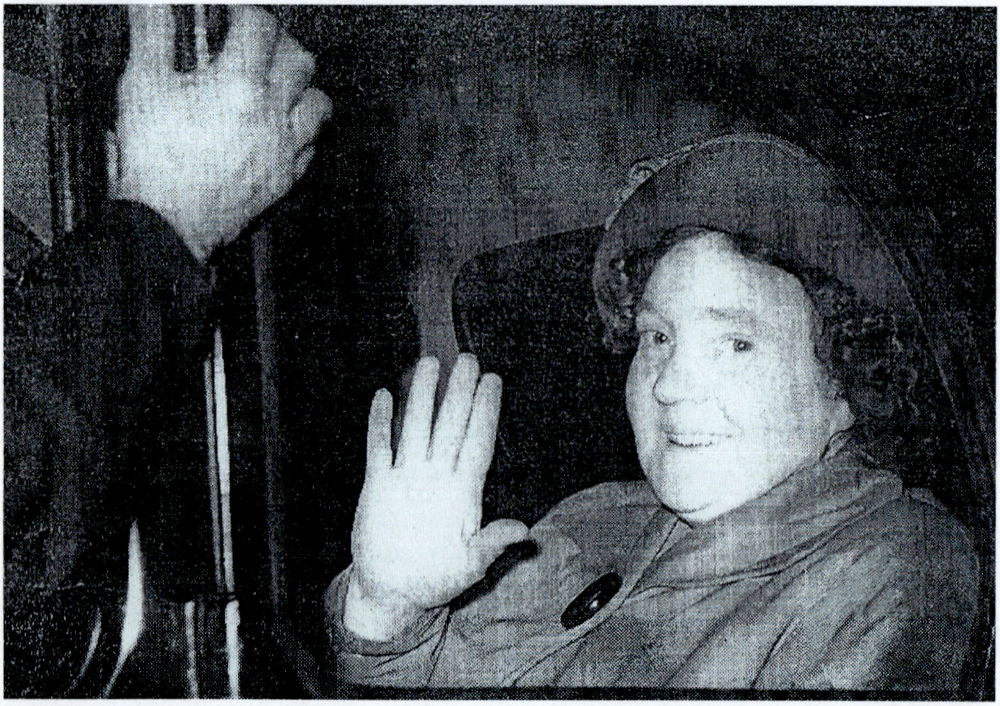

Above: John Lee at the time of the murder, and his victim Miss Keyse from Aberdeen Evening Express, 3rd February 1885

Left: Lee after his release from prison

From Illustrated Police News, 13th December 1884

Roy Fontaine

Lady Peggy Hudson, his employer

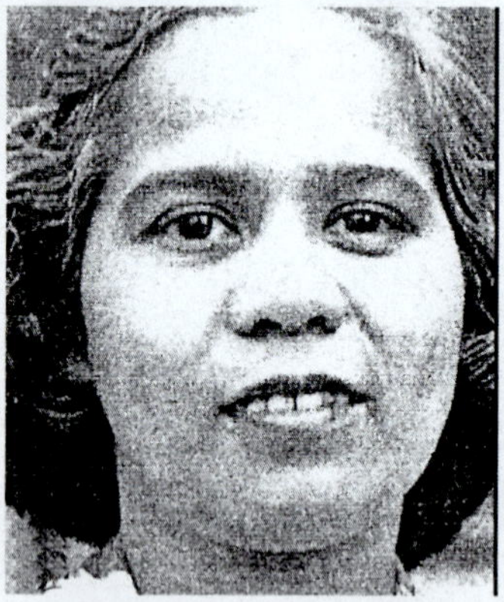

Roy Fontaine's victims, clockwise from top left:

David Wright
Dorothy Scott-Elliott
Walter Scott-Elliott
Mary Coggle
Donald Hall, Fontaine's brother

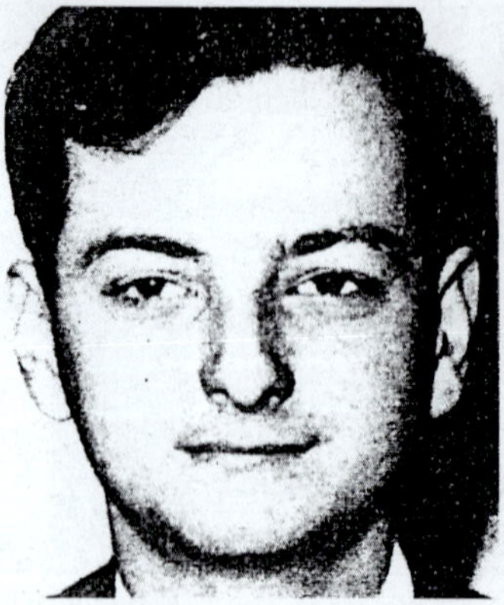

the night in the prison. Various officials arrived early the next day - the Vicar of St Mary de Lode, in which parish the prison stood, the Under-Sheriff of Herefordshire and the prison doctor. As it neared eight o'clock, a small group of women congregated near the door of the prison and watched the arrival of the prison Governor, Mr Whyte.

The Hereford Times described the scene in this way:

> A few minutes before eight o'clock the bell of St Mary de Lode commenced to toll and was still tolling as the hour struck. Amid the noise of the adjacent works, the bustle of the lorries in the square and the postman delivering letters at the Gaol almost at the moment of execution, there was nothing beyond the gathering of a small crowd to indicate that anything unusual was passing within.
>
> Charles Houghton, dressed in a navy blue suit which he wore at the trial, was visited by the Chaplain on the latter's arrival. A few minutes before eight o'clock Pierrepoint and his assistant entered the condemned cell and expeditiously carried out the pinioning. Immediately the folding door separating the cell from the execution chamber was thrown open and just a few steps took the condemned man on to the scaffold.
>
> Within a few seconds of his leaving the cell he had expiated his crime in the presence of the Under Sheriff of Herefordshire, the Governor, the prison doctor, the Chaplain and one or two warders. The warders leaving a few minutes past the hour was an indication that Houghton had paid the extreme penalty, for it is customary to disallow anyone to enter or leave the prison about the time of an execution.
>
> The small crowd remained outside the gates to witness the posting of the two notices, one confirming that the execution had been carried out and the other, signed by the prison doctor, to confirm that Charles Houghton was now dead. Several people remained to watch the departure of the officials a few minutes later before they, too, dispersed and went about their business.

To comply with the law, an inquest into Charles Houghton's death was carried out within the precincts of the prison before the coroner for North Gloucestershire, Mr James Waghorne, a jury of nine, the prison Governor, a doctor and three reporters. The jurors were obliged to view the body and confirm that it was the mortal remains of Charles Houghton. The Governor then stated that the execution had been carried out 'expeditiously'. The doctor also confirmed that death was 'absolutely instantaneous' caused by the 'dislocation of the neck'.

Thanking the jurors for their attendance, the Coroner was at pains to stress that both Charles Houghton and Major Armstrong, four years before, had committed their crimes in *Herefordshire*, not Gloucestershire - and the fact that they were executed in Gloucestershire was not to be seen as a reflection on the criminality of that county but simply 'owing to the closing of the county prisons of Worcestershire and Herefordshire'.

Which, in the circumstances, seems rather a heartlessly dismissive remark to make in view of the tragic events that had led to the death of three women - in the first case, Armstrong's wife, Katherine, and in the second, Ella and May Woodhouse - and the two men deemed responsible for their deaths. All were victims, one might say, of a violent and untimely death.

But why did the mild-mannered and friendly butler suddenly arm himself with a shot gun and blast the two elderly sisters to death? The question remains and may never be answered. One can only imagine how devastated Charles Houghton must have been at being told that, after twenty-one years of service, he was to leave Burghill Court by the end of the week. He had started work at the house in his early twenties; it was, therefore, not just a place of work but also his home. Equally hurtful was the fact that he had known Miss Ella and Miss May for so long and yet they chose to dismiss him so heartlessly - this must have been a stinging blow to his pride.

He was well-regarded by the other members of staff and had made many close friends in the village. It is rumoured that he had formed an attachment to one of the maids at Burghill Court - could it have been the young lady sitting on his left in the staff photograph, holding the black kitten? Was the idea of leaving a sweetheart too much to bear or was he, nearing middle-age, too wily where the ladies were concerned for that to have caused him much distress?

Employment, however, was a different matter. At the age of forty-five and with a drink problem, it was most unlikely he would have found another job as a butler in the area. In the period between the wars many of the families who ran large households found they could no longer afford the luxury of a butler and relied instead on the services of women, young girls or unskilled lads willing to work for less money.

Dismissal at his age left Charles Houghton with two options - being sent off to the estate in Yorkshire (clearly he found this idea abhorrent though his relationship with Gordon Woodhouse is unknown) or to stay in the area and seek some menial employment. Unskilled, as far as we know, in any other field, Houghton was also homeless and would have been forced to live in cheap lodgings which, after the relative luxury of Burghill Court, would have been uncongenial, to say the least. But it was more than that; he had prided himself on his position as butler and no doubt considered himself a cut above the other servants, a person in authority, someone who could command respect. Clearly the prospect of ill-paid drudgery and basic, probably shared, accommodation, was too much for him to contemplate. His resentment and anger towards the two sisters who could so easily reduce him to this state after twenty-one years drove him over the edge. It was too much, he *had* to retaliate, express his suppressed anger and take control of a situation that had devastated and humiliated him. It was the action of a cornered man, hurt, defeated, dangerously out of control and determined to bite back.

Louisa Merrifield

Rum and Rat Poison

When Mrs Sarah Ann Ricketts, a cranky, seventy-nine year old widow, advertised for a housekeeper in March, 1953, the applicant she chose was a homely-looking soul called Louisa May Merrifield. Peering between the folds of the net curtains, Mrs Ricketts must have felt reassured when she saw her walking up the garden path to The Homestead, a neat little bungalow in Devonshire Road, Blackpool. She could see straight away that there was nothing flimsy or flighty about Mrs Merrifield. She looked solid, dependable and as strong as an ox - just the sort of person to look after a cantankerous old lady like herself. Louisa was one of those broad-beamed, corseted, bespectacled women who love nothing better than a good laugh, with a nudge and a wink and plenty of saucy gossip.

Although it had not been her intention to take on a married couple, Mrs Ricketts got on so well with Mrs Merrifield - they had a real giggle and a natter while they drank their tea - that she was persuaded to employ the woman's husband, Alfred, as well. She had to agree that he would be very useful for all those troublesome little jobs about the house. Perhaps Mrs Ricketts missed having a man about the place - both her husbands had killed themselves - and felt it would be nice to have a bit of male company. Mind you, she must have thought, he was no spring chicken - at seventy, he was not much younger than she was, and a good bit older than his wife. Louisa had said she was forty-six but she was one of those post-war women who looked much older than their years, the chronically middle-aged. Yet, although Louisa Merrifield may have looked like a frumpy old maid, her looks were deceptive. She had been married twice before - Alfred was her third and most recent acquisition.

Louisa's background was also a little surprising for a woman who might easily be mistaken for the motherly sort. She was born in Wigan, in 1906, and had four sisters. Her father, Job Highway, was a miner and although the family were strict Methodists, when Louisa reached her teens, she defected to the Salvation Army. Intellectually, she was never very bright and on leaving school she worked as a mill-hand and later as a cook.

In September 1931, when she was twenty-five, she married an iron-worker called Joseph Ellison; they had lived in a large house, had a fairly stable lifestyle and produced nine children, four of whom survived - two boys and two girls. But Louisa soon found out that it was not easy bringing up a family on her husband's wages of £4.10s. a week. For a few years after the marriage, however, she did her best and it would seem that Louisa was all set to lead an obscure, uneventful life like millions of other housewives. To supplement the family income she even made two attempts at running small shops, but failed.

Nor, it seems, did she make a very successful mother. During the war years, she neglected her children in favour of having a good time; finding housework a bore she much preferred to go out to dance halls where she could drink, chatter and be the life and soul of the party. Her neglect did not go unnoticed. By 1945, the local authority had taken all four children into care. The following year, Louisa was arrested for stealing ration books from her neighbours and selling them on the black market. As she could, or would not, pay the fine she was sent to prison for eighty-four days.

Some time later, Louisa was given a second chance to prove herself a good mother - but again failed, for in 1949, the two girls and the younger boy went back to the children's home and the older boy was simply left to fend for himself. That same year, Louisa met a retired colliery manager, Richard Weston. It is perhaps difficult to fathom why but he seems to have taken a shine to Louisa. She found him attractive, too, for although he was seventy-eight, there were compensations, like a smart semi-detached house and £800 in the bank. He also had a wife but this did not stop Louisa from calling at his home and when, fortuitously, Mrs Weston died soon after, Louisa invited Richard to become a lodger in her house in Park Road, Wigan, and, no doubt, sharpened up her cooking skills.

On 3 October 1949, literally within weeks of Richard moving in, Louisa's husband, Joseph, died of an ulcerated leg and tuberculosis and she was free at last. Not that she remained single for long for, within two months, she had married Richard Weston:

'Such a nice man,' commented Louisa, at the time, 'and plenty of money too.'

She soon persuaded him to sell his house for £1,500 and put the money in the bank with the rest of his savings. Marriage to Louisa, however, proved too much for the old man, for eight weeks later, he died of a heart attack. By this time, all the money had gone and Louisa claimed to be so broke she couldn't even pay the £31 owing for the funeral expenses. Where the money went remains a mystery for the couple were regularly drawing £200 each week until Weston's death yet appeared to live in far from lavish style.

Thwarted yet again, Louisa was, nevertheless, still determined to find the security she craved and within a week of burying her second husband, she met Alfred 'Pop' Merrifield on a hospital ward. Although he was nudging seventy at the time, less than mentally alert, with impaired hearing and ulcerated legs - was this unpleasant condition a pre-requisite for catching Louisa's eye? - he was a dapper, chirpy sort of chap, the father of ten children. Having travelled the world for most of his life, when he met Louisa he was looking for a companion for his remaining years - and Louisa, with her non-stop chatter, rather domineering personality and forthright manner, seemed just the sort to take him under control. Yet Louisa seems to have made another foolish choice for Alfie Merrifield was entirely dependent on his old age pension and the National Assistance Board.

They were married in August, 1950, and soon ran into financial trouble. It could be that Louisa continued to enjoy her nights in the pub and between them they soon got through Alfie's pension each week. Before long they had to sell their furniture but still ended up owing a lot of money. Only a year after their marriage, they were so badly in arrears on their rent that they were evicted. Gone were any fancy ideas about retiring and settling into comfortable security. They both realised that, to carry on as they were, they, or at least Louisa, would have to go on working to survive.

So it was that they moved from Wigan to Blackpool in April, 1951, hoping to find domestic work with one of the town's collection of wealthy old ladies. Louisa took a number of jobs, private nursing, cooking and such like. But she never lasted in any job for long and they were continually on the move in search of work. Having been widowed twice already without reaping the benefit, Louisa was becoming more canny. She took out some life insurances on 'Pop' Merrifield and kept up the premiums secretly - for he disapproved of the whole idea. She took out several modest policies and even tried to insure him for £3000 but was unable to meet the premiums.

Before finding the job with Mrs Ricketts, they had moved from one drab lodging house to another twenty times in their search for the ideal position - bickering, it seems, most of the time. Then they had seen Mrs Ricketts's advertisement and now, at long last, they had found just what they were looking for - work for both of them and the chance to live in a lovely little bungalow. They moved in with Mrs Ricketts at The Homestead on 12 March, 1953 - it was a move that would end in murder.

At first, the three got on so well that two weeks later, on 24 March, Mrs Ricketts asked Mrs Merrifield to call at the office of a solicitor, Mr Darbyshire, with instructions to draw up a new will. She wished to leave The Homestead to Louisa. This news threw the housekeeper into a state of great excitement. It was a miracle, a dream come true. She could hardly believe it. Luck such as this rarely fell to the likes of Louisa Merrifield. How she and 'Pop' must have clutched each other with glee, knowing that, some day, soon perhaps, their days of pinching and scraping would be over. No more trying to stretch out Alfie's pension each week; there would be no more skivvying for other people, no more bowing and scraping just to keep a roof over their heads. At last, the dream of so many people in that stringent post-war period, was now within their sights - they would become house-owners.

Seeking out some of her familiars, Louisa couldn't resist telling them of her good fortune and such was her relief and joyful anticipation that she let her tongue run away with her.

'Where I have been living,' she confided to one of them, 'an old lady has died and left me her bungalow worth £3,000.'

Warming to her new role as householder, she went on to suggest that she and Alfred might augment their income by raising a mortgage to buy a nursing home.

But Louisa was being precipitate. Mrs Ricketts was still alive and, moreover, she had changed her mind again. She now wished to name 'Pop' Merrifield as joint beneficiary. Her solicitor arrived at The Homestead on 31 March, with the will ready for her to sign. Her signature sealed her fate. Mrs Merrifield sat down the same day and wrote to a former employer telling her that she had been left *'a lovely little bungalow - and thank God for it'.*

During the evening of Thursday, 9 April, Dr Burton Yule received a visit from Mrs Merrifield in his surgery in Warbeck Hill Road. She was worried about her employer, she said, and feared that she might die of a stroke at any moment. Would he, she asked, call round and examine her and at the same time certify that she was of sound mind when she signed the will. After all, she twittered, Mrs Ricketts had left everything to her and she didn't want 'any trouble with the relatives' when they found out.

Despite describing her, amongst other things, as *'a tiresome type of woman'*, Dr Yule agreed to see Mrs Ricketts but the old lady refused to submit to an examination. She disliked and distrusted doctors, particularly Dr Yule, who, she said, always expected to be paid in cash.

On Monday, 13 April, when Mrs Merrifield called to pay his bill with a cheque, he refused to accept it and, knowing Mrs Ricketts's peculiar ways, declined to make any assessment of her mental fitness, at least for the housekeeper's benefit.

Having drawn a blank with Dr Yule, Louisa went straight over to the surgery of a Dr Albert Wood, who had treated Sarah Ricketts three years before. When she told him that the old lady was ill and had been unwell *'for some time'* he promised to pay her a visit the next day. Mrs Merrifield seemed agitated.

'What happens if she dies during the night?' she asked.

A little concerned by this remark, Dr Wood decided to call that same evening. He was not only surprised to find that Mrs Ricketts was perfectly well but also annoyed with Louisa for calling him out unnecessarily.

The following day, 14 April, Mrs Merrifield managed to persuade Dr Page, Dr Wood's partner, to visit The Homestead. Arriving in the middle of the morning he found Sarah Ricketts dying. The doctor was rather shocked to find 'Pop' Merrifield having his lunch close to the bed where the old lady lay in a coma. His wife, he said, had gone out to look for a doctor. Seeing the condition of Mrs Ricketts, Dr Page suggested they contact Dr Yule, her regular physician, as quickly as possible. Mrs Merrifield did subsequently telephone his surgery three times, but he was out. When he finally arrived at the bungalow, Mrs Ricketts was dead.

In the circumstances, the doctor naturally refused to sign a death certificate and reported it to the coroner as a suspicious death. He ordered an immediate post-mortem examination which was performed by a Dr Manning. His investigations made it clear that the cause of death was poisoning by phosphorus, a component of rat poison.

Mrs Merrifield's behaviour immediately after Mrs Ricketts died was odd, though not necessarily sinister. As soon as Dr Yule had left the house, she gathered up all her, Louisa's, personal documents, insurance policies - and an unwashed teaspoon - crammed them all into a handbag and hurried to a shop on the Promenade where her friend, Alice Hands, worked. She left the bag with her 'for safety'.

Naturally, in the course of their enquiry, the police questioned both Louisa and 'Pop' Merrifield. In her statement to Detective Superintendent Colin MacDougall, Louisa insinuated that Mrs Ricketts had been fond of a drink.

'She used to have egg and brandy about three times a day,' she said, sanctimoniously, with no mention, of course, of her own alcoholic propensity. As for 'Pop', he told the police that, four days before Mrs Ricketts had died, Louisa had expressed concern about her condition. She had told him that the old lady ought to see a doctor, adding that she 'didn't want to get into trouble if anything should happen to her suddenly'.

Her employer's unexplained death and her interrogation at the police station did not, however, inhibit Louisa. Far from it, for she continued to tell friends - and even strangers she met in the street - about her expectations.

To a journalist from the *News of the World*, she gabbled:

> 'I believe Mrs Ricketts made a will a few weeks ago, and she said we would always be able to live in comfort here.'

During their enquiries, of course, it didn't take the detectives long to establish from Louisa Merrifield's friends that she had told them all about the contents of the will some time before the old woman's death.

They also learned that Mrs Ricketts, on the day before she died, had already begun to have serious doubts about her new housekeeper and her husband. She had told George Forjan, a delivery man, that they would have to go. She also mentioned to him something about changing her will. It soon became clear that this statement, in conjunction with many more made to the police during the initial murder enquiry, might well lead to 'Pop' and Louisa Merrifield's arrest.

Soon after lunch on Thursday, 30 April, Mrs Merrifield's solicitor, Mr John Budd, and his clerk, arrived at The Homestead. It was a warm, sunny afternoon and holiday makers strolled along the promenade close by. As they talked with Louisa inside the bungalow,

'Pop' Merrifield, dressed in a blue suit and homburg hat, paced about in the front garden. Just before 2.20.pm, the police arrived.

Superintendent Colin MacDougall, a Scotland Yard Murder Squad officer, was in charge of the investigations, assisted by Sergeant Nick Carter and Blackpool's C.I.D. Chief, Inspector John Dunn. No sooner had the police entered the bungalow, than a small group of ladies from the neighbourhood, curious to know what was going on, began to gather outside.

About an hour later, they watched as Mrs Merrifield emerged - wearing a tweed coat and thick grey stockings - to be driven to the police headquarters in one of the police cars. Her husband and her solicitor followed in the second police car and, soon after her arrival, she was charged with the murder of Mrs Sarah Ann Ricketts. To this, she said, 'I am not guilty.'

Later that evening, a distressed 'Pop' Merrifield returned to the police station with a suitcase of clothing for his 'Louie'. He was told that she would appear at the Magistrates' Court the next day but was refused permission to see her. So it was that he returned to The Homestead alone that night, to reflect on all that had happened and pray for poor Louie's early release.

Several hours before the proceedings were about to begin on the following day, Friday, 1 May, a huge crowd of women had gathered around the entrance to Blackpool Magistrates' Court. More than two hundred people, protesting loudly, were turned away and 'Pop' Merrifield had a job to push his way through the door of the court to see his wife formally charged with murder. When the Clerk of the court called *'Put up Mrs Merrifield',* he leaned over the dock, waving his wife's reading glasses, but he was not allowed to hand them to her. The hearing lasted for little more than a minute. Having confirmed her identity and pleaded not guilty to the charge against her, she was remanded in custody. As she turned towards the cells, her husband grasped his silver-topped walking stick and called out:

'Keep your chin up, Louie!'

Outside the court, the dapper old man waved his brown trilby hat, which had a green feather stuck in the band, to the crowd. Before returning to The Homestead, he went shopping, closely followed by journalists who regaled their readers the next day with the riveting news that 'Pop' Merrifield had cooked himself a simple meal but was still bemoaning the fact that *'they didn't let me see my Louie'.*

Something else was worrying the old man. The handbag his wife was being so furtive about, leaving it with her friend, Alice Hands, and not saying what was inside. On 4 May, determined to see for himself, he collected the bag from Alice and, on seeing its contents, took it to his solicitor, for, he said, *'his own safety'*.

It was not until ten days later, on 14 May, at the start of the Committal hearing, that Merrifield was allowed to visit his wife in the cells at Blackpool Magistrates' Court. But he got more than a cuddle from his Louie - to his amazement, he, too, was arrested and also charged with the murder of Sarah Ricketts. The following morning, as he was brought up from the cells, 'Pop' Merrifield smiled and waved merrily to the court officials, saying: 'Good morning, gentlemen'.

It was the first time the pair had appeared in court together and, after pleading Not Guilty, they sat side by side on the solicitors' bench, as though taking the air on the sea-front, sucking boiled sweets as they listened to numerous witnesses testify against them.

The *News of the World* described Louisa Merrifield as a *'stocky, brown haired woman, hatless and wearing a pale blue coat, who sat for most of the time with her hands folded in her lap. Her husband, his sparse white hair ruffled, smiled at witnesses and occasionally whispered to his solicitor, Mr John Budd.'*

Dr Albert Wood, one of the doctors who had visited Mrs Ricketts prior to her death, was too ill to give evidence in court; so it was that, during the afternoon session, the Merrifields were driven in separate cars to the doctor's home on the corner of Warbeck Hill Road, about two hundred yards from The Homestead. Police patrolled the road outside as the prisoners were led into a room next to the doctor's surgery. They were allowed to sit next to each other by a window, carefully guarded by a wardress and a nurse from Strangeways Prison.

Then Dr Wood entered, wearing a red jersey and carpet slippers;

he was attended by his own doctor who sat behind him as he gave evidence. Clearly very ill and speaking in little more than a whisper, he told the prosecutor, Mr Prys Jones, that Mrs Merrifield had begged him to visit Sarah Ricketts on April, 13 because, she insisted, the old lady was very ill. Seeing that he was reluctant to make the call, she had protested:

'What happens if she dies during the night?'

He did eventually call on Mrs Ricketts after his surgery and, in his opinion, in spite of a chronic bronchial condition, the old lady was in good health. He told her there was nothing to worry about and prescribed sedative capsules as she seemed *'nervy'*. The old lady, clearly uneasy about something, asked him to call again the following morning but the doctor had said he would ask his partner, Dr Page, to make a visit.

'I got ready to go,' went on Dr Woods, 'and at this point Mrs Ricketts asked Mr and Mrs Merrifield to leave the room. She did not give any reason while they were present. Mrs Ricketts asked me to shut the door after them. I then had a conversation with Mrs Ricketts and when it was finished I made my way out through the hall. Mrs Merrifield mentioned something about a will to me but I was rather annoyed at having been called out and said I was not interested in her domestic affairs.'

Questioned by John Budd, the solicitor acting for the Merrifields, the doctor admitted that when he examined Mrs Ricketts on 13 April, the day before she died, he found no evidence of any symptoms of phosphorus poisoning - that is, a garlic taste in her mouth, a burning sensation in the throat, pain in the stomach or extreme thirst.

This said, the hearing was adjourned and resumed at the Magistrates' Court the following Wednesday. The inquiry lasted for three days, during which time a great many witnesses were questioned at some length. As a result, both Louisa and 'Pop' Merrifield were committed to stand trial for the murder of Sarah Ricketts at Manchester Assizes.

The trial was opened on Monday, 20 July 1953 and lasted for eleven days. The case came before Mr Justice Glyn-Jones, with the

Attorney General Sir Lionel Heald, QC, representing the Crown. Before embarking on his opening speech, he explained his presence as prosecutor:

'The crime of murder is a very grave one, but murder by poisoning has always been regarded as a particularly heinous form of crime because of its secrecy and treachery. There has always been a custom that the Law Officers of the Crown, or one of them, should appear in poisoning cases for the prosecution'.

Louisa Merrifield was defended by Jack di V. Nahum, QC, who, in the intervening weeks, had tried to stress the need for his client to curb her chattering tongue and appear less flippant in the face of such a serious charge.

The Attorney General then spent two hours outlining the details of the case against the Merrifields. He began by explaining that, as in the majority of poison cases, the charge rested purely on circumstantial evidence - evidence which was, he suggested, particularly strong in this case. He emphasised the unexplained fact that, despite Dr Woods's evidence that Mrs Ricketts was perfectly fit on the afternoon of 13 April, when Dr Yule was called to the bungalow the next day, the old lady was dead.

It was also beyond dispute, he said, that death was caused by poisoning with yellow phosphorus, usually found in rat poison.

> 'A one ounce tin [of Rodine] costing one shilling contains ten grains of yellow phosphorus - enough to kill five people if used skilfully. The other main ingredient in Rodine is bran, and bran was found in the body of Mrs Ricketts.'

It was also an undeniable fact, he went on, that the only other persons in the house at the time the old woman swallowed the poison were Louisa and Alfred 'Pop' Merrifield.

The prisoners, suggested Sir Lionel, knowing full well the contents of their employer's will, had every reason to hope to inherit as soon as possible - and, he emphasised, they had the *'exclusive opportunity'* to kill her. Indeed, Louisa Merrifield had boasted about the bungalow several days before the will had been signed. He would produce witnesses, he assured the court, to testify that she had spoken of her *'good fortune'* well before Mrs Ricketts's death.

Sir Lionel then drew the jurors' attention to Mrs Merrifield's actions after Mrs Ricketts had died and referred to the mysterious handbag given to Alice Hands. This bag, Sir Lionel told the court, was eventually collected by Mr Merrifield and given to his solicitor, John Budd, who at first refused to hand it over to the police, saying it would jeopardise his relationship with his client. When they did eventually take possession of the bag on 27 June, they found, amongst a pile of personal papers, a used teaspoon. When analysed, the substance adhering to the spoon was found to contain sugar - it may have been either rum or jam.

'I should like to tell you at once,' went on the Attorney General, 'there was no suggestion of phosphorus being on that spoon'.

This, in itself, he explained, was of no significance, as phosphorus was very quickly evaporated and would leave no trace. What *was* significant, he suggested, was that, if it had been used for a perfectly innocent purpose, Mrs Merrifield had felt it necessary to hide the spoon in the first place.

After commenting on the loophole in the law by which such a dangerous poison might be so easily bought over the counter for the price of a shilling, the prosecution turned to the witnesses in the case. The deposition of Dr Wood - who had died shortly after giving evidence in his house - was read to the court after which a number of witnesses were called.

One of the first was Mrs Aline Cawton of Bolton Street, Blackpool, who confirmed that, on the day that Mrs Ricketts had died, Louisa Merrifield called at the shop where she worked and left a handbag which she asked her to give to Alice Hands for safe keeping. Questioned by the Attorney General, she maintained that she did not look inside the bag and did not know its contents. Louisa, sitting tight-lipped in the dock, no doubt thought otherwise.

Mrs Cawton was followed into the witness box by another of Louisa's familiars - Mrs Esther Fagg, who lived in the same building as Alice Hands. She swore that on the following day, she had seen

Mrs Hands take a piece of paper from the bag, screw it up in a ball and throw it into a bucket of water.

'There was something about a £40 cheque written on it,' she said.

Yet when questioned, Alice Hands, of course, denied it. She had known Louisa Merrifield for eight or nine years, she told the court, and as to the contents of the handbag, Louisa had told her that there were some personal papers and insurance policies which she didn't want 'Pop' Merrifield to see.

'He had threatened to burn them if he could get his hands on them,' she said.

But after his wife's arrest, 'Pop' Merrifield seemed anxious to have the bag back, so she arranged to leave it, covered in brown paper in a carrier bag, on the cobble-stones on the Promenade for him to collect. She saw Merrifield pick it up but neither of them spoke. This cloak and dagger method of returning such an innocuous item seemed rather melodramatic and was never fully explained - unless, of course, the bag had contained something more sinister or incriminating when it passed into 'Pop' Merrifield's hands.

Next came Miss Mavis Atkinson, an assistant in Cotton's Chemist shop, at Victoria Bridge, Manchester. She identified Alfred 'Pop' Merrifield as the man to whom she had sold a tin of Rodine in March of that year. It was a product in fairly common use, however, for she said she had sold about twelve tins between January and April. She said that Merrifield had come into the shop with a woman and had also asked her if she could recommend a remedy for an ulcerated leg. At the time, he was wearing spectacles and a hearing aid. However, at a police identification parade held on 30 April, she had paused in front of Merrifield but failed to point him out because, she now maintained, she was too *'nervous'*. It was not lost on the jury that, although Miss Atkinson denied that she had seen photographs of Alfred Merrifield in the newspapers since that time - and that he was the only person in court wearing a hearing aid - her belated identification was, to say the least, flawed.

Her testimony was endorsed by the chemist, Harold Hague, who also claimed to recognise 'Pop' Merrifield in court, having previously failed to do so at two identification parades. He told the court that he had already sold two dozen tins of Rodine that year and, as he said this, 'Pop' Merrifield leaned forward in the dock and smiled broadly at him. The chemist went on to recall the conversation he'd had with Merrifield concerning his bad leg - the old man had been wearing spectacles, a loose mackintosh and a soft hat. Although he, too, said that he had been in the company of a woman at the time, neither he nor his assistant positively identified Louisa Merrifield as that woman.

Dr George Manning, the pathologist who had performed the post-mortem on Mrs Ricketts's body, testified that, in his opinion, death was caused by phosphorus poisoning and that this was taken during the night of 13 April. The jurors were asked to smell a sample of Rodine rat poison, after which they listened keenly as the doctor described the experiments he had done with phosphorus. The odour and taste, he informed them, was 'garlicky' but both rum and blackcurrant jam masked the taste very well. Although brandy also masked the taste, he found that he could still detect a slight smell of phosphorus. Yellow phosphorus, he went on, quickly evaporated and, in conjunction with oxygen, was immediately transformed into phosphates which were not poisonous. Although this was his first case of poisoning by yellow phosphorus, he was able to estimate that *'almost certainly more than one grain was involved'*.

The pathologist was followed into the witness box by Alan Thompson, staff chemist of the North West Forensic Laboratory, in Preston. He testified that there was no phosphorus in the sugary substance on the spoon that Mrs Merrifield had hidden in her handbag.

The Attorney General also called various witnesses who were only too happy to testify to Mrs Merrifield's careless bragging prior to old Sarah Ricketts's death. The court heard that to a Mrs Allwood she had confided her good fortune several days before the solicitor had even been informed that the old lady wished to change her will. And six days before the will was signed, Louisa had told another witness, David Brindley:

> 'I have had a bit of luck. Where I have been living the old lady has died and left me the bungalow.'

Again, on 30 March, Louisa had written to a Mrs Lowe:

> 'I am doing all right. We are landed. I went to live with an old lady and she has left me a bungalow worth £4,000.'

Furthermore, the jury heard that on the evening before Mrs Ricketts's death, Mrs Merrifield had met a woman called Elizabeth Barraclough whilst waiting in a bus queue. Although she was a perfect stranger, Louisa initiated a conversation by saying that she was very worried as the old lady for whom she was working was very ill. This was followed by a faintly ludicrous scenario of her, Louie, returning from a trip to Wigan to see her children and finding her husband in bed with the old lady!

'She said that half an hour later,' Mrs Barraclough testified, aware of the rapt attention of the court, 'her husband wanted to know if he could massage the old lady's legs for her and that was to try to get the will changed in his favour. She said if it happened again, there would be a row. She said: "I know what I'll do. I'll poison the old..... and him as well."'

Equally damaging to the defence was the evidence given by George Johnson, a funeral director. Mrs Merrifield, he said, called at his office two days after Mrs Ricketts had died and tried to arrange for her cremation, saying that the old woman had specified that she did not want to be buried with either of her husbands and did not want her daughters to know about her death. Johnson, however, told her he could only take instructions for the funeral arrangements from the next of kin.

The prosecution case was further enhanced by the appearance of Mrs Veronica King, for her evidence was devastating. She testified that, on the Sunday before Mrs Ricketts died, she had met Louisa Merrifield at a neighbour's house.

As she was leaving, Louisa said: 'I will go and lay the old lady out.'

Mrs King had then asked if somebody had just died and received this ominous reply:

'There's an old lady but she's not dead yet, but she soon will be.'

Dr Yule said that when Mrs Merrifield called at his surgery on 13 April, to pay a bill she did not mention that her employer was ill. In response to a message left at his surgery, he called to see Mrs Ricketts the next day by which time she was already dead.

'I came to the conclusion that she had been dead roughly an hour,' he said.

Perhaps suspecting suicide or accidental death, he looked for any tell tale signs. 'I looked round the room but could see no receptacles like tumblers, glasses or cups. Nor did I see any spoons or tins. Mrs Merrifield came in and I told her that I was extremely surprised - I had seen Mrs Ricketts alive on the Friday and she was now dead. She did not complain of any symptoms likely to cause sudden death. I said I could give no medical reason why she should die. I refused to issue a death certificate and said I should have to report the matter to the coroner.'

Cross-examined by Mr Nahum for the defence, the doctor again denied that Mrs Merrifield had mentioned that the old lady was very ill when she called at the surgery on 13 April. He did admit, however, that on the day Mrs Ricketts died, Mrs Merrifield had called him at his surgery at 12.20, 12.45 and 1.15pm, while he was out on his rounds.

Dr Ernest Page told the court of his visit to Mrs Ricketts about mid-day on the morning of 14 April prior to Dr Yule's arrival. Describing the scene at the bungalow he said:

> 'Mr Merrifield was having lunch from a table which was pushed right up against the bed in which Mrs Ricketts was lying. There was another place laid for Mrs Merrifield. Mrs Ricketts was propped up on pillows and she was very ill. I asked for the table to be taken away and, when I put my arm round Mrs Ricketts and said something to her, it was apparent that she was dying.... I advised Mrs Merrifield to send for Dr Yule as soon as possible.'

He had explained that, as he was not treating the old lady, he was not in the position to issue a death certificate.

Though the circumstantial evidence against the Merrifields

was undeniably strong, the forensic case against them was far from convincing. Phosphorus was *not* found on the used spoon in Louisa's handbag. Even if Louisa had used the spoon to feed the old lady a mixture of rum and rat poison, there was no way the forensic department could prove it. The tin of Rodine, alleged to have been bought by the Merrifields, was never found. Nor was there a single trace of phosphorus in the house - this in itself, suggested the prosecution, was suspicious.

Only if the poison had been administered criminally would it be necessary to clear away all trace of it. Its absence must therefore be indicative of the Merrifields' guilt for only they had shared the house with the poison victim and, therefore, had every opportunity to administer it, unobserved.

Both Mrs Ricketts's daughters, Mrs Ethel Harrison and Mrs Whittaker, also gave evidence, telling the court that their mother had been married twice and both husbands had killed themselves by inhaling gas. When certain difficulties concerning the old lady's relationship with Mrs Harrison was alluded to, she said: 'We were good friends, but we were better friends if I did not go too often'.

Also called to the witness box was Lavinia Bleazard, a lady who had occasionally worked for Mrs Ricketts. She insisted that the house was always very clean and entirely free of vermin; she had never seen any rat poison in the house.

The solicitor who drew up Mrs Ricketts's will was also called. William Arnold Darbyshire, confirmed that when Mrs Merrifield called on 24 March with instructions from Mrs Ricketts to draw up a will, Mr Merrifield was not included. When, on 31 March, he called at The Homestead for Mrs Ricketts to sign the document, the old lady had decided to include 'Pop' Merrifield as well.

The evidence given by the delivery man, George Forjan, was of extreme importance to the prosecution. He drove a van for a firm of wine merchants and said he used to deliver a bottle of rum once a week and a dozen bottles of Guinness a month to Mrs Ricketts at The Homestead. Twice in the last six months, he went on, he had also delivered a bottle of brandy. As soon as Mrs Merrifield moved into the bungalow, she ordered a bottle of champagne and a dozen bottles of stout for herself.

Describing his visit on 12 April, he said,

> Mrs Ricketts opened the door and I went into the front room where Mr Merrifield was. I had a bottle of brandy which I gave to Mrs Ricketts and opened it for her. She had not paid me for three or four weeks and started looking for money to pay me. She looked in the safe first and Mr Merrifield said, 'You looked there before. They are not there."
>
> Then she [Mrs Ricketts] turned to me and said:
>
> 'I don't know what they are doing with my money, George. I cannot pay you again.'
>
> She gave me a handbook and asked me to find out how much money she had in the bank so that she could pay me next week. I told her I could not understand bank books. Then Mr Merrifield stepped in and tried to help her but found out he could not understand bank books. He suggested he could go to the bank and find out for Mrs Ricketts.
>
> Mrs Ricketts told him that while he was going to the bank he could call on her solicitors because she wanted to change her will. Mr Merrifield said he could not go to the solicitors because it was too far for him. That moment Mrs Ricketts turned round and said: "What can I do, George?"
>
> She started to complain about her food and said she had not had proper food for the past three days.
>
> Mr Merrifield said that she was telling stories. He said: "You had three eggs."
>
> Mrs Ricketts said: "I cannot live on eggs only." Then she said to me: "They're no good to me. They will have to go out."

To this, the delivery man said that, prior to the Merrifields taking over the old lady's housekeeping, she had always paid her bills regularly and never owed money.

The validity of Mrs Ricketts's complaint to George Forjan - that the Merrifields were wasting her money and not giving her enough to eat - was endorsed by the evidence of Mrs Jessie Jensen. She said that on the evening of 12 April, 'Pop' Merrifield had told her that his wife 'had been out since one o'clock that afternoon and had come back at five in an awful state - slightly inebriated. She came with a tin of steak and that was the only ration they had for three days. She had spent the old lady's ration money. They had had a terrific row.'

Mrs Jensen went on to say that, at the time, 'Pop' Merrifield had referred to his wife as 'an old fool' and feared that her behaviour might lose them their job, which would be especially stupid now that the old lady had made a will in their favour.

When cross-examined by Mr Nahum, Dr George Manning described his findings during the post-mortem on Mrs Ricketts's body. He said that the stomach contained about four ounces of dark brown fluid and the stomach wall was very congested and inflamed. This was caused by some irritant substance. The condition of the liver indicated that a fairly recent toxic change had taken place, caused by some poisonous substance that could have been - either introduced to it or manufactured by the body itself - a condition known as auto-toxication. In his opinion, Mrs Ricketts died from a dose of phosphorus. If it was taken in one dose, then that must have been during the evening of 13 April. If, however, the poison was taken in several small doses, it might have been started in the evening and continued throughout the night. Rodine consisted of finely divided yellow phosphorus, bran and sugar, all of which were found in the body.

When Professor John Webster was called to give evidence for the defence, he gave a conflicting view. He was of the opinion that Mrs Ricketts did not die from poison at all; her death was due to natural causes - necrosis of the liver, brought on by a dietary deficiency due to alcoholic intake. He was not prepared to say whether, in his opinion, she had been given rat poison. What he *was* prepared to say was that, if this was the case, her naturally occurring liver disfunction caused her death before the effects of any poison administered to her. Mr Justice Glyn-Jones, wishing to clarify the point for the jury asked Professor Webster:

'Does this mean that, by coincidence, this old lady died so quickly after swallowing phosphorus that it had no time to enter her body?'

'That is correct,' replied Webster.

There was another possibility, suggested the professor. Mrs Ricketts may have been poisoned by contact with bottles from a brewery infested with rats. Unable to disguise his incredulity on hearing what he considered to be a preposterous theory, the Attorney General was heard to murmur:

'She might also have been struck by lightning.'

It must have been with some trepidation that, on Friday, 24 July, Mr Nahum called Louisa Merrifield to give evidence. Throughout the proceedings so far she had spent much of the trial sitting squatly in the dock, occasionally smiling and chattering, either to 'Pop' Merrifield, her solicitor or anyone who caught her eye. She seemed unaware of the gravity of her predicament. When called to the witness box, she dismissed the murder charge as being the result of jealousy on the part of gossip-mongers, who, she added smugly, were 'up to their necks in mortgages'.

After giving details of her early life, her two previous marriages and the years prior to going to work for Mrs Ricketts, she was questioned about the soiled teaspoon in her handbag. She told the court that she often carried items of cutlery in this way whenever she and Alfred were on the move from one job to another.

She went on to say that when she and 'Pop' Merrifield first went to The Homestead in March of that year, there was very little food in the house - only three boxes of breakfast cereal in the larder, some pots of jam and two rusty tins of fruit stored in a cupboard. Mrs Ricketts seemed to prefer a liquid diet for, she said, the old lady had a bottle of rum, a bottle of brandy and twelve bottles of Guinness in the house.

Inferring that the household was not only frugal but also casually run, Mrs Merrifield said that the grocer, milkman and coalman all used to walk into the bungalow unannounced. She soon put a stop to that, she told the court and, moreover, took over all the household finances, at least for the first three weeks.

Referring to Mrs Ricketts's consumption of spirits, she assumed a sanctimonious tone and said that the old woman drank steadily throughout the day - she would fill an egg cup with rum or brandy and sip from it whenever she wished - it was like a medicine to her. When George Forjan came with more rum and brandy Mrs Merrifield remonstrated with Mrs Ricketts, saying:

> I don't know what I'm going to do. If you are going to have all this drink, Granny, I can't carry on. If you are going to have all this drink I cannot give you the food I was giving you. I got chicken twice a week and fish three times a week. I made her good puddings and gave her egg custards. She was beginning to look well.

But the incident ended with the two ladies at loggerheads and it was eventually decided that Mrs Ricketts and the Merrifields would buy their own food and even store it separately.

Asked to describe the old lady, Louisa said:

> She was very nice when everything was going fine and she was getting all her own way. She was what you would expect an old woman of her years to be. She was whimsical, as we say. She was a very strong-willed woman and you could not make her do what you wanted her to do if she wanted her own way. The green grocery man came and said: "She will promise you the bungalow. She has promised it to everybody in Devonshire Road."

'She had lived in the place for thirty years,' Louisa told the court, 'and not one neighbour asked how the old lady was. I went down to the grocer with whom she had dealt for thirty years and no one in the shop asked how she was.'

Asked about her former employer's health before she died, Mrs Merrifield said she had often urged her to see a doctor but she had refused, saying she'd had a 'belly-full of them'. Louisa then told the court that she had nursed Sarah Ricketts through a 'mysterious' illness on her last night. The old woman was suffering, she said, from intense pain, thirst and coma. Though Louisa seemed unaware of the significance of her testimony, it was not lost on the jury that these were some of the symptoms of phosphorus poisoning.

When the prosecution demanded to know why, if the old lady was so ill, she and her husband had not sent for a doctor, Louisa replied that it was 3.15. in the morning, after all, and she didn't like to go out after dark. When asked the same question, 'Pop' Merrifield had claimed to be too crippled to walk as far as the doctor's house. However, it was later confirmed that he was able to make it to the bus stop, which was considerably further.

The subject of the legacy of the bungalow had first arisen, Louisa said, when they were listening to a band playing on the radio. Mrs Ricketts had said how much she admired the work of the Salvation Army. Louisa had then told the old lady about her association with the Salvation Army - how her first husband had been a regular bandsman and that although she did not wear the uniform she had been a Salvationist all her life.

When she told Mrs Ricketts the sad story - or rather, her version of it - of her children being taken from her and spending much of their childhood in institutions, the old woman had felt sorry for her and said she would leave her the bungalow, ensuring that the whole family would always have a home.

Questioned further, Louisa told the jury that Mrs Ricketts had disliked Dr Yule and refused to see him. Early in April, she received a bill from him for £1.11s.6d. She was annoyed, saying that the last time she paid him with a cheque, he had thrown it on the fire and demanded the money in cash. The feeling seemed to be mutual for, according to Louisa, when she called at the surgery to pay the bill, the doctor said: 'How is the old -------- getting on these days?'

It was then she told the doctor that her employer was not 'A1' to which the doctor replied: 'She's a funny old stick. I have known her for years. Has she made a will yet?'

Yet Dr Yule had denied that she said anything about her being ill. Louisa stressed that she asked the doctor to examine Mrs Ricketts, not, as alleged by the prosecution, to certify that she was '*compos mentis*', but because she was afraid she might die suddenly, as her second husband had done.

During that night, Louisa went on, she was 'up seven or eight times' attending to the old lady who was constipated and suffering from pains in her stomach. She took liquid paraffin mixed with jam spread on her breakfast cereal. That evening, she still had stomach ache and was coughing badly. On the morning of 12 April, Mrs Merrifield saw the old lady soaking a piece of cotton with glycerine to use as a mouth-wash as she said she had a nasty taste in her mouth. That evening, Mrs Ricketts mixed glycerine with blackcurrant jam and ate some fruit from a tin that had been in her cupboard for a long time - in fact, it was pre-war. In addition, she had her usual rum and brandy to drink.

Asked by Mr Nahum if there was ever a day when the old lady did not have her rum and brandy, Louisa replied: 'No, never,' she chuckled. 'I don't think there was ever two hours, never mind a day. She always took it neat in an egg cup.'

Those of a more sceptical mind in the court that day may well have considered this a classic case of the kettle calling the coal black if ever there was one.

On the Monday, Mrs Ricketts was still ill and complaining of stomach pain. Asked by her defence counsel to describe the old lady's last night on earth, Louisa said:

> I was up and down with her five or six times that night. She was in and out of the toilet. She was fumbling into drawers. I heard a tin of sweets fall all over the floor. I got up again. I sat with her for a few minutes. I heard her go to the bathroom again. She was under the tap. I asked her was she sick and she said: "No." I got her into bed again.
>
> She went to the toilet and she cried bitterly and said: "You don't know how ill I am." I got her into bed. She seemed to go a bit quieter. Next thing I heard her up again and she was in the hall on the floor. I picked her up. I got her into bed. She thanked both my husband and me for what we had done for her. Those were the last words she spoke.

Soon after three o'clock that morning, she lost her power of speech. According to Mrs Merrifield:

> Her teeth came out and I pushed them back and found she had about five pink cough lozenges in her mouth at once. She seemed to

> go quieter. She had a bottle of rum on the table, her egg cup full of brandy or rum. She had her tongue out. She could not speak. Almost asking, the way she would do, because she was thirsty. I just gave her a sip out of the egg cup which was prepared for by herself the night before. I gave her nothing until the time when she lost her speech.

In the morning, she went again for a doctor.

'After seeing so many people die,' she told the court, 'I knew it was up to me to get someone as quickly as I could.'

Dr Page reluctantly paid a visit about mid-day but told Mrs Merrifield to contact Dr Yule again. She did, in fact, call at the surgery three times that afternoon, without success. It was while she was out again looking for the doctor that the old lady had died.

At this stage in his questioning, Mr Nahum asked his client whether, at any time in her life, she had ever been told anything about phosphorus, the housekeeper replied: 'Never, sir.'

'Did you at any time cause to be administered or administer Rodine rat poison to Mrs Ricketts?'

'No, sir,' she said.

Finally he asked: 'So far as you could observe from the actions and words of your husband through the whole of these days to which we have been referring, did he ever administer anything of a poisonous nature?'

'No, sir.'

The following day, Monday, 27 July, the Attorney General began his cross-examination of Louisa Merrifield. One newspaper reporter describing the scene said that 'for three hours and 50 minutes plump Mrs Merrifield, speaking slowly but firmly, scorned a chair placed in the witness-box'.

Sir Lionel began by challenging the accused's insistence that she had not given Mrs Ricketts anything to drink until the early hours of 14 April, the day the old lady died. He reminded her that, in the statement she made to the police on 17 April, she had said that she had given the old lady sips from her egg cup full of rum or brandy throughout that night. To this, Louisa merely said that the old lady had prepared the contents of the egg cup herself the night before. What she had meant, she said, was that she had not given her Rodine to drink.

When asked if she had been fond of Mrs Ricketts, she said that she 'loved the old lady' but went on to say that she was a 'very immoral woman' in that she had been too fond of 'Pop' Merrifield. Asked to explain what she meant by this remark, Mrs Merrifield nodded towards members of the press and said, saucily: 'Is it all right to explain in front of these young men?'

Denying the Attorney General's suggestion that she had made up her mind to get the bungalow for herself from the moment she went to work there, Louisa also said that she had not mentioned the contents of the will to a soul before Mrs Ricketts's death. She could not understand why her neighbours had testified to the contrary - it must have been jealousy on their part. She further denied that she had ever insinuated that her husband was having an affair with Mrs Ricketts - nor had she ever threatened to poison anyone.

Furthermore, she said, she had never been to the chemist shop in Manchester nor set eyes on either Mr Hague or Miss Atkinson before. Nor could she remember ever speaking to Mrs Barraclough at a bus stop. In fact, she had never seen her before nor did she recognise any of the witnesses when she saw them in court. At one point, the Attorney General remarked:

'Don't you at times speak to people in an unguarded manner when you have had a drink?'

'I can have a joke with anyone when I'm sober. I never get drunk,' rejoined Louisa, unabashed.

'You know, don't you,' said Sir Lionel, 'that yellow phosphorus was found in Mrs Ricketts's body?'

'I don't know what colour it was.'

'You know what poison was found?'

'I heard so.'

'You know that, according to Dr Manning, the most striking sign of phosphorus poisoning is great thirst? You have said she suffered from great thirst in the early hours of the 14th?'

'She suffered from great thirst from the time of us going there,' Louisa quipped. 'She was always on the thirst for her brandy and her drink.'

'You told two people, I suggest, that you contemplated her death?'

'No, sir.' After a pause, Mrs Merrifield added: 'What do you mean by contemplated her death, sir?'

'To poison the old -------- , that is what you said?'

'I never poisoned Mrs Ricketts,' Louisa protested, 'I never gave her Rodine.'

'You said her last words referred to what you had done for her?'

'Yes.'

'Was not what you had done for her to poison her with rat poison?'

'No, sir, I loved her.'

It was only after Louisa Merrifield had been in the witness-box for a total of nine hours, over a period of three days, that she was allowed to leave. As soon as she stepped down and returned to her seat in the dock, on the afternoon of Monday, 27 July, her place was taken by her husband, 'Pop' Merrifield. His counsel began by referring to the allegation made earlier by Mr Hague, the chemist, and his assistant, Miss Atkinson - that on 10 March that year, he had come into their chemist shop in Manchester and bought a tin of Rodine.

'Definitely not, sir,' he protested, loudly. 'Perjured evidence, definitely, bolstered up by Scotland Yard men'.

'That will do,' snapped the judge.

Ignoring him, Merrifield turned to face the jury:

'This is a British court of justice, gentlemen,' he continued. 'I am giving my evidence in the fight for my life and my wife.'

When reminded of the allegation that he had bought a tin of Rodine in Manchester, he declared:

'I have not been in Manchester for five solid years. I have never left the precincts of Blackpool.'

He went on to say that he had never seen either the chemist or his assistant before in his life and had no more idea where the chemist shop was - he had, he quipped, 'no more idea than this spectacle case'.

He firmly denied their allegation that he had bought Rodine from the shop. They said he was wearing a light grey suit at the time - in that case, he said, it couldn't have been him, for although he did own a similar suit, it was in the pawn-shop in early March. When the court was shown a light grey suit, he laughingly declared: 'That's mine. Can I put it on?'

The judge was not amused and, once more, asked 'Pop' Merrifield to refrain from making jokes in court. Yet the old chap seemed to go out of his way to antagonise both judge and jury with his flippant replies. Despite the public reprimand, when asked about his ex-employer, Sarah Ricketts, he said: 'I thought she was a very, very heavy drinker for an old lady; in fact, I helped to drink some of it myself when she gave it to me,' he said, grinning broadly.

Questioned about the insurance policies found in his wife's handbag, he said he had never been in favour of heavy policies, only sufficient to 'bury a person decently but not of an excess to squander'. If he'd known about his wife's policies, he added, he would have destroyed them. Just before her arrest, when he pressed her to tell him what was in the handbag, Louisa had said: 'I have no fear of anything. There is nothing at all incriminating in that handbag.'

'Pop' Merrifield told the court, however, that he was 'very anxious' about this handbag for 'my own safety and I wanted to get hold of it to see if there was anything dangerous in it.'

But, when he had urged Alice Hands to give it back she was 'very windy about it'. She said: "Don't talk so loud; you never know who is hearing. I have got it in my room but how can I get it to you?"

The next day, Mrs Hands left the handbag on the promenade in a carrier bag and he picked it up. There was brown paper over the top, covering it.

'I never interfered with it in any shape or form,' he insisted, before suddenly bursting into tears. Despite frequently attempting to inject some levity into his evidence, his voice broke several times and he finally began to cry. When asked if he would like to take a short rest before carrying on, he replied: 'No, it's all right, but it is very hard work.'

A little later, Mr Nahum said: 'It has been suggested you were guilty of some impropriety with Mrs Ricketts.'

This did not please 'Pop' Merrifield, at all.

'A more infamous statement has never been made in a court of justice,' he replied, indignantly. 'It is definitely not true. Outrageous. Fancy getting into bed with an old woman of eighty. Look at my wife - a young woman.'

He denied ever telling Mrs Jensen that his wife had come back at five o'clock one afternoon *'in an awful state - slightly inebriated'*. Such a suggestion was, he said, yet again using his favourite adjective - *'outrageous'.*

'Did you say she came with a tin of steak?' asked Mr Nahum.

'It would have been a big mistake if she had!' he chortled.

This reply was followed by an outbreak of laughter in the court which further annoyed the judge. He turned to Mr Nahum,

'You might tell him,' he said, sternly, 'he would do well to remember his position and not make jokes.'

'I am not making jests!' came the jocular reply.

He was then asked: 'Did you ever see anything which led you to believe or suspect that your wife had administered or was going to administer poison to Mrs Ricketts?'

To this he retorted: 'If I had thought, my lord and gentlemen, if I thought there was any action of any description that my wife was going to do wrong to this old lady, I would certainly have prevented it, for my own sake.'

'Have you yourself in any way done or attempted to do anything to harm the old lady?'

The old man's response was dramatic. He raised his arms and clenched his fists above his head.

'There is a pair of fists, gentlemen,' he declared. 'If they do not open again all I did was to succour the old lady, not destroy her.'

Asked by the Attorney General if he had been fond of his employer, he replied: 'I was very fond of her. I had a good, comfortable home and nothing at all to worry about. That is why I was fond of the old lady.'

Asked why, if that was the case, he was able to sit so close to the old woman's bed as she lay dying, eating his lunch as though nothing was wrong, he looked puzzled and asked: 'Where else could I sit?'

Despite this odd reply, Merrifield was not pressed to elaborate or explain to the court why he did not choose to eat his lunch in one of the other rooms. When Sir Lionel intimated that neither the time nor the place could be considered appropriate, Merrifield said: 'Was I not perfectly entitled to have my lunch?'

To this, Sir Lionel wondered whether he might not have been too upset at the prospect of the old lady's imminent death to eat at her bedside. But 'Pop' Merrifield explained: 'She was not a blood relation of mine, but I was upset about her dying.'

'It did not interfere with your appetite?' enquired the Attorney General, facetiously.

'Yes, it did,' Merrifield replied. 'Definitely it did. You were not there to see the quantity of food I had.'

Asked why, if he was so fond of Mrs Ricketts, he had not fetched a doctor when it was clear that she was dying, Merrifield said: 'I am a cripple. It is definite that I should have my rest. Not only that but there was a capable lady there, my wife, to attend to her.'

Asked what he considered might have been in his wife's handbag that would constitute a *'danger'* to him, Merrifield simply said: 'My own safety.'

Voicing the suspicions of many present in court that day Sir Lionel suddenly said: 'Were you afraid it might be something like this?' as he produced a tin of Rodine from behind his back. Seeing this, Merrifield turned his head away, saying: 'Don't let me look at it. I have heard so much about it this last four months. I see it in my sleep.'

The next witness to give evidence was Professor John Webster, Director of the West Midland Science Laboratory and Professor of Forensic Medicine and Toxicology at Birmingham University.

Questioned for the defence, he disagreed with much of Dr Manning's evidence, saying that the degeneration of the liver mentioned by the prosecution pathologist was caused by disease - necrosis, not poison. In his opinion, Mrs Ricketts had died naturally, although he did concede that she may well have swallowed some phosphorus from rat poison as well.

He was medical advisor to the Home Office and therefore normally called for the prosecution. In this particular case, he had been given special permission to appear for the defence as it fell outside his regional area. Whether he thought that the poison was taken accidentally or with suicidal intent, he was not prepared to speculate. He put the probable time of ingestion at seven o'clock on the morning of 14 April, the day Mrs Ricketts died. She may even have taken further small doses after seven o'clock, went on the Professor, but these would not have been the actual cause of death.

Sir Lionel expressed his contention by suggesting that it was a 'fantastic hypothesis for a medical man to put forward'.

To this, the professor replied, frostily: 'You are entitled to your opinion, sir.'

The Attorney General also asked a number of questions about the detection of phosphorus, to which Professor Webster demurred: 'I am not a chemist. I have not the faintest idea.'

It was apparent that the judge shared much of Sir Lionel's scepticism regarding the suggestion that Mrs Ricketts may have taken the poison herself. 'Is the suggestion,' he asked, 'that she liked it so much that, after seven o'clock in the morning, she helped herself to more?'

Professor Webster did not reply and the hearing was adjourned until the following day, the ninth in the trial. Webster was recalled and there followed further discussion on the defence hypothesis that even if Mrs Ricketts had taken phosphorus - which, he emphasised, could have been little more than one grain, the minimum lethal dose - she had, nevertheless, died naturally, before the poison had time to invade her system.

'This coincidence of poison and death from natural causes,' he explained, 'is not a thing to be wondered at at all. It occurs every week in this country. The commonest poisons, apart from alcohol, to which the community are exposed, are the anaesthetics, which are poisonous. Deaths occur on the table which were formerly termed *'anaesthetic deaths'* and we now know a large proportion of these were not *'anaesthetic deaths'* at all. We find in a great many cases we can recover the anaesthetic from the organs though they died from natural causes, such as coronary thrombosis.'

Another expert, Mr Freshfield Leonard Cann, a Home Office chemist, was next to take the stand. After being questioned at length about the properties of phosphorus, his place in the witness box was taken by Dr Manning, recalled for cross-examination by the defence.

Mr Stanley Garlick, a Blackpool pawn-broker, also testified that Louisa Merrifield had pawned 'Pop' Merrifield's grey suit [and a brown one with white chalk stripes] on 9 February and subsequently redeemed them both on 14 March. This further negated the evidence of the chemist and his assistant who claimed he was wearing the suit when he visited the shop on 10 March.

Hearing his evidence, 'Pop' Merrifield put his head in his hands and seemed to be weeping, presumably with relief.

Later that day, Mr Nahum began his final speech for the defence but no sooner had he begun than 'Pop' Merrifield started to sob again; he slumped forward in the dock, clutching at the hand rail.

'I can't stand it,' he cried, pitifully. 'It's not fair. Let me go downstairs while you finish. I can't hear. You may as well let me go down.'

Louisa Merrifield patted her husband's shoulder as he was taken down to the cells to receive medication. When he returned fifteen minutes later, Mr Nahum was able to continue with his speech. Much of the suspicion that had 'not unnaturally accumulated like a rising mountain' against the Merrifields, he said, was caused by Louisa's own 'foolish talk'. But, he warned, people in this country were not convicted of murder on what they said, but on what they did.

> 'Let us not lose sight of the crux and kernel of this case - the two things which the prosecution must prove before either of these two accused can be convicted of murder. The first is that the dose of

> yellow phosphorus was introduced into the body of Mrs Ricketts and that dose actually caused her death. The second thing is that it was by the hands of the accused that the vital dose was introduced into her body.'

He went on to submit to the jury that the prosecution case had failed to supply the degree of proof necessary in a murder case. He also admitted that Mrs Merrifield had made a number of evasive statements whilst giving evidence and she had also accused some witnesses of lying, but, he went on, this was 'merely the vapourings of a woman in difficulties which, on the face of it, would tend to bear against her.'

Referring to Sarah Ricketts's will, Mr Nahum declared: 'Is there any merit in the suggestion that they murdered her rather than wait for her natural death - this old lady of eighty?'

As Mrs Ricketts was estranged from her daughters there was nothing unusual, he explained, about her leaving the bungalow to the Merrifields, who had been so kind to her. Nor must they put any sinister interpretation on the fact that Mrs Merrifield went to fetch the solicitor to execute the old lady's will and tried to get a doctor to establish that she was '*compos mentis*'.

On the contrary, he said,

> Let us visualise that these two people made up their minds to poison Mrs Ricketts. They buy a will form. They do not call a doctor. They get her to make a will in their favour and administer the poison to her. She dies. A strange doctor is brought in. She is a lady of eighty. They tell the doctor she fell ill in the night and they came down next morning and found her. May not that have been a pretty good way - the way the murderers would work if they really were murderers? The prosecution say that if you bring a solicitor and bring a doctor - Mrs Merrifield called in three - that is evidence of guilt. If you don't bring both that is also evidence of guilt. "Heads I win, tails you lose."

If Dr Manning was correct in saying that Mrs Ricketts died from a dose of yellow phosphorus, why, he asked the jury, did Professor Webster, 'a competent, honest, and distinguished professional man, another pathologist, come into court to contradict him?'

He reminded the jurors that Professor Webster was a man of almost unequalled experience in his highly specialised field - the pathology of murder - surely they must at least doubt Dr Manning's conclusions?

'I do not ask you to say Professor Webster is right or Dr Manning is wrong. As a result of hearing Professor Webster there is a chance, there is a possibility that Dr Manning is wrong about his conclusions, and that is enough for my purpose.'

It was, after all, he emphasised, the prosecution's brief to prove the Merrifields' guilt, not for the defence to prove their innocence.

'Beyond the finding of phosphorus in the body of the old lady and beyond the suggestion that the Merrifields were the only people in the house and must have administered the poison, there is not one scintilla, not one jot of evidence that the Merrifields did in fact administer the poison. You cannot rule out accidents of the most extraordinary kind'. Furthermore, he added, there was no proof whatsoever that the poison was administered criminally - it may have been taken by accident or, if it was a case of suicide, by design.

At this point, Mr Nahum referred to the current case of John Reginald Christie and Timothy Evans.[34]

'Was it not a fantastic coincidence that in the same house in Rillington Place there were two murderers - two stranglers?'

Turning to face the Merrifields in the dock, he said:

'Perhaps the long arm of coincidence and the long arm of the law struck at the same time and engulfed these two people?'

He also rejected the notion that his clients could have been feeding Mrs Ricketts with rum laced with rat poison throughout the night of 13 April. The old lady enjoyed her rum and would undoubtedly have noticed if it had been mixed with something as obnoxious as

34 John Reginald Christie was found guilty of the murder of seven women whilst living at 10, Rillington Place, Notting Hill. He was hanged at Pentonville Prison on 15 July 1953. Another tenant of the house, Timothy Evans, was hanged in 1950 for the murder of his baby daughter, Geraldine. He also confessed to killing his wife, Beryl, but later retracted his statement. Reg Christie, arrested three years later, admitted that Beryl had been one of his victims. In 1966, Evans was awarded a posthumous free pardon.

phosphorus.

'It would have been like asking someone to drink mud,' suggested Nahum.

Turning then to the actions of Mrs Merrifield before and after the death of Mrs Ricketts.

'If Mrs Merrifield was a murderer about to kill her victim,' he suggested, 'what would be the two subjects she would avoid most in conversations? They would be death and death in connection with Mrs Ricketts.' Her remarks prior to the old lady's death were 'just the reverse of an indication of guilt'.

As for 'Pop' Merrifield, Mr Nahum described him as a 'guileless, tragic simpleton', no more capable of concocting or taking part in a murder plot than a child. Referring to the failure of the chemist and his assistant to pick out Merrifield in the police identification parades, he insisted that their subsequent 'recognition' in court was unreliable. It was also 'contemptible' for the prosecution to use it to make up for the deficiencies of their case. It also, said Mr Nahum, 'fell very short of the sort of identification which is required in a capital charge'.

The speech for the defence had lasted for four hours at the end of which the judge addressed a question to both defence and prosecution counsel:

> Supposing the jury find that one or other or both of these accused administered Rodine rat poison to Mrs Ricketts intending to kill her and that she died, not of rat poison but of natural causes, what is the proper verdict?

'My lord,' replied Nahum, 'it must be 'attempted murder.'

'I agree,' said the Attorney General, after which he began his closing speech for the prosecution by saying that 'poisoning has always been a crime of the deepest dye because of its treacherous and secret character'. Although the evidence was largely circumstantial this was a clear case of wilful murder. It could not be denied that phosphorus was found in the body of Mrs Ricketts as 'yellow phosphorus doesn't materialise out of the air', he said.

'There is a possibility that a dying rat came through the window and the phosphorus was deposited that way. How it got in Mrs Ricketts's throat is a further matter of speculation,' said Sir Lionel, sarcastically. 'I put it quite bluntly - suicide and accident are right out of the picture altogether - it can be nothing but murder.'

He rejected Professor Webster's theories as simplistic propositions. There was, he insisted, evidence to show that Mrs Ricketts had died of phosphorus poisoning, not natural causes. In her last hours, she had suffered from intense thirst and had complained of a nasty taste in her mouth - both were symptoms of phosphorus poisoning. He then reminded the jury that the Crown case consisted of a joint charge against both prisoners. One cannot say, 'Oh, well, he is a harmless old gentleman; we can let him out. I cannot ask you to do that. Not only is there evidence against Mrs Merrifield of the clearest kind but evidence that they acted together. They were both in the same house, both standing to gain from the old lady's death, both thoroughly callous about her, both more concerned with what they could get out of it than with any other consideration. I have no alternative but to submit to you that you must find both guilty of wilful murder.'

It was true that throughout their trial both Merrifields had come across as rather unfeeling and hypocritical persons, misguided perhaps, rather than evil, and it was difficult to imagine them in the role of murderers.

When the judge began his summing up on Friday, 31 July, he said that most cases of murder by poison must be established by circumstantial evidence alone. But this type of evidence, he said, was not necessarily inferior to direct evidence. In fact, in his opinion, it could be stronger. He directed the jury to bring a verdict of attempted murder only if they were not wholly convinced that one or both of the defendants had given the poison to Mrs Ricketts - that by doing so they had intended to kill her - and, moreover, that it was the phosphorus that killed her and not the condition of her liver.

Mr Justice Glyn-Jones went on to say that, having listened to Mrs

Merrifield giving evidence, she was a 'vulgar and stupid woman with a dirty mind' but this did not mean they should convict her of murder.

'If the evidence of the three doctors was believed - and there was no reason why they should lie - the onset of Mrs Ricketts's illness must have been sudden and severe. In that case,' suggested the judge, 'would not the Merrifields have taken urgent steps to get a doctor as soon as possible? Mrs Merrifield's answer was that 3.15. in the morning was not a very nice time to be in the streets'.

As for 'Pop' Merrifield, he had told the court that because of his ulcerated legs he could not walk to the doctor's house, a distance of some two hundred yards.

The judge went on to remind the jury of the scene described by Dr Page when he called to see Mrs Ricketts on the morning of her death. There was 'Pop' Merrifield tucking into his lunch, at a table laid for two, wedged up close to the bed on which the old lady lay dying.

'But,' said the judge, 'Be careful not to let that prejudice you too much - he may be no more than a stupid old man with all the insensitiveness of a stupid old man. He and his wife, on the other hand, may be entirely callous about the sufferings of Mrs Ricketts because they had determined to put her to death. They are the two sides you will have to decide.'

It was a fact that phosphorus was found in the body of the dead woman; this can only mean that there was a tin of rat poison in that house.

'Where,' asked the judge, 'was that tin? It may have been put in the dustbin, which was taken away on the Tuesday. It was true there was no tin of rat poison in Mrs Merrifield's handbag when it got to Mr Budd, the defence solicitor. What happened to the bag while it was in Mr Merrifield's possession?'

Had there been a tin of Rodine in the bag - was that the reason why Louisa was so anxious to give it to her friend for safe keeping? And why was 'Pop' Merrifield so anxious to get it back and check the contents for his own protection? Surely he wasn't just worried about some insurance policies?

As to the identification in court of Alfred 'Pop' Merrifield, the judge reminded the jurors that Mr and Mrs Merrifield could have walked into any chemist shop in Blackpool or Wigan and bought rat poison - it didn't have to be Cotton's, in Manchester.

'I would advise you, and as strongly as I can,' he said, 'to reject any identification or recognition in the Magistrates' Court or here'. He conceded that the chemist and his assistant had, most probably, seen photographs of Merrifield in the newspapers.

Finally, the judge addressed the conflicting opinions of the two pathologists, Dr Manning and Professor Webster, adding that, at the end of the day, the jurors must make their decision by using 'their practical common sense'.

The jurors retired at 3.52 pm to consider their verdict and returned nearly six hours later, at 9.35 pm. During their absence, the court had filled and 'fashionably dressed women sat on the courtroom floor and ate sandwiches whilst in the corridors outside men ate snacks. In their separate cells the Merrifields had their tea and supper while they waited for the verdicts.'

Shortly before nine-thirty, they were brought up from the cells. Louisa came first, between two wardresses, followed by 'Pop' Merrifield. Louisa turned round and put her arms out towards her husband but her guards restrained her.

Once the court was reassembled, Mr Justice Glyn-Jones asked for the jury's verdict. He was told by the foreman that they were agreed in the case of one charge only. Taking Louisa Merrifield first, the clerk announced the verdict of Guilty.

The two wardresses caught hold of the prisoner's arms as she whispered: 'No. No.'

Louisa Merrifield had been so sure that she would be found Not Guilty that, before she left the prison to attend court that morning, she had laughed and joked with the other prisoners, telling them, as they curled her hair for her, that she wouldn't be coming back.

As the jurors were unable to agree on a verdict in the case of Alfred 'Pop' Merrifield, the judge ordered him to stand trial again at Manchester Assizes in November. He tried to reach his wife but was held firmly by his guards and led towards the steps to the cells. He stumbled as he went and seemed confused and kept asking: 'What happens? What do I do now?'

His footsteps could be heard echoing down the underground passage to the cells as the judge slowly placed the black cap on his head. He asked Mrs Merrifield if she had anything to say before sentence was passed.

In a whisper, she replied: 'I have nothing to say.'

Then Mr Justice Glyn-Jones said, gravely: 'You have been convicted on plain evidence of as wicked and cruel a murder as I ever heard tell of.'

This said, he sentenced her to death and as he said the words, 'May the Lord have mercy on your soul', Louisa swayed visibly.

Then, ashen-faced, with set lips and no tears she left the court with the two wardresses supporting her.

Louisa was taken to the condemned cell at Strangeways Prison whilst 'Pop' Merrifield went back to the hospital wing to await his re-trial.

But, according to a reporter from the *Daily Mirror*, in his view 'it is most unlikely that Merrifield will stand trial again. The sending forward to the next Assizes of a prisoner over whom a jury had disagreed, is a legal formality. But it is unlikely that the Director of Prosecutions will offer any evidence and Merrifield will probably be discharged when he appears again.'

As the old chap climbed into a Black Maria outside the court he leaned heavily on his guard and asked, 'Where's Louie?'

Crowds of people had gathered in the dark outside, only a few yards from the garishly-lit Piccadilly area of the city; some had waited for hours to catch a glimpse of the prisoners and had come prepared with camp stools and a supply of food.

The trial had cost the tax-payer £6,000, although the Attorney

General did not receive a fee. Mr Nahum was paid only £32 for his services under the Poor Persons' Defence Act. The judge extended his thanks to him, his junior and John Budd, the defence solicitor, for their handling of the case. An appeal, which would have to be lodged within ten days, was being considered, although the Court of Criminal Appeal had just closed for the holiday season and would not sit again until 1 October.

The vacation judge was, by some strange coincidence, Mr Justice Glyn-Jones, so he would not be able to take part. The proposed re-trial of Alfred Merrifield also posed some interesting legal problems. Louisa Merrifield's execution had been set for Tuesday, 18 August - if her defence did launch an appeal on her behalf and it was refused, would she be given a stay of execution until October so that she could be called as a witness in her husband's re-trial? Her solicitor announced that 'the re-trial raises an unprecedented issue[35] - whether the Home Secretary will permit a condemned person to give evidence in a public court. It is an amazing position. Mrs Merrifield is a competent witness under criminal law and she could be called. But it would be a most painful decision to have to reach and would be made only after very careful consideration.'

The appeal on behalf of Louisa Merrifield was submitted to the Home Secretary, but dismissed on Thursday, 3 September, although she was not told until the 16th. Two days later, on Friday, 18 September, at nine o'clock in the morning, Louisa Merrifield, the garrulous housekeeper, was hanged by Albert Pierrepoint.

Whist preparing his memoirs, he wrote that he had no qualms about hanging her. He described her as 'square-faced, thin North country mouth, eyes glinting behind oval National Health spectacles, she looked a typical 'Mum' in her frock that you could pick from the racks of any cheap department store; her hair scraped thin by morning curlers, which she had tried to frizz into some semblance

35 In fact, a similar situation had arisen in the case of Christie and Evans. The Home Secretary had refused permission for Christie, already condemned to death for the murder of at least seven women, to appear as a witness in the Timothy Evans trial. His evidence was taken down in his prison cell a few days prior to his execution.

of a modern style. Homely shoes and lumpy ankles.'

On the afternoon before her execution, Louisa Merrifield was brought from the women's wing at Strangeways to the condemned cell, which was in the men's part of the prison. Pierrepoint stood in the darkened doorway of a disused cell in the corridor and watched her pass. The peepholes of the men's cells had been latched from the outside to prevent the inmates from seeing her pass.

But, according to Pierrepoint, they could hear her for, even now, on her way to the condemned cell, still chattering loudly and laughing:

> Her tongue faltered only once, and this was when she caught her first glimpse of the men's gaol, its dark, damp walls and circling iron stairways sealed off by tunnels of netting. I saw her lift her face and stare upwards and all around her. Her eyes widened behind her spectacles. But all she said was: 'My - its gloomy, isn't it?' and laughed a bit nervously.
>
> Two women prison officers in blue uniform were with her, the governess of the women's prison and a Salvation Army chaplain. She walked slowly, taking her time. I stood in my darkened doorway and she almost brushed past me. She did not see me watching her. The condemned cell waits at the end of this long, cold corridor. Its doorway is exactly like all the others. I heard its iron door rumble open, and then clang shut.
>
> My assistant and I went to another room, had a few bottles of beer and were early to bed. I am told that Mrs Merrifield had a bottle of beer, too, and sat enjoying it for some time after we were both asleep.
>
> At half-past seven next morning I went to the execution chamber for another testing of the apparatus. The condemned cell was through the next wall. Then I had breakfast of bacon and eggs, and so did she.
>
> Just before nine am, I entered her cell. The door was flung open for me. The two women warders stared at me with white faces. So did the governess. Mrs Merrifield was sitting at the table with her back towards the door, but she twisted around in her chair and looked at me silently, very pale.
>
> They were in the middle of some game of cards. The cards dropped from her fingers onto the table. Four women - all white-faced and silent - stared at me. I felt like an intruder at some very private affair. It is always the same when a woman is to be hanged. The female

prison officers who guard her grow strangely fond of her. They seem almost as if they want to get up and defend her from me. It is always a disturbing moment - so silent and tense - when I walk into the condemned cell of a woman.

"Come on, love," I said to Mrs Merrifield. She didn't move. I said it again, in a friendly, appealing voice. She looked up at me so pitifully that I almost hesitated. I have known so many women like her. The garrulous life-and-soul of a pub party, making jokes, talking loudly. The sort of woman who thinks that nobody can get the better of her in an argument. She must have given many people 'a piece of her mind' with scathing remarks, as she tried to do in court, several times, to the prosecuting counsel and was bewildered when it didn't work.

She stared up at me and licked her mouth slowly. She seemed to be on the brink of arguing, even then. But it was too late for any more arguments. And as if she suddenly realised it, her shoulders drooped. Her mouth turned down at the corners, like a child about to cry.

For the third time I said: "Come on, love, it's all right." This time she stood up very slowly. I pinioned her arms with my strap, which is designed specially so that this can be done in a half-second. I carefully removed her spectacles, warm from her face, and put them on the table. She would never need them again.

I led the way through the condemned cell door into the waiting execution chamber. She began to walk after me, then paused. I had heard her footsteps hesitate and turned back with the thought that she had faltered, but she hadn't. She was just looking back at the two blanched women who had guarded her.

"Thank you, my dears, for all your kindness," she said. They smiled tensely and turned their faces to the wall, away from her.

A further four paces and she was inside the execution chamber. Before she had time for more than the briefest glimpse of it, I had guided her onto the chalk-marks and dropped the white hood over her face, the rope with it, and pulled the lever. She dropped out of sight into death. She had not spoken a word to me.

There seems to be a certain element of pity in this account of Louisa Merrifield's death. The death penalty for murder came to an end with the passing of the Murder (Abolition of Death Penalty) Act

1965, although repeated calls are made in Parliament for its return. It is worth reflecting, therefore, on the words Albert Pierrepoint wrote in the preface to his autobiography, *Executioner: Pierrepoint*, when it was published in 1974:

> It is a fact which is no source of pride to me at all – it is simple history – that I have carried out the execution of more judicial sentences of death, (outside the field of politics), than any executioner in any British record or archive. That fact is the measure of my experience. The fruit of my experience has this bitter after-taste: that I do not now believe that any one of the hundreds of executions I carried out has in any way acted as a deterrent against future murder. Capital punishment, in my view, achieved nothing except revenge.

Although a Salvation Army officer, Major Lesley Gale, had kept vigil with Louisa Merrifield in her last hours she did not confess to the murder of Sarah Ricketts. A large crowd, numbering about five hundred, had gathered outside the prison to await the posting of the notices of execution on the gates.

As for her husband, 'Pop' Merrifield, although the Attorney General eventually decided against a re-trial, the murder charge against him remained. For a while after his wife's execution, he continued to live in the bungalow left to him by Mrs Ricketts. That he was entitled to the building was strongly contested by the old lady's two daughters but it was eventually agreed in June 1956 that he should receive one sixth of its net proceeds after the sale of the property. He died on 24 June, 1962, having worked in one of Blackpool's many sideshows for a number of years. Did he, one cannot help wondering, after it was all over, even joke about the fate of poor Louie?

John Lee

The Man They Could Not Hang

The case of John Henry George Lee is one of the most remarkable in the history of crime, not so much for the murder for which he was convicted and sentenced to die - that of killing his elderly employer, sixty-eight year old Miss Emma Ann Whitehead Keyse - but because he survived three attempts to hang him.

John Lee was only fifteen when he first went to work for the Miss Keyse. She had lived for most of her life in The Glen, a delightful thatched villa in Babbacombe Bay, near Torquay, Devon. Originally known as Babbacombe, the house enjoyed wonderful views of the English Channel, whilst the densely-wooded slopes behind provided a stunning backdrop to complete the idyllic scene.

Miss Keyse so loved the house that she called it 'paradise on earth' and, it was said, boasted about visits made by Queen Victoria and the Prince Consort during the early years of their marriage though these fanciful claims were but wishful thinking and cannot be substantiated.

Miss Keyse's life, nevertheless, had been one of privilege. As a typical Victorian spinster, she was well-intentioned, a stickler for routine and the maintaining of standards, a regular worshipper at St Marychurch and renowned for her charitable works. She took her Christian duty very seriously and prided herself on her philanthropic endeavours. She was the type of lady who would donate money to buy bibles and bras for heathens in faraway places. She also felt that some of the local youths needed her guidance and John Lee became one of her protégés. Born in 1864, John was the son of a clay miner and part-time farmer from the village of Abbotskerswell, near Newton Abbot, and Miss Keyse originally employed him as a general dogsbody. The rest of the household consisted of Miss Keyse, Eliza and Jane Neck, two elderly sisters who had served her as maid-companions for nearly fifty years, and the cook, Elizabeth Harris, Lee's half-sister, who had taken over from another sister, Millie, two years before. Disconcertingly devoid of any sense of gratitude, Lee was 'continually getting into mischief'. It was understandable, of course; he was young and bored with living at the beck and call of fussy old women and, moreover, in a sleepy Devonshire village. He was naturally keen to see more of the world which he knew lay beyond the cluster of fishing boats moored in the harbour.

Eighteen months later, realising that Lee would never make a suitable page, Miss Keyse managed to get him and another boy placed on board HMS *Implacable*, docked at Devonport. However, once the novelty had worn off, John grew to dislike life at sea and for the next two years made such a nuisance of himself he was eventually branded as 'incorrigible' and dismissed. After leaving the Navy, he was employed as a railway porter at two different stations but proved unsatisfactory in both.

Having always concerned herself with John Lee's welfare, Miss Keyse found him a position with a local dignitary, Colonel Brownlow, who lived in a mansion house on the outskirts of Torquay. It was while he was working there that his criminal life really began. He was caught pawning some of the Brownlow family's silver while they were abroad. When charged, he pleaded Guilty and served six months' imprisonment with hard labour in Exeter Prison.[36]

It was while he was there that kindly Miss Keyse, hearing of his fate, contacted the prison chaplain to plead on his behalf. When he was working for her, she said, Lee had been 'honest, truthful and

36 Hard Labour, introduced in 1864 as an alternative to Transportation which was expensive and difficult to supervise. It included turning the crank under a 12lb pressure up to 10,000 times a day or walking the treadwheel to a height equivalent to that of Ben Nevis. Both were abolished in 1898. Women and children were more likely to be put to 'oakum picking', a painful task untwisting old, tarred marine rope, that could result in fingers literally worn to the bone.

obedient'. So convinced was she of his innate good nature that 'with the true charity and benevolence of a Christian lady she offered him temporary asylum until he could get a position'. She agreed to take him back if he was prepared to do odd jobs for 2/6 a week.

According to the *Torquay Directory*:

> Miss Keyse did everything in her power to find him a situation. She pleaded personally with tradesmen in Torquay to take him on. To these she urged that it was very cruel not to give the boy a chance to retrieve his character. The poor lady declared that Lee had faithfully promised never to err again, that he would shut up shop, do errands, clean boots, in fact, do anything to earn an honest living, and she was so satisfied of his earnestness that she offered to become guarantee for his honesty. All these efforts failing she endeavoured to get him to emigrate.[37]

Lee, however, remained at The Glen. As the only male member of the household, he was designated the pantry, which was little more than a bed-space. And so it was that John Lee, now aged twenty, was given a second chance. Although the pay was low, even by late Victorian standards, Lee, having a criminal record, was fortunate indeed to find a live-in job with a kindly employer. He seemed to have settled at last and started courting a local girl called Katie Farmer.

Then, tragically, on Saturday, 15 November, 1884, everything changed. In the early hours of the morning, the cook, Elizabeth Harris, was awakened by the smell of burning and her cries alerted the rest of the household. While the old maid, Jane Neck, ran to wake her mistress, her sister, Eliza, followed by the cook, hurried downstairs to find the house ablaze. John Lee, having pulled on his trousers and socks, came running from the direction of the pantry.

After telling him to fetch their neighbour, William Gasking, the landlord of the nearby The Cary Arms, Eliza went into the pantry to fetch some water. But Lee did not go to fetch help straight away; instead, he ran up the broad staircase towards a room known as 'the

37 Unless otherwise stated all quotes are taken from the *Torquay Directory* (later re-named *The South Devon Journal*).

honeysuckle room'. By now, the house had filled with smoke and he came across the servant, Jane, who, having found her mistress's bed empty, was feeling her way towards the banisters. At the same time, she heard her sister calling from below, saying that Miss Keyse was in the dining room - *dead*. As John Lee guided the old maid towards the top of the stairs, he caught hold of her right arm with his left hand.

As soon as Jane reached the dining room, she was faced with a ghastly sight. The body of Miss Keyse was lying on the floor; her right foot and part of her body were badly-scorched and her clothes were still smouldering. She had terrible injuries to her head and her throat had been cut. Surrounding the body were piles of half-burned newspapers and there was a strong smell of paraffin. Despite the attempt to burn the body beyond recognition, most of the flesh remained intact and Emma Keyse was easily identified.

In a state of shock, Eliza continued to throw water over the upholstery while Jane went over to the window, intending to climb out and run for help. As she opened the shutters, shards of broken glass crashed to the floor at her feet. Several panes had been broken. John Lee, having by now returned to the house with William Gasking, said that he'd smashed the window to let some of the smoke out. It was on the splintered glass, he said, that he had cut his left arm. The blood from the wound had run down to his hand. This seemed to account for the bloodstained print, later found on the right sleeve of Jane's nightdress. He had used his left hand, he said, to guide her to safety at the top of the stairs.

Within minutes, several other men, coastguards, fishermen and firemen, had arrived and between them they managed to extinguish the fire. Once the smoke had cleared a little they found a large pool of congealed blood in the passage leading to the pantry. When the police arrived, more blood was found, not only on the oil-can - which had contained paraffin - but also on a knife and a towel. When their initial investigations were complete, they were already convinced that John Lee was the culprit. They dismissed the idea of any of the three women being responsible for such a vicious crime. The Neck sisters were gentle souls of nearly seventy and the cook, Elizabeth Harris, was pregnant at the time.

About ten o'clock that morning, after he'd returned from an errand to Chelston, John Lee was arrested 'on suspicion of being concerned in the death of Miss Keyse' and taken to Torquay Police Station. The old lady had been so well-respected that when news of her murder reached the local inhabitants their feelings ran high. The local newspaper, the *Torquay Directory,* took up the story with a vengeance, writing blatantly biased and scathing reports about John Lee even before he was brought before the Magistrates.

On Thursday, 20 November, Miss Keyse was buried in the family vault at St. Marychurch. As a mark of respect, every shop and business was closed and most people wore black. The *Torquay Directory* described the scene in this way:

> Owing to the difficulty of access down the steep road to the house it was arranged that the cortege should form on the top of the hill. The coffin had been conveyed to the summit by relays of bearers and soon after twelve o'clock the carriages began to arrive; several hundred persons were already there...

The coffin was placed in a hearse having open panels and was covered with a number of beautiful and costly wreaths and other floral tributes of affection and esteem from relatives and friends. The remains of the deceased lady were enclosed in three coffins, consisting of a shell, a leaden coffin and a coffin of polished oak, the latter being fitted with brass furniture. The inscription on the plate was as follows:

> Emma Ann Whitehead Keyse, aged 68 years: died 15th November 1884.

Local feeling and the reporting of such sorrowful scenes alongside derogatory descriptions of young John Lee succeeded in ensuring that those involved in the Magistrates' hearing, which was held at Torquay Courthouse, set out with a pre-conceived idea of his guilt. At least one magistrate on the Bench was a local man whilst the others had undoubtedly either read the newspapers or heard all about the tragedy from friends and neighbours. The whole area was agog with news of the murder and the inhabitants talked of little else.

The coroner's inquest, opened at St Marychurch Town Hall on the day after the funeral, attracted huge crowds. Whilst waiting in an anteroom Lee stood at the window and watched with 'infinite amusement' the crowds pushing and shoving to get in.

Once inside, the crowds sat on the edge of their seats 'eager to hear more of the ghastly details of the atrocious crime'. Whenever there was a particularly gruesome piece of evidence 'the assembly of people in the body of the hall would at once show the eagerness of their curiosity by pressing forward on tiptoe and in a few cases stepping on the seats'.

One of the jurors at the coroner's inquiry was the Vicar of St Marychurch, Rev A.B. Wrey. Unable to curb his feeling of outrage at the death of such a prominent - and no doubt generous - church member, he delivered an emotional sermon on the Sunday after the funeral, referring to Miss Keyse as 'the one who served God so well'. He went on to bemoan the fact that she had 'fallen victim of a heartless, cold blooded, stealthy murderer', knowing that he and his entire congregation, had already made up their minds that John Lee was guilty. The Vicar was so pleased with his impassioned oratory that he had it printed in leaflet form for the edification of his grieving flock.

The Magistrates' hearing, held concurrently over several days, was subject to a number of adjournments and much of the evidence given was duplicated at the coroner's inquest. John Lee was represented by Mr Reginald Gwynne Templer, a solicitor from Teignmouth – more of whom later. The court was told that when examined soon after the murder, Lee's left forearm showed 'some superficial cuts' and both his coat and trousers showed traces of blood and smelled of paraffin.

The case for the prosecution was outlined by Miss Keyse's solicitor, Mr Isidore Carter. He produced a bloodstained hatchet that was found just inside the dining-room door, suggesting that it may have been the murder weapon - the obtuse end being used to bludgeon the old lady's head and fracture her skull. A pair of the prisoner's socks, smelling of paraffin and with some hair stuck to the soles, had also been found rolled up in a box in the pantry. A bloodstained knife was also produced; this had been found amongst some papers in a drawer close to Lee's bed. It had been freshly wiped in earth as though someone had tried to clean it. The fatal wound to the old lady's throat had been made with a sharp knife - with a single stroke, from left to right, cutting the flesh to the bone.

The elderly maid, Eliza Neck, was called as a witness and told the court that, on the Friday before the murder, Elizabeth Harris, the cook, had been feeling unwell and had gone to bed about five o'clock in the afternoon. John Lee, who was under orders to be in by ten o'clock, had been to post some letters at seven o'clock and spent the rest of the evening with his girl-friend, Katie Farmer. He and the two old maids had attended evening prayers as usual conducted by Miss Keyse in the dining room before retiring for the night.

Eliza saw John Lee asleep in his bed about half past twelve when she went to fetch something from the pantry. She then performed all her household duties much as she did every night; after putting a hot water bottle in Miss Keyse's bed, she went back downstairs to make her a cup of cocoa which she always left on the kitchen range. This done, Eliza went upstairs again, to the room she shared with her sister and Jane soon followed, leaving Miss Keyse in the dining-room.

The court learned that, surprisingly perhaps, the only fire in the house was in the kitchen, even though it was mid-November and there was a bitter wind blasting in from the sea. Despite the cold, Miss Keyse often stayed up late, writing letters or copying passages from the scriptures into her journal. She also wrote notes to John Lee with his instructions for the next day which she would leave in the pantry.

Eliza told the court that after Elizabeth Harris had smelled burning and raised the alarm, she, Eliza, had hurried downstairs in her nightclothes to find the place so filled with smoke she couldn't see properly. She had heard John Lee coming from the direction of the pantry:

'What's the matter?' he'd called.

She'd also heard her sister, Jane, who was still upstairs, calling out her mistress's name. Eliza ran to the pantry to fetch some water and it was only when she came back that she went into the dining room and saw the body of Miss Keyse. She did not notice any broken window. She had then sent Lee to fetch Mr Gasking from The Cary Arms, who, she informed the court, arrived with his trousers on over his shirt and his braces hanging down.

When asked to recall the night of the murder, the other maid, Jane Neck, told the court that it was her duty to lock up at night.

'I closed everything except a window in the dining room which was always kept open by Miss Keyse's request.'

She explained later that she meant the shutters were left open, not the actual window as her mistress liked to hear the striking of the church clock.

> I shut the front door, the conservatory door and the door leading from the first hall to the second or middle door and fastened the latter with a bar. I also fastened the back door and likewise the kitchen door... I saw Miss Keyse at half-past twelve; she was writing her diary in the dining room. She was in the same dress as when she read prayers - in evening dress. There was a lamp in the room and I put down a candlestick with matches on the sideboard which she lighted before she went upstairs.

It was clear that Miss Keyse must have gone to bed as usual that night for her half-empty cup of cocoa was found by her bedside the next morning. Describing the horror of the night's events Jane said that, awakened by the cook, she had rushed to Miss Keyse's bedroom:

'The bedroom was full of smoke and the furniture and curtains were in a blaze,' she told the court. 'I thought Miss Keyse was in bed. I pulled off the clothes and called "*Miss Keyse*!" but she was not there.'

Then she had heard her sister calling up the stairs saying that Miss Keyse was in the dining-room - dead. She tried to find the stairs but couldn't see through the thick smoke. It was then that John

Lee had appeared; she thought he was heading in the direction of the 'honeysuckle room'. He stopped to help her by taking hold of her right arm and steering her towards the staircase. Questioned about the blood she found on the right sleeve of her nightgown the following day, the maid insisted that there was no blood there when she put the garment on that night and the only way it could have got there was from the blood from Lee's injured left arm running down to his hand.

Questioned further, however, Jane made a vital addition to her testimony. She said that a little later that evening she had gone out to the veranda hoping to summon help from one of the fishermen on the beach. But it was so dark John Lee had to catch hold of her to prevent her from tripping over the flower pots.

'It was possible,' she said, 'that it was then that the blood got on my dress as the prisoner had just previously helped Gasking carry out the body.'

Shown a sharp-bladed knife, thought to be the murder weapon, the old maid said she used one just like it to take the grease off the candlesticks - but hers was blunt. Miss Keyse had a similar knife, she said, but it was kept very sharp for use in the garden and was usually kept either in the front hall or in the pantry.

In answer to further questions, the old woman said that as soon as she went into the smoke-filled dining-room she opened the shutters so that she could get out and raise the alarm. When she drew back the shutters, she saw that four panes of glass had been shattered. Questioned about her mistress's stock of silverware (which was only used when they had company) Jane said that it was kept locked in a box in her bedroom and the key was kept in another room. There were, however, some other pieces of silver in the 'honeysuckle room'.

The cook, Elizabeth Harris, was also called as a witness to what happened that night. She said that John Lee came upstairs as soon as she raised the alarm and tried to put the fire out in the 'honeysuckle room', using water from a butt outside. He had smashed the top with a stone so they could get to the water more quickly.

After the womenfolk had finished answering questions, the men who had fought the blaze that night were called to give their version of events. William Gasking, landlord of The Cary Arms, told how he had been awakened at four o'clock in the morning by the prisoner. He had quickly dressed and hurried to the house which was well ablaze. Seeing the body of Miss Keyse in the dining room, he urged Lee to help carry her out of the house but the lad started 'dithering and chattering' and seemed reluctant to handle the corpse. Losing patience, Gasking told him to hold his tongue and help. As they lifted the body, Lee stumbled and Miss Keyse's head dropped down. They found a piece of carpet and wrapped it around the body to make it easier to carry.

'There was plenty of light from the fire in the room,' Gasking said. 'We carried her out of the back door and took her off to the shed.'

Once they had covered the body with another length of carpet and secured the door of the shed, they went back to the house to tackle the flames. Shortly afterwards, the coastguard, Thomas Pearce, and his men joined them. Pearce described the efforts of Gasking, Lee and himself to get the flames under control. He recalled asking Lee to fetch a hatchet to break through some laths in a partition to prevent the flames from spreading. Thinking the hatchet was kept in the woodshed, he was surprised when Lee returned almost immediately. Whilst tackling the fire, he had not noticed anything wrong with Lee's arm although he did notice that he tired easily. About five o'clock that morning Lee volunteered to run over to Compton to inform Miss Keyse's sister, Mrs Maclean, of the tragedy. It was suggested that he would be more useful staying at the house but he seemed anxious to leave.

When questioned about this, Mary Hatchford, Mrs Maclean's maid, said that John Lee reached the house about five-thirty that morning. He shouted outside the window to wake her and then told her that The Glen was on fire and Miss Keyse was hurt but, when pressed as to her condition, he admitted that she was dead. He then begged Mary to break the news to Mrs Maclean, as he said he couldn't do it himself. Yet when Mary Ann Bolder, the cook, joined in the conversation, Lee was less reticent, saying that his mistress was burned to death. Then he rolled up the sleeve of his coat and showed the women the cut on his arm, sustained, he said, when he broke the window in the dining room.

When John Lee returned to the house, he helped the men douse the embers and clear away the debris. By the time the fire was out and the police had taken charge, it was eight o'clock and Gasking went home for his breakfast. Similar accounts were given by the other men who helped fight the fire that night and all agreed that Lee worked as hard as the rest to bring the fire under control. Several confirmed that, at one stage, the lad was knocking down parts of the burning ceiling with a long pole, apparently unhampered by the gash in his arm. He did, however, seem 'excitable' and frequently drew attention to his injuries; but it was not until the fire was put out and he had returned from Compton that his half-sister, Elizabeth, washed and bound his arm for him.

Damning evidence was to come, however, from another witness, William Richards, described as a 'letter carrier of Babbacombe' who had known Lee for six years. He recalled a conversation they'd had a few weeks before, in which the lad had told him that he had recently quarrelled with Miss Keyse. During the argument, he had told her he was fed-up with his job and wanted to leave. Miss Keyse, who had lived at The Glen for fifty years, told him that the house was about to be sold to a gentleman who might possibly keep him on.

'If my mistress does not get me a good place soon,' Lee had confided, 'she'll b........soon wish she had and I'll put an end to one before I leave.'

Lee, said the witness, was quite sober when he said this; the postman warned him that this was dangerous talk, especially if anything should happen to the old lady - but he said he didn't care.

The cook, Elizabeth Harris, also recalled a conversation she'd had with young Lee:

> We were talking about leaving Miss Keyse's service and I said: "What would you do if she did not give you a character?" [a reference] He said: "If she will not I will lay the place in ashes."

To this, the cook had replied, "Don't burn me with it."

"I'll let you know," was Lee's flippant reply.

Elizabeth also remembered the time John Lee came into the kitchen in tears. It was the morning of 28 October, the day on which he had quarrelled with Miss Keyse.

'I asked him what he was crying about,' she said. 'At first he made no answer and afterwards he said Miss Keyse was only going to pay him 2s. a week. I said I thought the agreement was 2s.6d. a week and he replied he did not know as he did not make the agreement; he added that he would not stop another night and that before he left Torquay he would have his revenge. Another time, he said that Miss Keyse had been grumbling or quarrelling and he said that if she had been near some place he would have pushed her down over. Then another time, he said he would set the place on fire and watch it until he was arrested. He used to speak of Miss Keyse as 'the old woman''.

The medical evidence given at the inquest and the court hearings was fairly straightforward. Drs Steele and Chilcote, who had both examined the body of Miss Keyse, were adamant that her death was a case of murder, not suicide. Even if she had been able to inflict the initial blows to the head, her injuries would have caused her to collapse; in this state she would have been quite unable to cut her own throat. Dr Chilcote suggested that the square-shaped wound to the side of the head might have been caused by the blunt end of a hatchet. Such a severe blow would undoubtedly have caused unconsciousness and, in all probability, Miss Keyse had died of loss of blood from the deep gash to her throat.

Further evidence was given by PC Meetch; he was the first officer on the scene, by which time the fire was well under control. He was shown the body of Miss Keyse in the shed and, on seeing the gaping wound to the throat, he had sent for Sergeant Nott and Dr Chilcote. Shortly after eight o'clock that morning, while he was sifting through the debris upstairs, he was approached by John Lee, who was trembling noticeably.

'You're shaking,' Meetch had said, to which the lad replied: 'Yes,

I'm cold; this is a bad job, for I've lost a good friend.'

Sergeant Nott confirmed that newspapers scattered about the dining room and around the body of Miss Keyse, smelled strongly of paraffin; so, too, did her nightclothes and the carpet under the body. He produced four plain gold rings taken from Miss Keyse's body and a diamond one from her bedroom, where, he added, he noticed that the bell-pull had been unfastened as though Miss Keyse had rung for assistance during the night.

The local press exploited every aspect of the affair and reported on each session of the Magistrates' Court which was packed with up to six hundred spectators at any one sitting.

On Wednesday, 26 November, under a heading *'The Babbacombe Tragedy'* the *Torquay Directory* told its readers that:

> ...the interest in the dreadful murder was in nowise diminished. A variety of speculations and theories have been put forward to explain sundry apparent inconsistencies in the evidence. It is said that the police have obtained the right clue and are pushing it to its logical conclusion. The police are naturally reticent as to what their line of action is but the main thread of the evidence is so unmistakably clear that they have no difficulty in following it.
>
> At present, only one side of the case has been heard. The public are anxiously waiting to hear the nature of the defence. It is an axiom of English law that every man is supposed to be innocent until the contrary has been actually proved.
>
> There are now two courts occupied with the investigation - that of the coroner and his jury, and, secondly, the magistrates. The question before the former is to ascertain the cause of death of Miss Keyse; the latter have to determine whether the weight of evidence adduced is sufficient to warrant them in committing Lee for trial at the Assizes on a charge of murder.

The article went on to say that:

> ...the police have been indefatigable in their investigations, and have brought to light many facts which are likely to have an important bearing on the case. It has been surmised that more than one person was concerned, if not in the tragedy itself, at least in its preparation and arrangement. There have been various rumours afloat on this

> point, and even persons have been named without any warrant whatever. It appears, however, that several articles have been missed from the house; these articles have been traced to St Marychurch, and are said to have been sold by the prisoner Lee.

With reprehensible bias, the paper went on to describe John Lee's appearance at the Magistrates' hearing:

> When brought into Court he had a very jaunty air, looked round with a half-vacant expression, and took his seat where directed by the police with the utmost composure. A sort of leer passed over his face at times as witnesses gave their evidence but he exhibited no sign of any feeling of horror at the narration of the witnesses, nor did the production of the poor lady's clothing, half-burnt and saturated in paraffin, or the murderous hatchet, extort from him the least manifestation.
>
> Lee's personal appearance is by no means prepossessing. He is tall, well-built, and has a powerful frame; he seems to be very muscular, and evidently possesses great strength. His lower jaw protrudes and droops; he has thick lips and half-open mouth; his nose is straight with an upward tendency. His head recedes behind almost to a point, and his black hair dishevelled and with no attempt at a parting, either in the middle or the sides, descends over his low forehead to the eyebrows. There is a peculiarity about his eyes; they lack lustre and expression, and are such as may be met with in our lunatic asylums. Altogether his appearance does not indicate any ordinary degree of intelligence.
>
> But personal appearances and accidental circumstances have nothing to do with the case in hand; they are simple surroundings which may or may not have their influence in the crime which the coroner and a jury are now investigating.

Then, after saying that 'the prisoner may be assured of having a fair and impartial examination', the article pre-supposes a Guilty verdict by adding 'whatever the result of the verdict of the jury may be, that will be further analysed by the Grand Jury at Exeter'. A verdict of Not Guilty would, of course, exclude the necessity for a further trial.

Before long, everybody was getting in on the act. On the same day that the *Torquay Directory* ran an article on John Lee there was the following advertisement:

[38]

Other newspapers ran similar advertisements and on 28 November, the *Torquay Directory* described the final sitting of the inquest at the Town Hall, remarking on the crowds that had waited from an early hour to gain admission and commenting on the number of females present.

After hearing a great deal of repetitive evidence, the Coroner felt satisfied that the jury had heard sufficient to allow them to come to a conclusion as to how Miss Keyse had met her death. He reminded them to set aside anything that had read in the newspapers or any of the gossip that was rife in the area and form their judgement entirely on the evidence they had heard.

He also instructed them that their duty was twofold - firstly, to ascertain whether Miss Keyse had died by natural or violent means - and secondly, if they determined the latter, 'by whose hand that death had been caused'.

Referring to the opinions of Drs Herbert Chilcote and William Stott Steele, he said that the blows to the old lady's head had been dealt first, after which the fatal gash to the throat was inflicted. In addition, he referred to the evidence of the Home Office analyst, Dr Thomas Stevenson, who had confirmed that the stains on the carpets, the knife, the hatchet, the oil can and the clothes of John Lee were all those of human blood.[39]

38 Another offered photographs of John Lee 'direct from life'. Mr Collis warned the public against buying 'Vile and Spurious Copies'. Below his advert was another from Pearce's Photographic Studio, Torquay, offering a genuine photograph of John Lee, 'considered the best likeness out'.

39 Current DNA testing procedures would have established whether it was Lee's blood from his arm on the sleeve of the maid's nightdress. If the blood belonged to Miss Keyse it could have been transferred as he helped Gasking carry her body from the house. Only if it could have been proved that the blood on the nightdress was the victim's and it came from Lee *before* he had lifted the body could it be classified as incriminating.

Finally, before asking the jurors to consider their verdict, he asked them to take into account the evidence of the cook, Elizabeth Harris - that Lee had said he would have liked to push Miss Keyse over a cliff after they had quarrelled and, moreover, had threatened to burn The Glen to the ground. He urged them to be 'unflinching' in naming the person they felt was responsible for the death of Miss Keyse so that the perpetrator might be committed for trial, charged with her murder.

It only took the jury fifteen minutes to consider its verdict. It was that Miss Keyse had been wilfully murdered and that John Lee was guilty of the murder.

John Lee's trial was scheduled for the Devon Winter Assizes, which were held at Exeter Castle. The case was not heard until Monday, 1 February, of the following year. The choice of presiding judge did not bode well for John Lee. Mr Justice Manisty had such a backlog of work that he was too busy to study the details of the case. He opened the proceedings by warning the court that 'it had been utterly and absolutely out of his power to give the attention to it which was necessary clearly to understand the case.... but he did not think it was necessary as there was quite enough to get a general notion of a case of that kind...'

To this disconcerting announcement, he added that, despite this, he felt confident that the jurors would 'give their attention to the case without any assistance on his part, with the single exception that it seemed to him from the little he did know of the case that it was one in which they should return a true bill'. So much for the impartiality of the law.

The prosecution was led by Mr Collins, QC, and Mr Stonehouse Vigor, instructed by Miss Keyse's solicitor, Mr Isidore Carter. Mr Walter Molesworth St Aubyn, former Conservative MP for Helston, Cornwall, led the defence but it transpired that John Lee's solicitor, Mr Reginald Gwynne Templer, having represented him at the

Coroner's inquest and the Magistrates' hearings, had, in the interim, become so mentally disturbed that his younger brother had been obliged to take over the case for the defence.

John Lee faced two charges, that of the murder of Miss Keyse and for 'attempting to set fire to a house with three persons in it'. He stood in the dock adopting an air of indifference; his appearance, however, was less dishevelled - his hair had been trimmed and brushed for the occasion and he wore a grey flecked coat.

On hearing the charges against him, he pleaded Not Guilty, whereupon Mr Collins opened with a lengthy resume of the case. The court learned that, although Miss Keyse had told John Lee on the evening before the murder that he could go to Compton before breakfast the next day, she evidently changed her mind, for a note was found on the little table at the foot of Lee's bed in the pantry:

> John, it will be better to do some raking of the paths before breakfast, and go to Compton after.

Mr Collins went on to remind the jury that, in a drawer in the pantry, the police had found an old, but very sharp knife which Miss Keyse kept for work in the garden:

> There were marks of blood on the knife; two pieces of paper upon which it was lying were also stained and a drop of fresh blood had trickled on to the underside of the drawer. In a cupboard on the further side of the prisoner's bed, to which no one could have access without disturbing the occupant of the bed, an oil can was found. Jane Neck would say that this can was nearly full on the Friday evening. She had used it and, on putting the can back into the cupboard, she had corked it and placed an inverted funnel on the cork. When the can was found by the police, it was empty, the cork was out, and there were marks of blood on the can. The prosecution suggested that the contents of the can must have been used to saturate the paper and other articles in the dining room and the carpet on the stairs.

As to the injuries inflicted by the murderer, the prosecution informed the jury that the medical men were of the opinion that 'the throat had been cut when the deceased was nearly, if not quite, dead, because under these conditions the blood would not spurt, but would slowly trickle out into a mass, such as the police found. Every drop of the poor woman's blood must have been drained out of this fearful wound'.

The police had measured the distance from the scene of the murder to the pantry in which John Lee was sleeping. From the door of the pantry to the pool of blood was five feet nine inches. From his bed to the spot where Miss Keyse was struck down, was less than eight feet. The door of the pantry was usually left open and there was a gap of nearly two feet above the partition.

Finally, Mr Collins referred to a letter that the prisoner had written to his sweetheart, Katie Farmer, in which he described his mood of restlessness and dissatisfaction with his job. This, he said, would be read in full during the proceedings.

The Crown called a number of witnesses who reiterated the evidence they had previously given at the inquest and before the magistrates. Questioned by Collins, Eliza Neck said that her late mistress had been very kind to John Lee and never complained when he came in late in the evening.

Next came Elizabeth Harris, looking 'much careworn'. Cross-examined by Mr Molesworth St Aubyn, she admitted that she was an unmarried woman. In deference to her pregnancy, she was offered a seat in the witness box but declined. Questioned at some length about the events of that fateful Friday night, she said that she had gone to bed in the afternoon because she was feeling unwell. She also said that she waited half an hour between first smelling smoke and raising the alarm. Unfortunately, Mr Molesworth St Aubyn did not pursue the point and the cook was allowed to leave the court without giving any explanation for the delay.

Whilst listening to the witnesses, John Lee 'seemed almost bored by the whole proceedings, and the only time when he evinced anything like keen interest was on the few occasions when the witnesses slightly contradicted themselves, contradictions which drew from the prisoner something like a smile of contempt. His uneasiness, however, was manifest when allusions were made to the blood marks on his clothes which the wound in the arm would not explain, and when the reference was made to his failure to make any sign until the servants called him.'

On the second day of the trial, Tuesday, 2 February, crowds had gathered outside Exeter Castle from an early hour; those who had been turned away the day before were especially determined to gain admittance. At half-past nine the jurors, who had stayed at the White Hart Hotel overnight, were escorted into the court by the Sheriff's officers, followed half an hour later by the judge. Every eye was turned towards John Lee as he was brought up from the cells and placed once more in the dock. He sat with the 'almost serene indifference which characterised him the previous day, and looked around the Court with as little concern as if he had been a mere spectator instead of the principal figure in the trial.'

Another reporter noticed that Lee greeted an acquaintance sitting in the public benches with a smile and a wink.

The proceedings began with the calling of Sergeant Nott to give evidence. He emphasised the fact that the violent slaughter of Miss Keyse occurred within eight feet from the prisoner's head as he lay in his bed in the pantry. In addition, the noise of the affray must have passed easily through the pantry partition and the smoke from the fire must have floated through the gap at the top. There was no way that the prisoner could not have been aware of the desperate struggle in the passage. Faced with these facts, the jurors had to ask themselves - why didn't John Lee raise the alarm?

The police were of the opinion that the house had not been burgled although the window in the dining room had been broken from the outside - when the shutters were opened, the shattered glass fell inwards, crashing to the floor.

Asked to describe the blood stains on the prisoner's clothes, Sergeant Nott said that there was blood inside the left sleeve of John Lee's coat, corresponding with his arm injury, and on the left leg of his trousers. As he spoke, Lee listened attentively and 'looked more serious' than before. It was at this point that the prosecution saw fit to read the letters that had passed between the prisoner and his sweetheart, Katie Farmer, who sat near him in court:

The Glen, Babbacombe, 10th October 1884.

My Dearest Katie, - I write to tell you I am very unsettled in what I am going to do in my future life. I am tired of service, and I am going to look out for something else to do, which might not be to your liking. And, my dear, don't let me keep you from going anywhere that will be for your good. My dear, you may get a better chance going away, and we may not be always the same as we are now, in love. I implore you, if you think we shall not come together, let us break off our engagement before it is too late. I am beginning to love you so much that it will break my heart if we should leave in time to come. Do let us break it off at once. My dearest, let what we have gone by die out of our thoughts, but our love never can. You have been the kindest I ever met with in my love and all things. I shall ever love you the same. I shall leave the town as soon as possible. I shall feel it very much my darling. If I had kept your company when first I seen you I would have married you and made you happy, but I am unsettled now and don't know what my fate may be. Good-bye, my sweetest love, from one who will ever love you the same.

John Lee.

Clearly shattered by his letter, Katie penned this lengthy and heart-felt reply:

My Dearest Love, - Your letter to hand, which has caused me the greatest pain and grief. What can you possibly mean by telling me one time you will not leave me, and then writing to know if I wish to break off the engagement? It is no use to tell. I cannot make it out, as you are undecided as to what you intend to do for the future. Are you also undecided about me? I tell you now, the same as I have told you before, that our engagement shall not be broken off with my consent.

As to what you intend to do in the future, if it was your lot to crack stones in the street, and would ask me to be your wife, I would not say no. Have a little pity for me and think how dearly I love you. Perhaps if I had loved you less you might have valued me a little more.

As to my getting a better chance away, do you think I want anyone better than the one I love? If you knew how you were deceived you would never mention it. Why not have told me last night when I mentioned about my going away? What you write, then, would not come so hard for me.

There is one thing I wish particularly to know; that is, do you think I

> wish you to marry me before you see your way clear? No, my darling, I am quite prepared to battle my way in the world til you think fit to make me your wife. I will never be the one to grumble at waiting for you.
>
> You say that you love me more and more and that it would break your heart to leave me later on. Jack, I think if we part you would be the cause of grieving me to death and breaking my heart. After what you said on Monday I never dreamt of your writing me now in the same strain as your last letter was written in.
>
> But never mind, I freely forgive you. At the same time I will not give you up. My mother will naturally come into your mind. Would to God it had been my funeral you went to instead of hers. Then I should never have got your letter and you would never have written it - she was my only friend but I have always depended upon you to be something more than a friend. You have been my chief support in all my troubles and have helped me to bear them better than I could have done else.
>
> Before concluding may I say I shall very much like to see you once more, as I have something to say which cannot be written. You ask me if I would be annoyed if you sent me a present. You must fancy me annoyed with you, which you know could never be. Nothing will give me more pleasure than to receive anything from the hands of one I love so devotedly. Whatever it is it shall die with me and my love. Grant my last request by coming down to-morrow evening, [Wednesday]. Accept my fondest and truest love, and believe me ever your true love.
>
> Katie Farmer.
>
> Please excuse this scrawl, as I am very unwell today.

Superintendent Barbor followed Sergeant Nott into the witness box. He, too, confirmed that the window panes in the dining room had been broken from the outside and told the court that 'a piece of skin adhering to the glass corresponded in size with the largest wound on the prisoner's arm'.

Dr William Steele expressed the opinion that the wounds to Miss Keyse's head could have been caused by the blunt end of the hatchet; likewise, the vicious gash in her throat could have been caused by the sharp gardening knife found in the pantry.

Dr Herbert Chilcote, though, disagreed on two of these points; he thought the head of the hatchet produced in court was too large to account for the wounds and that the garden knife was too small to have caused the lethal severance of the throat.

The analyst, Dr Thomas Stevenson, discussed his findings at some length. After a thorough comparison, he felt sure that the hairs adhering to the soles of John Lee's socks had come from the head of the deceased - the texture and rather unusual red colour were, in his opinion, exactly the same.

The absence of any vigorous cross-examination by the defence counsel, Mr Molesworth St Aubyn, was extraordinary if, that is, the newspaper accounts were accurate. If their coverage can be believed, statement after statement passed without challenge. John Lee was entirely at the mercy of a totally passive defence and the prosecution's case against him was formidable.

On the third and final day of the trial, Wednesday, 3 February, Mr Collins summed up the case for the prosecution.

'The house was clearly fired,' he said, 'and the murder committed by someone in the house, and the first person seen when the old servant came down was the prisoner, on whose hands there was at that time blood, as was shown by Neck's nightdress, on which the prisoner put his hand.'

Even this ambiguous and misleading statement failed to elicit any response from Lee's defence. He went on to suggest that John Lee, knowing he had his mistress's blood on him, had broken the glass and deliberately cut his arm.

Mr Molesworth St Aubyn rose to make his speech for the defence, one that was brief and totally lacking in conviction. He admitted that there was 'the gravest and strongest suspicion against the prisoner' but it was purely circumstantial. No one had seen John Lee kill Miss Keyse and then set fire to the house. He drew the jury's attention to the fact that the cook, Elizabeth Harris, was pregnant - could her lover, he asked, have been the murderer? That was the sum total of the defence and John Lee didn't stand a chance.

The judge, Mr Justice Manisty, who, by his own admission, was not in full command of all the facts in the case, nevertheless declared that it had been thoroughly investigated and the trial fairly conducted. As for the feeble defence, he suggested that it was unlikely that someone other than the prisoner had committed the murder. Was it possible, he asked, for someone to fetch the paraffin can and knife from the pantry without the prisoner waking up? Having said this, the judge reminded the jurors that if there was any reasonable doubt as to the prisoner's guilt, they must return a verdict of Not Guilty.

Not surprisingly, the jury returned a verdict of Guilty, one which evidently met with the judge's approval for prior to sentencing Lee to death, he told him:

> You have been found guilty of as cruel and barbarous a murder as was ever committed and the jury have found you guilty upon evidence so conclusive that, I am sorry to say, I cannot entertain a doubt as to the correctness of their verdict.

Thereupon he donned the black cap and, facing the young man in the dock, he passed the sentence of death. Lee's response was measured and direct; he looked straight back at the judge and said: 'The reason, my Lord, why I am so calm and collected is because I trust in my Lord, and he knows that I am innocent.'

There was, of course, a concerted effort to obtain a reprieve. In addition to the petition sent to Sir William Harcourt, the Home Secretary, orchestrated by Mr Molesworth St Aubyn, John Lee's family and the Vicar of Abbotskerswell, there was, according to the *Torquay Directory*, a written statement from Lee implicating others in the crime. It was said that he told members of his family and the vicar the names of two persons involved in the murder. Despite this, no further investigation was ordered and the plea was rejected.

John Lee was confined in a condemned cell in Exeter Prison to await his fate. He was allowed the comparative luxury of a bed, a table, three chairs and a copy of the Bible.[40] Guarded twenty-four hours a

40 A newspaper report said that during Lee's imprisonment awaiting trial 'time hangs very heavily on his hands and his only occupation has been reading the books supplied by the police from their library, varied now and then by exercise in the quadrangle'.

day, he was, nevertheless, fed reasonably well and allowed to take exercise twice a day. Whilst in prison, he wrote a number of letters to members of his family, some of which were printed in *The Exeter Gazette*. Although heavy with religious dogma - probably drummed into him by Miss Keyse - they were remarkably philosophical for such a young man to write and totally lacking in self-pity:

> Her Majesty's Prison, Exeter, 6th February 1885
>
> Dear Father and Mother,
>
> A few lines hoping this will find you much better after the shock. I hope you will bear up as well as you can. I am quite happy and well, and am quite prepared for my home above. You must trust in God the same as I have. You see how I have borne it up. I do not know whenever I was happier than I am now, because I know where I am going to. It is a pity you should have stopped to hear the sentence passed. I heard you crying behind. I hope you got home all right.
>
> I know you feel it more than I do, but you must not think of things in this world, you must pray to God to meet me in heaven. I will pray for you the little time I have to live, you must pray to God to help you. Do not think I am unhappy, you do not know how happy I am, you would be surprised to see me. Do trust in God and you will see the difference in the worldly man and the spiritual man.
>
> Dear Mother, if you think you would like to see me before I die you must write and tell the Governor of the Prison, and tell him the day that you will come up, or else you cannot see me. You can write to me at any time. Give my love to Milly, and tell her I have trusted in the Lord, and she must do the same and meet me in heaven. I am happier than I should be if I was out. What does it matter about a few years in this world? We must all leave it some time. You can all come and see me, only let the Governor know. I cannot think of any more to say at present, so I must say good-bye and we must trust in God.
>
> From your affectionate son, J H Lee
>
> NB.- The day is fixed for the 23rd of this month. Good-bye

The following week, John Lee wrote to his sister, Millie:

> Dear Sister,
>
> Your letter to hand this morning was received with much pleasure, and gave me great comfort to see that you are still the same kind

and loving sister who is always willing to do anyone any good. I have always noticed that you have not trusted the world altogether. I think you said Miss Keyse taught you to look above for help. I think she gave us both very good counsel. She never went to bed without praying for us, and I hope we shall all meet in heaven.

We shall know the truth of this case, it is the same as you say, it is hard to be punished when one knows that I did not do it, but I will trust in the Lord and ask him to give me strength to bear it all. This world's punishment is nothing after all to a better home above.

Dear Sister, I hope we shall meet in heaven. We must trust in the Lord and ask His forgiveness for all our sins.

Dear Sister, I shall be very glad to see you and father when you please to come. I was very glad to hear mother got home all right. It's a heavy blow for you all, you must help mother and father.

Though Mr St. Aubyn worked very hard for me, but there is no doubt that the truth will come out after I am dead. It must be some very hard-hearted persons for to let me die for nothing. All the witnesses will and must appear before our Saviour, for what they have said against me, and to answer for my life, they little think of it now; but the time will soon come for them, and I hope they will be prepared to meet our Saviour.

I thank God I am not blind so as not to know what I have seen and what I have done. They have not told six words truth, that is, the servants and that lovely step-sister, [Elizabeth Harris] who carries her character with her!

Give my love to mother and father and yourself; we must trust in the Lord, he will help us through all our trouble. He has helped me so far and He will help me to the end. Have you heard from K.F, [Katie Farmer]or seen them, you know who I mean.

Good-bye, my dear sister, for the present.

From your affectionate brother, who is dead to the world.
J.H.Lee.

The date for the execution was Monday, 23 February. On the previous Saturday, James Berry, the hangman, journeyed by train to Exeter from his home in Bradford, Yorkshire. One reporter described Berry as a 'slight-built, drab-whiskered and a rather under-sized man', whilst another said he was of 'medium height and strongly made'. He was, in fact, 5' 8", weighed 13 stones and was married with young children. Though an ex-policeman, he was a religious man, a teetotaller and not entirely without pity. He often sent 'inspiring' poems to his intended victims and, when he retired, he became a committed evangelist. He had been appointed as a public hangman the previous year, when he was only thirty and his appointment with John Lee was to be his nineteenth execution.[41] Yet no amount of experience could have prepared him for the dramatic events that were to follow. His attempt to carry out the sentence of death was to guarantee John Lee a unique place in the annals of crime and, within the realms of folklore and legend, lent him that status of a hero - he became the underdog who beat the system, *the man they could not hang*.

On the night of 22 February, the night before his execution, something extraordinary happened. John Lee wrote some final letters, received the Last Sacrament and then lay on his bed, seemingly resigned to his fate. He fell asleep, 'the last before the long, peaceful sleep of death', and had an extraordinary dream - he was standing on the scaffold, the hood was in place, the rope around his neck, the bolt was drawn - but nothing happened. The sequence was repeated three times.

The following morning, as soon as he awoke, he told the warders about the strange dream and it was later recorded in the prison log book. Soon after John Lee had eaten his breakfast of tea and toast, the prison chaplain, Rev John Pitkin, who had come to his cell twice a day 'for instruction, meditation and prayer', arrived to comfort him for the last time.

He had clearly made every attempt to get Lee to make a confession during these sessions for in a letter to the Home Secretary he wrote

41 James Berry, executioner 1884 to 1892. He devised a Table of Drops based on the weight of the prisoner and the length of the rope to ensure death was by dislocation of the neck, not strangulation. Some truly atrocious 'bunglings' were recorded, occasionally resulting in decapitation. During his career as a hangman he executed more than two hundred persons although, like Albert Pierrepoint, subsequently professed to condemn the practice of capital punishment.

that 'after pressing John Lee, for the 50th time almost, to tell me the name of the man whom he states as being at The Glen with his half-sister on the night of the murder of Miss Keyse, he yesterday said he would not swear to him, but he believed him to be Cornelius Harrington, a Babbacombe fisherman. His half-sister, he said, can give the man's name'.

The possibility of this man's involvement in the crime was, apparently, investigated, but Harrington said he had been at home on the night of the murder.

A little after seven-thirty, the dreaded figure of James Berry appeared in the doorway. He and his assistant swiftly, and without speaking, pinioned John Lee's arms behind his back. What followed next can best be described from articles in *The Western Morning News* and the *Torquay Directory*:

> What under ordinary circumstances would have proved the closing scene in the Babbacombe tragedy was enacted in the Devon County Prison yesterday morning, when John Lee - whose indictment, trial and condemnation for the terrible crime of the 15th of November are yet fresh in the public memory - was brought to the scaffold to undergo the dread sentence of the law. The details of the scene which accompanied the official efforts to deprive Lee of the life he had forfeited were of the most harrowing description, and are, probably, without a parallel in the history of such events in this country....
>
> Since his condemnation, Lee has entertained no hope of reprieve and appears to have resigned himself to the certainty of his terrible doom.
>
> This fact, however, does not appear to have operated in a manner which might have been expected upon one so young, or indeed from anyone occupying so terrible a position. The apparent indifference which characterised him in every stage of the proceedings connected with the unravelling of the crime has been maintained by the convict during his occupation of the condemned cell. His health was not visibly affected either by confinement or the anticipation of his fate. He partook of his meals with heartiness and evinced little of the depression which would be naturally looked for in a case of one so situated.
>
> When visited by his mother and other relatives his demeanour was

> by no means indicative of a man who realised, much less dreaded, the approach of death by hanging. While persistently asserting his innocence he assumed a cheerfulness, and even jauntiness of manner, which to his friends was not less painful than surprising. In bidding his last farewell he betrayed not the slightest emotion - not even when his grief-stricken mother finally embraced him and reluctantly withdrew from his cell...

The article refers to the refusal of the Home Secretary to issue a reprieve and tells its readers that, despite this, John Lee still protested his innocence and 'without a single expression of regret. On the contrary the culprit darkly hinted that the perpetrator of the horrible crime was the lover of his step-sister, Elizabeth Harris.'

In fact, in a later edition, the paper was more explicit:

> It is understood that Lee has written a confession occupying two pages, acknowledging his guilt, but implicating his half sister and another person.
>
> The execution was fixed for eight o'clock. At 7.30 the approaches to the exterior of the gaol were barred to all but the representatives of the Press, who were admitted by ticket and ushered one by one into a large room immediately within the portals of the main entrance of the building. At five minutes to eight the reporters, ten in number, were stationed within the main corridor at a point to be passed by the culprit on his passage from the condemned cell to the place of execution.
>
> A few seconds later the procession, headed by the Chief Warder [Mr Rainford] entered the corridor. The Chaplain [Rev. J. Pitkin] and the Schoolmaster [Mr Libby] came next and were immediately followed by Lee, who walked with pinioned hands between a couple of warders. The Prison Surgeon [Mr Caird] and the Governor [Mr Cowtan] also accompanied the procession, while other warders and beside them, Berry, the executioner, brought up the rear.
>
> The slow and deliberate tread of Lee and his companions and the tolling of the prison bell, added to the impressive tones of the chaplain *as he repeated* portions of the burial service, combined to make the occasion one of deep solemnity. The look of the doomed man during what was literally regarded as his march to the grave, bore no sign of anything like fear. He walked with firmness and with head erect...

> The scaffold, which was the same as that employed in the execution of Anne Tooke about five years ago, had been removed to another part of the building. It was sunk into the ground and formed, in fact, the flooring of a small brick shed ordinarily used for sheltering the prisoners' van....
>
> From a beam across the interior of the shed the hangman's rope depended, immediately beneath and in the centre of the floor being the trap from which it was intended to drop the prisoner. The gloomy and repulsive character of the gallows was, if possible, intensified by its enclosure within brick walls.
>
> As Lee walked into the building and, by the direction of the executioner, placed himself on the fatal planks, there was no faltering or sign of fear. He cast a glance at the rope above him as if to assure himself that its fastenings were perfectly secured and then inaudibly muttered something to Berry as the latter adjusted the noose around the culprit's neck. There was even a dash of Bravado in the unhappy man's demeanour as he glanced at the ghastly paraphernalia of death.
>
> A white cap was, in the usual manner, placed over the head and face of the convict, and as the closing words of the burial service died away on the lips of the chaplain, Berry, at a given signal, drew the lever. The only response was a grating sound and a slight movement of the trap upon which the culprit stood.

The *Torquay Directory* told its readers at this point that the two warders standing either side of Lee, firmly pressed their feet on the trap door in an attempt to push it open.

A second and third attempt was made to draw the bolt but with no more success than attended the first effort. Something was evidently wrong, and Berry, assisted by some of the warders, made an examination of the apparatus, having in the meantime withdrawn the rope and cap from the culprit's neck and face and moved him a little forward. In this terrible position Lee never flinched, but stood erect as before, his countenance having undergone no visible change. But not so with the officials, whose hurried movements and pale faces betrayed signs of deep anxiety and even terror.

The apparatus having again been prepared, Lee's legs were once more pinioned and the rope and cap adjusted. Again the fatal sign was given and the loud click of the lever once more startled the witnesses to this terrible scene. The bolt having once more defied the repeated efforts of the hangman, Lee was freed from the fatal noose and removed, this time to the back of the building in full view of a further trial to put right the stubborn machinery.

By this time the convict had become an object of the supreme sympathy of every man present. Still seemingly unmoved by the lingering torture thus added to his terrible fate, the condemned man surveyed the preparations which were going on before him. After a suspense of several seconds he was once more placed and Berry ran hurriedly to the back of the shed to drop him. As the bolt again and again refused to yield, Berry made a desperate effort to force the trap down by stamping it with his feet. Fortunately for himself the effort was unsuccessful, otherwise in all probability the executioner would have fallen with his victim.

As the convict had once more to be set aside, a feeling of inexpressible horror plainly depicted on their countenances, seemed to seize every one present. After a hurried conference of the officials Lee was conducted to the interior of the prison. In the meantime the services of a carpenter were procured, and by the process of planing it was sought to remedy the cause of the previous failures. This occupied something like five minutes, when for the fourth time the condemned man was placed in readiness for execution. The hope that every possibility of failure had this time been averted was quickly removed for the apparatus seemed, if possible, more rigid than ever. The impossibility of proceeding with the execution under the circumstances were too obvious to require further thought and Lee was accordingly returned to his cell.

The result of this extraordinary episode was that any further attempts to hang John Lee were abandoned and James Berry caught the next train back to Bradford, undoubtedly frustrated and perplexed by all that had happened. The scaffold was duly tested a few days later, using the appropriate weight - *and worked perfectly*. Berry was not held responsible for the fiasco - blame was put instead on a heavy shower of rain on the Saturday before the scheduled execution, which had caused the wooden parts of the structure to swell and become jammed.

The crowds waiting outside the prison to see the black flag hoisted - a signal that the execution had been carried out - were greatly perplexed when, after half an hour, they saw the reporters hurrying through the prison gates, anxious to get back to their newspaper offices and relate the whole incredible story.

Meanwhile, after lengthy discussions with the Governor, the Under-Sheriff caught the 10.05 train to London to see the Home Secretary, Sir William Harcourt, armed with a report on the abortive attempt to hang John Lee and a request for the sentence to be commuted to life imprisonment. With commendable speed and efficiency the Governor of Exeter Prison received a telegram later that same day, informing him that 'the prisoner had been respited and that a commutation of the death sentence would follow'.

Later that same day, the Home Secretary raised the matter in the House of Commons and informed its members that an official reprieve had been signed. News of the commutation reached the prison Governor the following day and, predictably, the press covered the ensuing debate over the decision at great length, many deploring Harcourt's decision not to attempt another execution which sparked further exchanges both for and against the reprieve.

As for Lee's state of mind at the time of his ordeal, according to *The Western Morning News*, the strain of such a terrible experience caused 'a certain amount of physical prostration'.

The *Torquay Directory*, however, described his condition in more detail - 'his face was ghastly, his hands were blue with cold; he tottered as he was helped from the scaffold and was so near fainting that he could not without assistance raise his foot sufficiently to mount the step over which he had to pass into the interior of the gaol'.

Once Lee was back inside his cell, the Governor, who was greatly affected by what had happened, offered him stimulants - probably brandy - but Lee refused and had soon recovered his composure, accepting the extraordinary events of that morning with his usual stoicism. He was given a second breakfast, a beef steak and half a pint of port, and then allowed to walk for a while in the exercise yard.

The day after the attempted execution, Lee's inadequate defence counsel, Mr Molesworth St Aubyn, in a letter to Rev John Pitkin, had the gall to write:

> What a terrible time you must have had with Lee! I am one of those who was never satisfied of his guilt. What a marvellous thing if he turns out to be innocent! At any rate he must have a nerve like iron. What will become of him now I wonder? If you can give me any details I should be glad.

In all probability Rev Pitkin, and others of a superstitious and religious turn of mind, chose to put the whole fiasco down to divine intervention, convincing themselves that the attempts to hang John Lee were doomed to failure simply because he was innocent of the crime - yet there was never any evidence to prove Lee's innocence and, furthermore, were this the case, the failure of the gallows would have been an occurrence of some frequency for the many innocent men and women who have been successfully hanged.

Most newspapers favoured the theory that heavy rainfall over the weekend prior to the attempted execution had caused the woodwork of the gallows to swell and become jammed - despite the fact that the prison carpenter, for all his frantic hammering and planing, failed to solve the problem.

Unable to offer any plausible explanation, a rumour soon circulated that James Berry had been bribed to abort the attempt by rigging the apparatus in some way. Yet this seems most unlikely as Lee's family and supporters were by no means wealthy and there was never any evidence that James Berry had ever accepted bribes in this way. He was required, of course, to make an official report on the failure and reprinted his subsequent letter to the Under-Sheriff of Devon in his autobiography published in 1892.[42] He put the blame squarely on the inadequate strength of the ironwork catches on the

42 *My Experience as an Executioner.* James Berry. Introduction by Jonathan Goodman. David & Charles Reprints.

trap-door. He admitted, however, that he had failed in his duty by not inspecting the apparatus before the scheduled execution. This does not explain, of course, why the trap-door opened perfectly well when Lee was not standing on it.

Two prison officers were sent by the Home Office to investigate the phenomenon. Their subsequent report, complete with diagrams, favoured Berry's theory, stating that they were 'perfectly satisfied that the cause of the failure to act was due to the fact that one of the long hinges rested on a draw-bolt one eighth of an inch too much'. Had Berry tested the apparatus using a dummy weight, this fault would have been detected in advance.[43]

Many local people, however, preferred a more esoteric explanation - that John Lee belonged to generations of witches and that no member of his family could hang; it was even rumoured that a white dove appeared above the prison walls when the trap-door failed to open. In later years, Lee always maintained that all sorts of bizarre happenings occurred in his parents' cottage on the night before he was due to hang and that his mother, Mary Lee, had dreamed that his life would be spared by the breaking of the rope.

As for Lee's own dream that Sunday night, the Rev John Pitkin described the whole incident in a letter to Lord Clinto, Chairman of the Exeter Quarter Sessions:

> Her Majesty's Prison, Exeter. April 8th 1885
>
> My Lord - The following are the particulars which your Lordship has requested me to supply of the dream of John Lee. After the attempted execution of Lee on February 23rd 1885 I went to his cell and spoke to him about the extraordinary event that had happened to him. He replied that on the night before his execution he had a dream which had shown him what would happen.
>
> At my request he related it to me. He said that in his dream he saw himself being led from his cell down through the reception basement to the scaffold which was just outside the basement door. He saw himself placed upon the scaffold and efforts being made to force the

43 Testing the apparatus in this way became standard practice soon after the abortive attempts to hang John Lee and was maintained until the Murder (Abolition of Death Penalty) Act 1965.

> drop which, however, would not work. He then saw himself led away from the place of execution, since it was decided that a new scaffold would have to be built before the sentence of the law could be carried out.
>
> He told me that when he woke at six o'clock on the morning fixed for his execution he had mentioned the dream to the two officers who were in the cell with him. These officers were not present when he told me this nor had they been with him since the attempt was made. They had, however, reported the dream to the Governor of the prison, to whom I also made a statement.
>
> I ought to add, my Lord, that John Lee did not attach much weight to the dream. Up to the time of his execution he had fully believed that he would be hanged. The dream did not come back into his mind while attempts were being made but only after he had recovered from the semi-consciousness into which he had apparently fallen.
>
> I am your Lordship's obedient servant,
>
> John Pitkin, Chaplain.

Pitkin also enclosed a copy of the statement made to the Governor of the prison by the two warders who sat with John Lee that night:

> At six am, when John Lee rose from his bed he said: "Mr Bennett, I have dreamed a very singular and strange dream. I thought the time was come and I was led down through the reception out into the hanging place but when they placed me on the drop they could not hang me for there was something wrong with the machinery of the drop. They then took me off the drop and took me [instead of the way I had come] around the A Wing and back through the A Ward to my cell."
>
> He told me in the presence of Mr Milford, who watched with me through the night.[44]

The document was signed by the Assistant Warder, Samuel D. Bennett and the Superior Officer, James Milford.

The chaplain was of the opinion that John Lee had, in fact, wanted to die and, whereas he had behaved with superhuman courage at the scaffold, he spent the next month at Exeter Prison making a

44 Quoted in *The Babbacombe Murder* by Frank Keyse.

nuisance of himself. Shortly before he was transferred to Pentonville Prison in London, the Governor received the following report from one of his warders at Exeter:

> Lee has shown a great deal of violence and insubordination, has repeatedly threatened the warders in charge of him and says he contemplates suicide...'

So truculent was he, that, after serving three months at Pentonville, he spent several weeks in solitary confinement at Wormwood Scrubs. By October 1885 he had been moved again, this time to Portsmouth where he was to spend the next seven years making hammocks and working in the prison laundry.

On Saturday, 6 August 1887, however, a little more than two years after the murder, the following extraordinarily speculative article appeared in *The Gloucester Journal*:

> A rumour of a most extraordinary and sensational character which, if true, would seriously shake public confidence in sentences pronounced on circumstantial evidence, is being whispered about amongst the clerks at the Home Office. Some years ago, a young man, a butler named Lee, was sentenced to death for murdering his mistress and benefactress, an elderly maiden lady at Babbacombe, near Torquay. This case attracted a lot of attention at the time and your readers will probably remember the facts well. I may remind them, however, that the lad, all through, stuck firmly to his innocence. On the scaffold there was a ghastly and shocking scene. Three times the hangman tried to do his duty...
>
> It is now said that, some months ago, one of Lee's fellow servants - the girl who at the trial was suspected of having an illicit lover - confessed to the crime on her deathbed and satisfied the authorities of Lee's innocence. The unfortunate man was subsequently released and pensioned for life at 30s a week but not till he had given a solemn undertaking to the prison chaplain not to reveal the truth. The Home Office justify their extraordinary action in the matter on the ground that, if the facts were known, circumstantial evidence in capital cases would practically become a dead letter; and it is most undesirable as ninety cases but of a hundred conclusions deduced therefrom are correct.

The article, however, carried the following editorial comment:

> *The Pall Mall Gazette* has made enquiries and is assured that Lee is still at Portland Prison where he is likely to remain for the rest of his life.

In fact, records show that Elizabeth Harris gave birth to a daughter, Beatrice, in the Union Workhouse at Newton Abbot on May 24th 1885 after which she travelled to Australia where she died in 1926.

John Lee remained in prison serving the last fifteen years of his sentence at Portland, no doubt 'breaking stones' as young Katie Farmer had predicted. As a life sentence was generally given as twenty years, Lee naturally expected to be released in 1905. Unfortunately, the Home Secretary at the time of his conviction had been of the opinion that Lee should remain in custody for the rest of his life. Lee, of course, reacted badly. The Governor reported that *'he has become generally discontented with everything and everybody and seems to think that any trivial incident is specially designed with a view to annoying him and any tyranny specially directed against himself'*.

In 1906, as the press began to agitate on his behalf and public interest was once more engaged in his case, questions were raised in the House of Commons. Rumours of his imminent release soon followed but they proved to be false. Petitions were presented to the new Home Secretary, Mr Herbert John Gladstone, and Mr A Nicholson, MP, wrote an article which sought to convince him that Lee's guilt was never proved and that his half-sister, Elizabeth, had been shielding the real culprit. But his efforts were to no avail.

Lee's mother, Mary Lee, who had visited her son regularly over the years, sent a personal letter to the King begging for his release. His Majesty's Private Secretary passed it to Gladstone without comment. But Mrs Lee refused to give up and on 13 October she wrote directly to the Home Secretary from her cottage in Abbotskerswell:

> I humbly beg mercy from you towards my dear son John Lee that has been confined in His Majesty's Prison for over 20 years as he has had such a good record and I do humbly beg for mercy under the new Criminal Law for a father's feeling towards my Dear Son and his poor

aged mother, a poor old broken-hearted widow.

Later that month, John Lee asked the Governor for various concessions now that he was, in effect, serving overtime. He sought permission to buy liquorice and peppermints - which was refused - and to see his mother for a full hour instead of the customary thirty minutes, which was granted. The following year, 5 September 1907, he wrote to the Governor:

> Your petitioner humbly begs that in the eventually [sic] of his being released at any time that you would be so kind as to allow him to grow his hair some little time before his discharge so that he may go out looking a little bit respectable...

The authorities did allow Lee to grow his hair and presented him with a set of dentures. His freedom was less easily gained though pressure for his release was sustained. In a letter dated 15 August, 1907, Herbert Gladstone wrote this letter to Sir Mackenzie Chalmers, Under-Secretary of State for Home Affairs:

> Lee is now 43. Imprisonment for the rest of his life would inevitably mean sooner or later - and from recent reports probably soon - mental and bodily decay. Then perhaps a decision to release him would be arrived at and he would leave prison a wreck of a man. I cannot think this would be right. If it is decided that he should be released it is best to do it at once.
>
> I have today again consulted with Mr Asquith on the case and he agrees with the view that I have formed - that he may be discharged on licence at the end of the year, say before Christmas. It may be well to transfer him from Portland to Dartmoor at once.
>
> As to when he should be informed this depends largely on the opinion and advice of the prison authorities. Clearly strict conditions must be made otherwise the Press and the Music Halls will get hold of him. It may be impossible to prevent the Press from making use of him but he can be stopped from making public appearances should he be tempted by offers sure to be made to him.

After much procrastination involving a great many letters passing between prison officials and various government departments, John Lee was finally released on 18 December, 1907. He was given a gratuity of £6.17s.7d. before being escorted to the police station in Newton Abbot and then taken by cab to his home in Abbotskerswell for an emotional reunion with his widowed mother.

Naturally, his release was headline news and reporters were permanently gathered outside the cottage waiting to besiege him and his family whenever they ventured outside. Had he been tempted to consider any of their lucrative offers for an exclusive account of his experience on the gallows, he was unable to accept. Released on licence, he was bound by certain conditions, one of which was that he should not 'take part in any public performance or deliver any lecture or speech or in any way exhibit himself at any meeting, assembly or place of entertainment'.

For the first six months or so, he was also obliged to report to the police station at Newton Abbot every month, giving the press the chance to follow close on his heels.

But it was the *Lloyd's Weekly News*, one of the country's most popular Sunday newspapers, that came up trumps. On 29 December, 1907, only eleven days after John Lee's release, they began a four part 'ghosted' serialisation of his story. This doubtless caused their sales to rocket for it was the news sensation of the year. As part of the second instalment on 5 January, 1908, the paper printed a letter from John Lee:

> Before I go on with my story this week I want to express my heartfelt thanks to *Lloyd's News* and its readers for all that is being done in my interests. Since last Sunday I have received hundreds of Christmas cards, letters and gifts from all parts of the country. I am astonished at the kindly sympathy with which the simple narrative of my sufferings has been received. How I would like to take all those dear people by the hand! I am only a poor unhappy man. But I have a heart and it is overflowing with gratitude. God bless you all in 1908.

Lee was also kept busy signing photographs of himself and, it appears, fending off the attentions of adoring females who were blatant in their pursuit of him. An article appeared many years later in the *Torquay Directory* on Wednesday, 11 March 1936, shortly after the death of Isidore Carter, the solicitor who did much to secure Lee's conviction. It contains the reminiscences of a tailor called Frank Wood and fully illustrates Lee's peculiar fascination for women.

At the time of Lee's release, Wood was newly married and kept a small outfitter's shop in Queen Street, Newton Abbot.

One day he noticed three strangers walking down the street - all three were tall, strong men 'so heavily built as to be remarkable. One had obviously just been released from prison for he wore a suit of rough prison cloth and the two men on either side of him were just as unmistakably warders'.

The following week, leaving his wife in charge of the shop while he attended a Trades Exhibition, Wood returned to find an enormous crowd gathered outside 'swaying to and fro and talking excitedly'. He saw that his wife was talking to the man he had previously seen under escort.

'He still wore his prison suit,' recalled Wood, 'and his fair hair and tremendous stature was a figure to be noticed'.

The man introduced himself as John Lee, 'a name which was almost a byword in those parts'.

The outcome of the meeting was that Wood agreed to make Lee a suit which required him to visit the shop on a number of occasions - this gave him the opportunity of witnessing Lee's special charisma at close quarters.

'Everywhere he went,' he said, 'a crowd followed him - a crowd largely composed of women, who almost went mad with excitement when they saw the tall figure in the streets. Young girls rushed to kiss his hand while others begged for a handshake or a smile. Everywhere the throng followed him and the man who had undergone one of the greatest ordeals of all time was beginning to feel the strain. He went into Mr Wood's shop and chatted to the tailor, asking if he might stop a while until the crowd dispersed. But the crowd would not disperse and at last, in desperation, Lee escaped unnoticed by the back door. But he had found a haven of refuge from the curse of the mob and in the days to come was often to be seen in the tailor's shop. There he would sit and converse on many things, always maintaining that he was innocent of the crime for which he had been convicted...

Months wore on and Lee became a constant visitor. He would take the children out on occasions and buy them fruit and sweets. Frequently, he invited Mr and Mrs Wood to tea at his mother's house in Abbotskerswell. His invitations became more insistent and at last they went. Mrs Lee was a dear old lady and her son seemed very fond of her and swore that he would never leave her but would support her to his dying day.

The article, however, finished by saying that Mr Wood:

> ...was not particularly fond of John Lee, finding him a bit of a braggart and a boaster and a hypocrite as well. Still the crowds pursued him and still his life was surrounded by a throng of staring, curiosity-maddened women. Mrs Wood, who did not like him, was ashamed of her own sex and took care to keep out of his way when he paid his frequent visits to her husband. Always he carried a bunch of white flowers in his hand and posed as a martyr - more sinned against than sinning.

He was as proud of his terrible experience on the gallows as a schoolboy is proud of his prowess at football and would recount with gusto to the wondering tailor how he could hear the men hammering at the scaffold and how the trap would go down perhaps an inch and he would stand on the tip of his toes so that he would not choke. But always he maintained that he never killed Miss Keyse and said that a grave error of justice had been made.

His fascination for women was enormous. On one occasion while Mrs Lee, his mother, and Mrs Wood were in the garden of his home in Abbotskerswell, he called Mr Wood on one side and produced a bundle of fifty or sixty letters from a cupboard. All the letters were from women, married, unmarried, middle-aged matrons and young girls, who all sympathised with him. Lee was by no means averse to their advances and would often return after a trip and recount in his boasting way of the good time he had had. In Newton Abbot, tradesmen's wives, milliners' assistants and stolid country milkmaids were all under his spell and fought with each other to get closer to him.

Despite the scores of women who propositioned him, Lee formed an attachment to a local girl, Jessica Bulled, a nurse in charge of the female mental ward at Newton Abbot Workhouse. The *Torquay Directory* stated that she had fallen 'under the spell of that strange fascination which Lee had for women; she consented to marry him and go away and no one could dissuade her. An old doctor friend, who still lives in Newton Abbot, spent hours begging her to forsake him but, in spite of her parents who were almost broken-hearted at the loss, the two were married...

John Lee and Jessie Bulled were married by special licence on 22 January, 1909, at the Congregational Church in Newton Abbot. Still the crowds followed him and the attentions of the press, once welcome, had now begun to pall. A few weeks later, John Lee wrote to the Home Secretary:

> Your petitioner complaines [sic] that now he his [sic] married and trying to live a quite [sic] and respectful [sic] life the papers will not let him.

The couple were thought to have left the area soon afterwards, possibly going to live in Durham. But in 1911, they were in London where Lee was thought to be working as a barman in Ye Old King's Head, London Bridge. Within months, however, he had left the country - it was rumoured that he went to America, possibly with a young lady in tow. By February, 1912, his wife and two young children, Aubrey and Victoria, were destitute and inmates in Lambeth Workhouse.

Speculation that John Lee had eventually made his way to Australia was endorsed by a highly romanticised and inaccurate silent film made there in 1917.[45] It was shown throughout England during the 1920s and Lee, having returned home, was said to have made several personal appearances dressed in his prison clothes. When it reached Newton Abbot, the film played to packed houses and members of his family were given special seats in the auditorium. But the crowds

45 *The Life Story of John Lee.* A copy of the film is held in The National Film Archive at the British Film Institute. A folk singing group, Fairport Convention, issued a record entitled *John Babbacombe Lee.*

that gathered outside the cinema hoping to see Lee himself were disappointed for he failed to make an appearance. Likewise, in one week thousands of people had flocked to a Cardiff cinema eager to see the man who had become a folk-hero and a living legend.

Details of the remaining years of Lee's life are uncertain but, according to the result of recent researches by Mike Holgate and Ian Waugh, the date of his death has been recorded as 19 March, 1945, in Milwaukee, USA, and he was buried at the Forest Home Cemetery, aged eighty-one.

So what did happen that stormy night at The Glen? The most probable scenario seems to be this - having carefully copied some religious verses into her diary, Miss Keyse gave her attention to the arrangements for the following day. She had already told Lee he could go over to Compton before breakfast [possibly to see Katie Farmer] but, after giving the matter some thought, she changed her mind.

As was her usual habit, she wrote him a note and, opening the pantry door, left it on the little table at the foot of his bed. In it, she said he must rake the paths instead of going to Compton as planned. He had been extremely truculent lately, more so than usual, and very restless. He seemed to resent being in service and she probably knew he would be very angry when he read her note. He really was an ungrateful young man and chose to forget that she had only taken him back as a concession, part of her Christian duty to help those less fortunate than herself - and since then she had done everything she could to find him another situation which was nigh on impossible with his criminal record.

Having delivered her note, she closed the door quietly behind her and lit the candle which had been left as usual on the sideboard by the old servant, Jane. Then, having collected her cup of cocoa from the range in the kitchen, she climbed the stairs to her bedroom, next to the room where the two elderly maids were sleeping. The cook,

Elizabeth Harris, was supposedly asleep in another room further along the landing, having gone to bed at five o'clock that afternoon.

Putting on a woollen bed-jacket over her nightdress - the wind was blasting in from the sea directly at the house - the old lady propped herself up in bed and began to drink her cocoa. Before she had finished it, she was disturbed by a noise - was it a shutter banging in the wind or someone moving about downstairs? Getting out of bed, she unfastened the bell-rope, and pulled. As the bell would presumably have rung in the pantry she would have expected John Lee to answer immediately. To her annoyance, there was no response. The old lady picked up the candle-stick and made her way downstairs....

But what did Miss Keyse find when she reached the passage near the pantry door? It was here that she met her assailant - someone who brutally attacked her with a hatchet or something similar and then, as she lay defenceless and almost dead, viciously severed her throat with her own gardening knife. The killer had then dragged the old lady's body into the dining room, scattered paraffin-soaked papers by her side and set them alight.

Was the person who sprang out of the darkness that night John Lee or someone else? Could it have been, as Lee himself said on a number of occasions, the lover of his half-sister, Elizabeth Harris?

Over time a controversial case such as this inevitably gathers a litany of rumour, speculation, supposition and debate. The mystery was rekindled in 1936, when the prosecuting solicitor at Lee's trial, Isidore Carter, died. The *Torquay Directory* printed an article retelling the story of '*The Babbacombe Murder*', fifty years before, once more relating the strange incident at a local funeral. Two lads and their father were amongst the mourners at the burial of a young man who belonged to a well-connected family and had died hopelessly insane. The two boys recalled that as the coffin was lowered into the grave they heard their father make this ambiguous comment:

'Today,' he said, 'we have buried the secret of the Babbacombe murder.'

Readers of the *Torquay Directory* were also told that soon after

John Lee was released in 1907, he went to see Isidore Carter. During their subsequent conversation, the solicitor insinuated that Lee had been wrongly convicted and that the real culprit, or as he put it - the man for whom Lee had 'stood in' - was a young man from a well-connected local family who had died 'hopelessly insane'. In Mike Holgate's study of the case, *The Secret of the Babbacombe Murder,* he suggests that the murderer was Reginald Gwynne Templer, the solicitor who had represented John Lee during the inquest and Magistrates' hearings (and, it was said, bore the cost of the proceedings) before becoming of unsound mind prior to the murder trial and too ill to function. His brother was obliged to take over the case. Reginald Templer died insane in Thomas Holloway's Sanatorium, Virginia Water, in Surrey, in 1886. Why Carter hadn't come forward with this information earlier and paved the way for Lee's release remains a mystery. One can only conclude that he, and others, were rewarded handsomely for their silence.

Was the mad young solicitor Elizabeth Harris's lover, and the killer of Miss Keyse? He was known to have been a frequent visitor to The Glen and was it perhaps an argument between the two lovers that had awakened the old lady? And then, suddenly confronted by an angry Miss Keyse, who, of course, would have recognised him immediately, he panicked and lashed out? Was the old lady felled by blows from a gentleman's stick, not a hatchet at all?

Or were Lee, Elizabeth and her lover in the process of robbing Miss Keyse of her silver when she disturbed them? Coming across her unexpectedly in the passage way, did Lee knock her down with a stunning blow and did the crazy young man come up behind her and slit her throat to make sure she did not regain consciousness and denounce him?

If Elizabeth *was* accustomed to entertaining her young man at The Glen when the old lady was in bed, then surely Lee must have known about it - he probably let him in. And did the lovers, perhaps, use the pantry for their love-making? They would hardly have risked going upstairs. Whatever the reason - illicit love or larceny - the three were disturbed and Miss Keyse's death was the result.

Another speculation was that John Lee and Elizabeth Harris had found out that Miss Keyse had left the old maids, Jane and Eliza Neck, a thousand pounds each in her will - equivalent to at least £40,000 today - and that he and his sister, Elizabeth, were to receive nothing. Their understandable resentment was deemed to be the reason behind the murder. Perhaps they had felt justified in stealing the old lady's silver but had not contemplated murder at all.

Undoubtedly, if Lee wasn't the killer, he knew who was. There was no way such a vicious attack could have happened within eight feet from where he was lying without his knowledge. Did he, in fear of his own life, do as he was told - help to set light to the house and wait for his sister to raise the alarm? And had she, in turn, been told to wait for half an hour before calling the other servants, not only to give the flames time to take hold and spread but also to ensure that her murderous lover was well clear of the house?

Or did Lee, in fact, kill Miss Keyse? Had he planned all along to rob and murder her and then burn the place down as he threatened? It was said that he was 'of a revengeful disposition and morbidly disposed'. He was certainly difficult and resented being in service - yet could his rage at having to rake the paths instead of going to Compton have been so great that it sparked off such a terrible surge of violence?

Certainly, he was feeling unsettled and anxious as demonstrated in his letters to Katie Farmer and during his conversations with his sister and the postman. Had he, perhaps, been caught stealing again, just like he had been at Colonel Brownlow's house? It was rumoured in the press that Lee had been trying to sell various articles from The Glen - and was that why Miss Keyse, at the end of her tether, decided to punish him by docking six pence from his weekly wage?

John Lee would have found this form of punishment particularly harsh as he had recently become engaged to Katie Farmer and, it appears, had every intention of marrying her as soon as he could afford it. Did the girl already realise that Lee, earning a pittance and unable to save any money, had already begun to steal from Miss Keyse? And did she half-expect him to be arrested at any moment?

Or did she suspect that he was planning a robbery at The Glen? Is that why she said she would love him even if he ended up 'breaking stones in the street', a common form of hard labour for convicted prisoners?

But why was it so important that Lee went over to Compton that morning? Did Katie live there, in service with Miss Keyse's sister, Mrs Maclean? Was she another participant of the family's charity? In one of his letters to her, John Lee mentioned the fact that Miss Keyse gave her good advice on coping with life and regularly prayed for them both. Did John Lee have a special reason for meeting her so early? In a letter written a month before the murder, Lee suggested breaking off their engagement and going their separate ways. With Lee in fear of imminent arrest for the petty thefts - and with the memory of his previous prison sentence fresh in his mind - had he decided it was time to get away while he still had the chance? And, having failed to break off his engagement to Katie, who refused to give him up, had they decided to run away together? Was that why he was so anxious to go over to tell Mrs Maclean about the tragedy - so that he could see Katie Farmer at the same time and tell her what had happened and, perhaps, revise their plans?

Was John Lee the killer? So long after the murder we can only speculate but there is one vital piece of the puzzle that may have exonerated him had his defence bothered to investigate it. Lee seems to have been *left*-handed for, on the night of the murder, when he put his fist through the dining-room window when the house was ablaze, he used his *left* hand, not his right. And when he guided the old maid, Jane, to safety towards the stairs on the night of the tragedy and later, through the flower pots on the veranda, he used his *left* hand, not his right. He was also using his *left* arm, despite the injury, to hack away at the burning laths and stab at the ceilings with a long pole whilst helping to fight the blaze. Either forensic science was not sufficiently advanced in 1884 to establish whether the savage cut to Miss Keyse's throat was made by a right-handed or a left-handed person or the matter was never investigated. It was established, however, that the fatal gash was made from left to right which, if inflicted from behind - as is usual in order to pinion the victim and establish sufficient leverage - would indicate that the killer was, in fact, *right*-handed.

As to the blood on old Jane Neck's nightdress - she testified that she did not notice it until the Sunday after the murder - how then could she possibly have known whether it had got there when Lee caught hold of her arm at the top of the stairs when the alarm was raised or later, when he helped her negotiate a path between the flower pots on the veranda? If it was the latter, he was probably splattered with blood as he helped William Gasking to carry the blood-soaked body of Miss Keyse from the house to the shed. Gasking had testified that the badly-battered head of Miss Keyse had flopped over as they lifted her body. In the circumstances the presence of Miss Keyse's blood on his clothing in no way proved that he was the killer.

John Lee's guilt or innocence was never proved. His bitterness towards his half-sister, Elizabeth Harris, was evident from his letters to his family and he said all along that she and another person were involved. Despite this, she was never cross-examined effectively and her lover was never apprehended and required, at least in public, to explain his movements on the night of the murder. It would not have been the first time that money and privilege saved a young man from the gallows.

As for John Lee, the newspaper reports were clearly wrong in their assessment of him. He was certainly wayward, misguided and truculent - he may even have been a killer - but he was not an ill-educated or belligerent oaf.

His letters show that he was literate, solicitous and possessed some intelligence. He had also managed to inspire the love of a sensible girl, one who was able to write coherently and express her feelings well. And yet, for all that, he seemed unable to claw himself off the lowest rung of society and fulfil a purpose in his life. Yet he bore the ordeal of his trial and the torturous fiasco on the scaffold with truly remarkable courage - and, by beating the system in the most extraordinary way, he has made his unique mark in criminal history and will be forever remembered as the man they could not hang.

Roy Fontaine

A Bloodthirsty Jeeves

On 2 November, 1978, nearly every newspaper in the country featured accounts of the murder trial at the Old Bailey of fifty-three year old butler, Archibald Thomson Hall, alias Roy Fontaine. Far from being bowed by his grave position, he had appeared in court the previous day confident and immaculately dressed - and, as details of his extraordinary lifestyle as a notorious jewel thief emerged during the trial, some reporters likened him to a 'Walter Mitty' figure whilst others dubbed him 'the monster butler', 'a bloodthirsty Jeeves' or 'the butler who served up evil'.

Most of the headlines at the time were blatantly sensational. A front page article in the *Daily Mirror,* entitled 'SEX SECRETS OF KILLER BUTLER', for instance, claimed that Fontaine had enjoyed homosexual affairs with three MPs. In addition, it claimed that Fontaine had once threatened to 'bring down the Government' by exposing their names.

As previous convictions are classified as inadmissible evidence, few people knew, however, that the man in the dock had, at Edinburgh High Court in May of that year, already been found guilty of murdering two people in Scotland - a businessman named Mr Walter Scott-Elliot and a young man called David Wright. Now, along with his accomplice, Michael Kitto, he was charged with the murder of three more, this time in England - Mrs Dorothy Scott-Elliot, Mary Coggle and his own brother, Donald Hall.

But who was Roy Fontaine? There was no doubt that he was an extraordinary man, imaginative, intelligent and cunning. He was also a hustler and a conman, a man who lived a lie. Even his name - Roy Fontaine - was a fabrication, a fanciful pseudonym adopted in honour of his favourite film star, Joan Fontaine. He hated the name he had been given - Archibald, after his father - and cursed his parents for giving him a label that seemed to him ludicrously unsophisticated, especially as he grew older and graduated from being a petty pilferer to becoming a master criminal, jewel thief and brilliant impersonator.

Fontaine came from solid, working-class stock but had, from the age of thirteen, been on the wrong side of the law. Yet it was only when he turned fifty, after spending half of his adult life in prison, that he turned to the ultimate crime - murder. He was accustomed to living on his wits and used his considerable talent for impersonation to hustle his way through life, always on a knife edge, at odds with society and constantly thinking up schemes to confound and challenge the establishment.

He was born Archibald Thomson Hall on 17 July, 1924. At the time, his parents were living in a small flat in a drab tenement block in McLean Street, Glasgow. His father and namesake worked in a GPO sorting office and his mother, Marion, was a waitress. A little later, the Hall family moved to slightly better accommodation in Albert Street, near Queen's Park. Young Archibald was an only child until the age of seven when his parents adopted a baby girl called Violet. Far from being put out by this addition to the family, Archibald, junior, took to the child straight away and they became close friends - a friendship that proved as strong as any blood tie and one which was to endure throughout all the traumas in later life.

Roy, as he insisted on being called, was always an imaginative boy and when he reached his teens he liked nothing better than to dress Violet in his mother's clothes and adorn her with all the jewellery he could lay his hands on. Violet was to say later that her brother always 'had a very strong artistic streak. When I was around seven or eight he exercised infinite patience and hours of his spare time making dresses for my dolls. In retrospect, considering he was then around fourteen, this appears to me now as perhaps the first feminine trait in his character that could have led in later years to homosexual tendencies. Often, when mother and father went for a walk, we used to remove the silk bedspreads. I used to stand on a chair or table and he pinned these around me, producing quite exotic creations. To complete my temporary elegance he put flowers in my hair, draped one of mother's necklaces around my neck and pinned brooches in precisely accurate positions'.[46]

Roy was to say later that he was always fascinated by jewels and wanted 'to hold them' in his hand. 'I wanted to possess them,' he explained. 'To me they were the most beautiful things in the world.'

The feminine side of his nature also showed itself in other ways. Unlike most teenagers, he was extremely fastidious, always kept his hair and finger nails clean and insisted on fresh bed-linen daily. He enjoyed cooking, housework and arranging flowers to make the home look attractive and, moreover, unlike most men, he was a kindly and patient nurse when anyone in the family fell sick. Yet, despite this and the even temper he displayed within the family and his close circle of friends, at the age of thirteen he was brought before the Glasgow Magistrates' Court for 'malicious mischief', although the actual offence is unknown.

It was soon after this that the country was shattered by the outbreak of the Second World War. In 1939, Fontaine's father was conscripted into the army and drafted to France where he came under enemy fire. After being badly wounded, he was brought back to England for treatment and convalescence. Once he had recovered, he was sent to an army base at Catterick, in Yorkshire, where he was eventually joined by his family.

Whilst he had been away, however, Roy, still only sixteen, had embarked on an affair with a married woman of thirty-six. The woman, attracted by the lad's immaculate appearance and veneer of sophistication far beyond his years, took him to dine at some of the grandest hotels in Glasgow, thus giving him his first taste of a life far removed from that of his parents, friends and neighbours.

46 From '*The Monster Butler*'. Norman Lucas and Philip Davies.

Whilst at Catterick, Archibald, senior, was given a job as a telegraphist with the Royal Corps of Signals. Unfortunately, while he was there some confidential documents went missing and, during their enquiries, the military police searched Roy's room. Not only did they find the missing papers, they were shocked to find the lad's room decorated with Nazi swastikas and pictures of Adolf Hitler, whom he professed to admire, despite the anger and concern of his patriotic family. Soon after this incident, Archibald, senior, was discharged from the army on account of his injuries and the family moved back to Glasgow.

The renegade side of Roy's nature was, by now, well to the fore. At one time offering to collect money for the Red Cross, he managed to obtain two boxes and subsequently collected from a poor area in one box and from a wealthy catchment area in the other. Of course, when it came to handing over the box, he relinquished the one with the least money, keeping the other for himself. This despicable act was followed by a bizarre incident when he was seventeen involving a medical bag which he stole from a doctor who had called at the house to examine him. He ran off with it and was missing for two days. His sister, Violet, later recalled the stress this strange episode caused the rest of the family:

'I will never ever forget that ghastly night. We had no idea why he had done such a thing. We hunted him in the streets of Glasgow in pouring rain and then walked alongside the River Clyde fearing that we would sight his floating body. My father was at work and my mother cried incessantly. We were stopped by a policeman and asked why we were out on such a dreadful night and forced to explain that we were searching for my brother. As the hours passed, mother became more and more convinced that he had committed suicide by taking the drugs.' [47]

Roy was eventually found happily ensconced in a hotel near Gleneagles, in Perthshire. He no longer had the bag, insisted he hadn't taken any of the drugs but refused to say what he had done with them. Another incidence of Fontaine's odd behaviour concerned an

47 From '*The Monster Butler*' : Norman Lucas and Philip Davies.

old lady who lodged in the same house as the Hall family. He seemed genuinely fond of her and, as she was without friends, he did her shopping for her and spent time keeping her company. When the old lady died, a search was made of the flat during which a trunk containing at least £2000 in bank notes. It had been assumed that she had been living on a meagre income and it was possible that she had somehow forgotten how much money she had hoarded. It was well-known that throughout his friendship with the old lady, Roy always seemed to have plenty of money and the conclusion drawn by the less charitable was that he had helped himself from the coffers. It does seem odd, however, that he should leave such an unexpected haul to be discovered when he could so easily have taken the lot while he had the chance, without anyone being the wiser.

In May, 1941, Roy was in for a shock. His mother produced another son, Donald, whom he never liked, grew to despise and would eventually kill. On 11 August, three months after his brother was born, Roy received his first custodial sentence - sixty days imprisonment for theft and forgery. He was only seventeen years old but his life of crime had begun. His law-abiding parents were shamed by their son's criminal activities and this may have been the reason why they moved house so often. But the family remained loyal and Violet always spoke up for her brother, seeing the caring side of his nature despite his increasingly anti-social behaviour. She said later that he was always protective towards her and whenever she was late home in the evenings her quick-tempered mother was usually 'standing behind the door waiting to swipe me with her hand. On many occasions Roy shielded me, letting me duck past my mother beneath his outstretched hand.'

She also had fond memories of playing truant from school on a Monday so that she could spend an exciting day with her brother. He always insisted that she wore her best clothes and was clean and presentable - even making her wear gloves and carry a handbag. Roy always seemed to have money in his pocket and they would spend the morning window shopping in the city centre and drinking coffee in select restaurants. In the afternoon they would go to the pictures – either to the Odeon, La Scala or the Gaumont - sometimes they would visit all three, one after the other. At La Scala, film-goers were able to eat as they watched the film which gave Roy the opportunity to instruct his little sister in table manners. Violet loved these Monday outings but was a little irritated by the fact that Roy always insisted on calling her, not Vi as he normally did, but by the name of the woman with whom he was having an affair.

There can be little doubt that Roy's delinquent behaviour, though not violent, arose from some sort of personality disorder. On three occasions as a young man, when he was apprehended by the police, he was judged insane and sent, not to prison, but to mental institutions. The first time this happened was in January 1943; he was charged with a minor offence in Edinburgh but, having been found unfit to plead, he was sent to Glasgow's Hawkhead Mental Hospital for assessment. He absconded and, according to Scottish law, after remaining at liberty for twenty-eight days, declared himself free.

But not for long. In February the following year, Roy Fontaine was charged with burglary and sent to Woodilee Home for the Mentally Disturbed where he was regarded by one psychiatrist who was treating him as 'a menace to society'. On 25 April, Roy managed to abscond again and, once more, remained free for the requisite number of days.

Yet, before the year was out, he was charged with further house-breaking offences. At this point Fontaine was certified insane and ordered to be detained indefinitely at the criminal lunatic department at Perth Prison. Presumably he received further psychiatric treatment and managed to convince the authorities that he was mentally fit for he was released two years later, on 22 November, 1946 - only to be jailed the following year for forgery and house-breaking. During the subsequent proceedings at the Old Bailey, the question of mental instability was not raised and he asked for a further fifty-one cases to be taken into account.

In 1949, soon after his release, he was jailed for a further twenty-one months for theft, fraud and forgery. Again, in 1951, he received another sentence on five charges of house-breaking - he was only twenty-five and already on a crash course to disaster.

As Fontaine was bisexual, his long terms of imprisonment were made more palatable by engaging in homosexual relationships - usually with younger men who were attracted by his charming manners, sensitivity and knowledge of a world more sophisticated than their own. Whereas some prisoners spent their time playing cards and reading action novels or 'girlie' magazines, Roy Fontaine was different. As part of his trade as a thief and confidence trickster, he chose instead to use his time constructively by studying the world of antiques and becoming expert on furniture, gems, silver, crystal and porcelain. And, just in case he ever needed to employ his considerable talent for impersonation, he chose to educate himself in the ways of the ruling classes. He read countless biographies of famous people and studied books on genealogy, etiquette and elocution and became familiar with all the whims, habits and mores of the rich and landed gentry.

His single-minded approach to his craft paid off. After countless hours of study Roy Fontaine was more than qualified to seek employment as a butler, or gentleman's gentleman, when he was eventually released. Although once free, he usually sought legitimate employment, his intent was ultimately criminal. By infiltrating the world of the wealthy, he hoped to pull off a series of spectacular thefts from some of the country's richest families and so secure for himself the ultimate dream of every crook - to end his days in luxurious indolence in an exotic villa somewhere in the sun.

His dedication to this aim held him in good stead when, after his release in 1951, he managed to secure a post as butler to Mr and Mrs William Warren-Connel at their mansion, Park Hall, part of a nine hundred acre estate in Stirlingshire. As his parents were now separated, he managed to persuade the couple to employ his mother as housekeeper and she duly arrived to take up her post, with ten year old Donald in tow. She left soon after, however, when, much to Fontaine's disgust, the lad was caught stealing a number of trinkets from the gardener's cottage.

It was whilst Fontaine was at Park Hall that he performed one of his more audacious impersonations. During a period when his employers were away, he steamed open the mail - which was his usual practice - and found an invitation for the Warren-Connels to a garden party given by the Queen at her official Scottish residence, Holyrood Palace, in Edinburgh. The challenge was too great for Fontaine to refuse. This would be an excellent opportunity to test his skill as an impersonator, have some fun and take on the mighty echelons of the Establishment. Having determined to attend the function as Mr Warren-Connel, he hired a morning suit and drove to Edinburgh in his employer's Bentley, driven by John Wooton, who had been a fellow inmate at Wandsworth Prison. Supremely confident, he conducted himself impeccably, mingled with the aristocracy with ease, discussing cars, horses and gun sports with wealthy landowners and food, antiques and country houses with their wives. It was an afternoon's work that must have given him immense satisfaction.

The gardener at Park Hall, however, was not so easily fooled. He was to say later that he wasn't the least surprised that the butler was able to impersonate his employer so effectively:

'Fontaine was always immaculately dressed and oozed charm,' he said. 'I can quite understand how he managed to bluff his way into the garden party. However,' he added, 'I always suspected that he was not all he pretended to be and my feelings have been confirmed.'

The police also viewed Fontaine's employment at Park Hall as risky, to say the least, and warned the Warren-Connels that he was a known burglar and jewel thief. Despite this, the lady of the house was prepared to keep him on but Fontaine felt himself to be under surveillance from local people and the police and decided to cut his losses and leave. Characteristically, he spent the generous three month's salary he was given on a fortnight at a hotel near Gleneagles, living entirely on champagne and smoked salmon.

In 1953, Fontaine carried out an ingenious and highly lucrative theft from a prestigious antique shop in Edinburgh. Two of his accomplices, posing as wealthy Americans, were inspecting some jewellery, when the proprietor was called away to answer the telephone. On the other end of the line, Fontaine, posing as a foreign buyer, kept her engaged in conversation just long enough for his fellow crooks to escape with a sizeable haul of precious gems. Fontaine and one of the men headed for Torquay and, still pretending to be rich Americans, they were invited to a civic dinner at the Imperial Hotel, at which the Star-Spangled Banner was played in their honour.

Roy Fontaine was finally arrested in July of that year and sentenced to three years imprisonment. But, in 1955, he was at it again, performing one of his most outrageous stunts. This involved dressing up as an Arab sheikh and booking into a smart London hotel. He arrived in a chauffeur-driven Rolls Royce and gave every impression of being extremely wealthy. Once settled into one of the best suites, he expressed a wish to buy some diamond rings and arranged for several top jewellers to bring samples of their best gems to his hotel suite. When they arrived, the bogus sheikh was taking a bath and asked for the trays of rings to be passed through the bathroom door for him to inspect at his leisure. Needless to say, when some time had elapsed and there was no response save the sound of gushing water, the jewellers found the bathroom empty - except for some discarded clothes and empty jewel boxes. The open window told them all they needed to know.

Fontaine's criminal life continued. In January, 1956, he appeared at Buckinghamshire Quarter Sessions and was convicted of burglary, theft and illegal possession of a fire-arm. He received a harsh sentence - thirty years preventive detention and five years imprisonment, to run concurrently. He was sent to Parkhurst Top Security Prison on the Isle of Wight but, after failing to perfect an escape plan with one of the other inmates, he was transferred to Nottingham Jail. His mother and sister visited him throughout his numerous prison sentences (he made Violet bring his best bone china cup whilst he was on remand) and he always managed to appear optimistic and somehow hide the despair he must have felt in such grim surroundings. Yet he, of all people, an extremely fastidious man, must have found prison conditions especially hard after the lavish lifestyle he adopted outside.

In 1963, Fontaine was actually given parole for two days to attend his father's funeral. He had always prided himself on a moral code that meant not grassing on fellow prisoners and keeping his word. He promised the new governor, Bill Perry, for whom he had some respect, that he would return - and he did. During his hours of freedom he spent time with his family, bought little gifts for his mates inside, spent, he said, two hours in bed with an attractive young woman, and then went back to the prison, ten minutes before the deadline.

He was eventually released on 19 March, 1963, emerging from the prison carrying a tabby cat called Whiskey in a box. Having raised it from a kitten, it had been a great comfort to him during his imprisonment and he was devoted to it. The Hall family, remarkable for their loyalty to Roy, organised a huge party to celebrate his release and the following week he was able to attend his mother's marriage to ex-con, John Wooton.

Soon after this, Fontaine became involved with a woman called Phyllis Nye and together they applied for various posts as butler and housekeeper. In October, 1963, while Fontaine was still working for a retired diplomat, Nigel Law, he applied for the job of butler to Sir George Aylwen, a former Lord Mayor of London - Phyllis also applied for the job of cook. When Sir George asked Fontaine for testimonials, the crafty butler gave him Nigel Law's telephone number and suggested a suitable time to call. Then he hurried back to Law's house in Buckinghamshire and, when Lady Aylwen rang as arranged, posing as his employer, he gave himself a glowing reference.

At one time, he also worked for Sir Charles Clore, but not for long. He only lasted for five days for, after Clore had wisely checked Fontaine's background, he gave him the sack on 15 November, 1963.

On 13 January, 1964, Roy Fontaine was arrested again, this time receiving a further ten years preventive detention. He was sent to the top security prison at Blundeston, in Suffolk. Incredibly, he and two other prisoners managed to escape and remain free for two years. It was whilst he was on the run that Fontaine became involved with a young woman called Margaret, who was pregnant at the time. Whether or not Fontaine was using her as a convenient cover whilst hiding from the police, he seemed genuinely fond of her. They travelled all over England - Fontaine carrying out the odd theft here and there - and at one time they lived in a rented house by the sea at Eastbourne, mixing normally with their neighbours and making new friends. They later rented a house in Kent, and, once again, they lived as any other couple without exciting any comment - they enjoyed eating out and evenings in the pub and even joined the local country club. It was while they were here that Margaret's daughter was born - Fontaine was delighted and quickly fell into the role of an attentive and indulgent father-figure.

But the police were never far behind - after robbing a jeweller in Falmouth, he was chased but managed to escape arrest by hiding under a bed in his lodging house. Another time, he was involved in a car crash in London and was taken to hospital - however, when the police came to question him, he escaped through a window. For two years he gave them the slip and remained free, during which time he had a number of hair-raising experiences; he was finally arrested a few days after moving to Weston-super-Mare with Margaret and the child in 1966.

On 13 May, 1966, he was tried at Edinburgh High Court for some of the crimes he had committed whilst on the run - seven cases of fraud, four of theft and one of receiving stolen goods. For these, he was sentenced to a further five years' imprisonment - in addition to the ten years preventive detention already outstanding. Though she remained loyal to Fontaine for a long time, Margaret eventually decided to take her little girl and start a new life in Canada.

If Margaret and the baby failed to prevent Fontaine from a life of persistent crime, it was unlikely that anything could. He was incorrigible and seemed to court danger; he also had a flare for the outrageous and, despite his many years in prison, seemed unable to resist embarking on a number of audacious deceptions.

He conducted endless frauds during his career as a jewel thief, sometimes using a smartly dressed woman companion as a foil, and knew every trick in the book. Occasionally, they would run off with an item of jewellery after asking to inspect it near the doorway of the shop where, they said, the light was better. On a number of occasions he had acquired genuine pieces of jewellery on loan only to replace them with copies, leaving the owners none the wiser.

One of his most successful tricks was to book into an expensive hotel and surreptitiously let it be known that he was a titled gentleman who would prefer to be addressed as plain mister and be treated accordingly. Before long, an accomplice would appear in the bar and greet the bogus lord with a hearty,

'My goodness, if it isn't Lord So-and-So!'

On the strength of this staged exposure, he would be able to cash cheques and enjoy his stay at the hotel to the full before leaving without paying a penny.

On a personal level, from time to time during his bouts of freedom, Fontaine became emotionally involved with women - they found him charmingly attentive and gratifyingly generous. When he was paroled in January, 1972, he was sent to live in a prison hostel in Preston and worked with mentally disturbed patients at Whittingham Hospital, near Garstang. It was here that he met a fellow worker, Mary Coggle, who was to feature so tragically in his subsequent murder spree.

He also formed a close relationship with a local woman, a fair-haired widow called Hazel Patterson. However, on one of his frequent weekend trips to London in his Jaguar, he met thirty-nine year old Ruth Holmes, a sophisticated woman with a career in a fashion house and a flat in Kensington. They were married at Preston Register Office on 13 September, 1972. But his attachment to a young man he had known in prison and his on-going involvement with Hazel Patterson, tainted the marriage. When Fontaine was jailed again for two and a half years in September the following year, Ruth visited him in Wandsworth but left the prison in tears. Fontaine had told her, quite frankly, that it would be better for her to seek a divorce and make a new life without him.

After his subsequent release, he lived with Hazel Patterson for a while and, at the time of his trial for murder, she was referred to as his common-law wife. There was no way, however, that theirs could have been a conventional marriage in that Fontaine spent most of his time planning robberies, carrying them out, on the run or in jail.

After a spell in Wandsworth, Fontaine was sent to Long Lartin Prison, in Worcestershire, where conditions were more civilised. It was here that he formed a close attachment to a young man from Birmingham, David Wright, the man who, through events that were destined to get out of control, was to become his first victim.

Fourteen months later, Fontaine was paroled yet again and sent to live in a hostel in the Midlands. The place was so sordid and depressing, he absconded and was, once more, on the run. Unable to resist stealing, he was arrested on 16 June, 1975, and charged with receiving stolen documents and the illegal possession of a firearm.[48] Sentenced to two and half years, he was sent back to Long Lartin, only to be released in the spring of 1977.

Free once more, Fontaine was about to begin the series of crimes that would end in his being incarcerated for the rest of his life. He began to look for work as a butler, probably with a view to robbery. So it was that on Tuesday, 31 May, 1977, Lady Peggy Hudson, a seventy-two year old widow, was waiting on the platform at Carlisle railway station. Her husband, Sir Austin Hudson, a former Conservative MP, had died in 1956 and she had recently paid a fee of £140 to hire a butler through an employment agency. The man she had selected was due on the Inter-City Express and she had decided to welcome him herself before driving them both back to her home, Kirtleton Hall, an eighteenth century mansion near the village of Waterbeck, deep in the Scottish countryside north of Carlisle.

As the train drew into the station the old lady watched the passengers alight - she knew straight away which one was her new butler. Roy Fontaine looked every inch the part. Now aged fifty-three, he was a little rotund and his dark hair was receding but

48 Fontaine obtained some highly confidential papers addressed to the Prime Minister and tried to sell them to the Soviet Embassy but the offer was declined.

he had the precise, slightly arrogant carriage of the perfect butler. To complement his immaculate appearance, he spoke in clipped Scottish tones, in a manner that was assured but deferential.

Lady Hudson was impressed and, frankly, relieved. Since the war a good butler was hard to find, besides which, she was impressed by his knowledge of history, antiques, good food and fine wines and the country style of living. She felt they would suit each other very well. Fontaine moved into a small, furnished flat in the Hall and was given permission to use the car. He noted with satisfaction that the house was comfortable and well-appointed. Set amongst trees and surrounded by an extensive estate, it had an indoor swimming pool under a domed glass extension. More importantly, the old lady possessed a great many valuable antiques and some very expensive jewellery.

For her part, Lady Hudson seemed puzzled that a mature and accomplished man such as Roy Fontaine should be content to work in the depths of the countryside for a salary of £20 a week. When she asked him outright why he stayed, he told her that he preferred life in the country and hoped one day to purchase a small inn to occupy him when he eventually retired from service.

After Fontaine had been with Lady Hudson for a few weeks, he told her he had received a telephone call from a friend of his - a young man called David Wright, who was looking for work as a gardener. Might he, he wondered, invite him to stay at Kirtleton Hall for a few days? Lady Hudson readily agreed, not knowing that Wright was an ex-jail bird like Fontaine. The two men had enjoyed an intense affair whilst incarcerated in Long Lartin, during which Wright had learned of Fontaine's long criminal history and took careful note of this information in order to blackmail him later.

Lady Hudson seemed to like young Wright, a handsome thirty year old, sturdy, capable and well-versed in country ways. Before long, she offered him a job as gardener at the Hall and he gladly accepted. When they were both free, he and Fontaine would drink together in the Kirtle Inn, in the village of Kirkpatrick Fleming. Fontaine, his friend noticed, seemed to have plenty of money, frequently bought rounds of drinks and regularly put money in the charity box. As Wright liked to gamble on horses and was always short of cash, it wasn't long before he was asking Fontaine for money and threatening to tell her Ladyship that her new butler was, in fact, a professional jewel thief.

Fontaine was willing to buy Wright's silence for several weeks, giving him ten or twenty pound notes whenever he asked. Before long, however, Wright had become a nuisance, and, moreover, a dangerous one. Even more so when, realising that Fontaine intended to rob Lady Hudson, he decided to be part of the action. But Fontaine was a professional and refused to include him in any plans for the robbery, preferring to work with two of his established accomplices in London.

The plan was to orchestrate the robbery at Kirtleton Hall by proxy - in other words, when Fontaine was well away from the area and with a cast-iron alibi. He was very annoyed therefore, when, a little later, while her Ladyship was away in London, he was rummaging through her jewel box - possibly taking an inventory prior to the theft - and noticed that an antique ring worth several thousands of pounds, was missing. Confronted and accused of stealing the ring, Wright denied it. Fontaine, however, went in search of the ring and, finding it in the possession of Wright's local girl-friend, demanded it back.

Wright was incensed by this and the two men had a flaming row in the kitchen. In the early hours of the next morning, after drinking the best part of four bottles of stolen champagne, Wright crept up to Fontaine's room and, finding him asleep, fired a .22 rifle straight at his head. The bullet missed him by an inch and lodged in the headboard.

'I told you that we were going to rob Lady Hudson,' Wright shouted, so drunk he could barely stand.

Fearing for his life, Fontaine feigned acceptance and suggested that they rob the old lady when she was next away.

To this, Wright blurted: 'You're a bloody fool. That's a crazy idea. She has her most valuable jewellery with her so we wait until she comes back and then wipe up all the really expensive gear.'

At this point, Fontaine got out of bed and moved towards his assailant. Wright panicked and, swinging the rifle butt, he struck the butler on the side of his face, just missing his eye. Then, shocked at the sight of the blood pouring from the wound, he threw down the rifle and started to cry:

'What have I done? What have I done?'

He had no way of knowing that he had, in effect, signed his own death warrant. Fontaine was seething with anger. Not only was he physically under threat but his carefully planned theft was also in jeopardy. He dare not go ahead with the robbery whilst Wright was alive. Having spent most of his adult life in prison there was no way he was going to allow a drunken blackmailer put him inside again.

By dawn that day, Fontaine had washed the bloodstains in the bedroom, plastered over the bullet hole in the headboard and disguised it with boot polish. His methodical manner, however, belied his inner turmoil. As soon as Wright had staggered off to bed, Fontaine, in a panic, had rung his sister, Violet:

'He's trying to get me,' he blurted, his voice shaking. Realising how frightened he was, Violet suggested he get in the car and drive to her house straight away. He couldn't do that, he said, because Lady Hudson was away and he had to look after the dogs. By the morning, however, he had regained some of his composure and went about his duties as usual.

Later that day, as though nothing had happened, Fontaine asked Wright to join him on a rabbit shoot. Lady Hudson was extremely fond of her three dogs and insisted on feeding them fresh rabbit so Fontaine's suggestion that they catch a few before Her Ladyship returned was perfectly natural.

After firing at several young rabbits and using up all his shot, Wright sat down on a grassy bank and took out his cigarettes. He pointed to a large rabbit and told his companion to shoot. Fontaine, a few feet away, lifted his rifle and aimed at the animal - then suddenly turned and aimed it at Wright instead. He discharged four bullets into his head and back, the last of which killed him. The act of killing had shaken him - but it was done. Before returning to the house he covered the body with bracken. Although he later claimed he had felt remorse over his killing of Wright - and even cried whilst burying him - he said on another occasion:

'David Wright was filth, a dirty blackmailer and he deserved to die. I was doing society a favour when I got rid of him.'

Meticulous as ever, once back at the house, Fontaine returned the two guns to their usual place and replaced the champagne that Wright had drunk. He later went to meet Lady Hudson at the railway station at Carlisle, once more the perfect butler. When she enquired about the wound to his face, he explained that he had bumped it on the steps of the swimming pool. He explained the absence of Wright by saying that he had left to take a job elsewhere.

That same evening, Fontaine went back to the scene of the murder and dragged Wright's body to the foot of a ravine where he dug a shallow grave, concealing it with piles of turf and branches, weighted down with small rocks. He returned to Wright's grave several times during the days that followed, making sure anything that could be identified was removed and adding more bracken and stones on top of the body to ensure its concealment.

Though obviously unaware of the murder, Lady Hudson may well have noticed the change in Fontaine's demeanour. Something was wrong. She also overheard a dubious conversation between Fontaine and one of his criminal colleagues and her suspicions grew. She eventually decided to contact the police but, before she had time to do this, she received a call - as did the local police - from a man who said he was a CID officer. He warned the old lady that Roy Fontaine was a criminal of some notoriety. As a result, he was immediately sacked and the local police escorted him from the estate.[49]

The next day, 7 September, Roy Fontaine went back to London, only to return to the Scottish borders on Sunday, 16 October, to rent a cottage, Middle Farm, in Newton Arlosh, for £40 a month. He soon became a regular in the local pub, The Joiners' Arms, but

49 These calls were not made by the police. It was later suggested that the mystery call may have been instigated by one of Fontaine's ex-girlfriends with a grudge.

he wasn't his usual gregarious self - he had become more subdued and thoughtful. Having murdered a friend, he no doubt had much to think about during the long winter nights. No longer inclined to rob Lady Hudson after all that had happened he regularly scanned *Country Life*, *The Lady* and *Tatler*, looking for suitable posts and was fortunate to find an advertisement by Mr Walter Travers Scott-Elliot, a retired businessman and former Labour MP for Accrington. He and his wife, sixty-two year old Dorothy, were looking for a butler for their luxury penthouse in Richmond Court, in Sloane Street, Chelsea. The job was tailor-made for Fontaine, and, with his forged references and supremely confident manner, he seemed the ideal candidate.[50]

It didn't take Fontaine long to establish that the Scott-Elliots were very rich indeed. Besides their London home, they had houses in France and Italy and had recently sold a large estate in Scotland. Their London house was full of antique furniture, silver, porcelain, ivory and jade objets d'art and, to top it all, Mrs Scott-Elliot possessed several expensive furs and some magnificent jewellery worth many thousands of pounds.

They also held a number of international bank accounts which provided an irresistible challenge to the butler's fraudulent skills. He thought he had really hit the jackpot this time - especially when he learned that Mr Scott-Elliot was, at eighty-two, becoming forgetful and verging on senility. Born in 1895, he was the son of Scottish landowners; educated at Eton he went on to become a captain in the Coldstream Guards during the First World War. After this, he went to India and worked his way up to the position of Managing Director of the Bombay Company Ltd. It was during this time that he amassed his fortune and bought many of his rare Indian antiques. He returned to England in the early 1930s and was elected as the Labour Party member for Accrington in 1945.

In 1948, his first marriage was annulled and he married Dorothy,

50 In fact the porter at Richmond Court said that Fontaine 'looked like a millionaire himself. He was always impeccably dressed and used to speak to the staff here in clipped tones. It was hard to believe he was a butler'.

twenty-two years his junior and the daughter of a wealthy Calcutta family. Many of the priceless items the couple possessed were heirlooms from her family. It was too good to be true. Fontaine must have felt compelled to rob the Scott-Elliots - a haul such as this was impossible to resist - one last massive theft and then perhaps he could quit a life of crime and retire an immensely wealthy man.

With his charming manners and solicitous demeanour, Fontaine soon ingratiated himself with his new employers. He and Scott-Elliot got on extremely well; they were both snappy dressers and often went shopping together at Harrods and dined at the best Italian restaurants where, during the old gentleman's more lucid moments, they would discuss the finer points of his antique collection.

Yet, whilst he was skilfully establishing a rapport with the Scott-Elliots, Fontaine was steaming open all their letters and trying to assess the value of the treasure trove so nearly within his grasp.

Fate, however, was waiting to trip him up. On the evening of 8 December, Fontaine went for a drink with a petty thief called Michael Kitto, to whom he had been introduced by Mary Coggle, the woman he had met whilst on parole in Preston, seven years before. Thirty-nine year old Kitto, a Battersea-born drifter, frequented the Soho area and was on the run after stealing £1000 from a public house. He had recently met fifty-one year old Mary in a pub in Kings Cross. Originally from Ireland, Mary was little more than five feet tall, slightly built and usually wore a blond wig. Twice married and the mother of nine children, Coggle was now working as a cleaner and part-time prostitute and living on the fringes of London's underworld. Of particular interest to Fontaine was the fact that she also had a lucrative side-line in handling stolen cheque books. Kitto, never more than a petty pilferer, was impressed by Fontaine, the debonair cigar-smoking butler with the posh accent and a string of convictions behind him. He listened avidly as Fontaine recounted some of his more outrageous frauds, daring thefts and spectacular escapes whilst resisting arrest and he soon became a willing accomplice to the robbery of the wealthy Scott-Elliots.

Fontaine had already decided to use both Coggle and Kitto in his plan. Fully aware that he was mentally superior to both of them put together, he also knew he could manipulate them successfully and then dispose of them with equal ease when the job was done. He was no longer just a jewel thief - he had killed a friend to survive - he was now a cold-blooded murderer. The other two were in a different league altogether.

After they left the pub at closing time on that night, Fontaine suggested that Michael Kitto, who had nowhere to stay, should accompany him back to the Scott-Elliots' flat. He could sleep in his room, Fontaine said, and, at the same time, have a good look round the place and help assess the value of the haul. It was quite safe, Fontaine assured him, for he knew that Scott-Elliot went to bed early and slept soundly. He wouldn't hear a thing. And as for his wife, Dorothy, she wasn't even there - she had gone into a clinic for treatment for her arthritis.

Or so Fontaine thought - but he was wrong. After showing Kitto around the apartment, the butler opened the door of Dorothy's bedroom, probably to show him where the furs and jewels were kept. To his profound surprise, he saw that the lady of the house was sitting up in bed, reading. When she looked up and saw the two men, she was at first shocked and then angry, shouting at them to get out. In a panic, Fontaine swiftly crossed the room and, snatching a pillow, held it firmly over her face to stop her screaming. To prevent the struggling woman from breaking free, Michael Kitto joined in, pressing on the pillow until the struggling stopped. Dorothy Scott-Elliot was dead.

For a few seconds the two men stood rooted to the spot. The next moment they heard the sound of Mr Scott-Elliot shuffling along the passage towards his wife's room, wondering what all the noise was about. Fontaine, quickly switching to his role as gentleman's gentleman, gently steered the old man back to bed, saying that Mrs Scott-Elliot had woken from a nightmare but was now sleeping peacefully.

During the remainder of that dreadful night, Fontaine and Kitto frantically sought a solution. They were in shock. They had not intended to kill anyone - least of all Mrs Scott-Elliot, for they needed her to sign cheques. However, it was done - and they were faced with a dilemma. Whilst they had to get rid of Dorothy Scott-Elliot's body as quickly as possible, they also needed to keep her husband alive long enough to sign away his fortune. Whether at this point Fontaine had decided that they would eventually have to kill him as well is unclear but it seems unlikely that he would have risked letting him live long enough to realise what had happened and alert the police. As they couldn't risk leaving him in the penthouse, they had no choice but to take him on an horrendous trip to dispose of Dorothy Scott-Elliot's body. Fontaine, with his knowledge of the border area, decided to bury her in a remote spot on the Scottish moors.

So it was that the following morning, Roy Fontaine and Michael Kitto, still badly shaken by what had happened, but determined to go ahead with the robbery, hurried to meet Mary Coggle at the telephone exchange in Kings Cross, where she was working as a cleaner. She seemed unperturbed on hearing of Mrs Scott-Elliot's death; she was, however, very interested in getting her hands on some of the woman's finery and agreed to help them get rid of the body.

Back at the penthouse, Scott-Elliot had begun to ask for his wife and when Fontaine said she'd left the house early and would meet him at the Reform Club for lunch, the old chap, suspecting nothing, strode off to keep the appointment.

While he was out of the house, the three villains hired a silver-grey Ford Cortina under assumed names and, on his return, Scott-Elliot, feeling tired and confused, was tricked into signing a cheque to pay for it.

Later that day, Fontaine and his accomplices sneaked down the back stairs of the mansion block, carrying the body of Dorothy Scott-Elliot, wrapped in a blanket. Having deposited the bundle in the boot of the car, Fontaine brought down a number of small, instantly saleable antiques and then went back for Scott-Elliot. Explaining that his wife was waiting for him in the car and that they were all going on a long journey, Fontaine gave him a double dose of sleeping pills. As soon as the drug had taken effect, Scott-Elliot was half-carried downstairs and put in the back seat of the car.

Sitting beside him was Mary Coggle, wearing a £4000 fur coat belonging to his wife, and for a change, a dark wig. As Mrs Scott-Elliot had grey, almost white hair, the fact that the woman was dark-haired seemed to puzzle him for a moment. But, befuddled by the sleeping tablets on top of his normal medication, the old chap assumed that Coggle *must* be his wife and, after she had chatted to him for a few minutes, he slumped back in one corner and dozed off.

Throughout the long journey to Fontaine's cottage near the Scottish border, Scott-Elliot woke several times and even recognised various landmarks as they passed. He was still under the impression, however, that his travelling companion was his wife, Dorothy, and that Michael Kitto was a *bona fide* chauffeur. It was well past midnight when the party reached Middle Farm Cottage and Fontaine put his employer to bed.

The following morning, Saturday, 10 December, the thieving trio and their confused captive, headed across the border into Scotland, stopping twice - once at Lanark to buy a spade and fork and the second time to have lunch at the Drummond Arms Hotel, at Crieff, in Perthshire. Fontaine had the audacity to include Scott-Elliot, by now totally bewildered, in the luncheon party and getting him, of course, to foot the bill. Throughout the meal, Mary Coggle acted the part of the devoted wife and Fontaine and Kitto that of respectful servants.

After lunch, Fontaine ordered Kitto to drive further into snow-covered Perthshire and, having selected a secluded spot, made him help dig a shallow grave in the frozen ground by the roadside between Comrie and Dalchonzie. Mary Goggle, snugly wrapped in the fur coat, remained in the back seat of the car with Scott-Elliot, feeding him pills to make sure he stayed semi-comatose. Once the body of Mrs Scott-Elliot had been covered, the party stopped for refreshments at the Royal Stewart Restaurant in Crieff. This time, however, they left poor Scott-Elliot in the car as they ordered double whiskies and Bacardis to fortify themselves.

This done, they drove the hundred and fifty miles back to Middle

Farm Cottage where Fontaine put Scott-Elliot straight to bed. Then the extraordinary trio spent the rest of the evening discussing their next move over bottles of champagne and brandy and a large steak dinner. Fontaine made it clear that he considered it would be just as profitable to obtain the Scott-Elliot's money through forged cheques as it would to steal the antiques and jewellery. On the other hand, although Scott-Elliot was still signing cheques, he was becoming a liability - he would have to be killed.

On Tuesday, 13 December, they bundled the old man into the back of the Ford Cortina and headed north once more. But this time, Michael Kitto was told to drive to the Tilt Hotel at Blair Atholl, in Perthshire. Mary Coggle, still wearing the expensive mink coat as part of her impersonation of Mrs Scott-Elliot, booked three of the best rooms the establishment could offer. Fontaine and Kitto played the part of butler and chauffeur to perfection as they assisted in getting Scott-Elliot up to his room. He was given a meal and left to sleep while the three impostors ate in the dining room and stayed drinking in the hotel bar until the early hours.

The following morning, Wednesday, 14 December, the four had breakfast together in the dining room of the hotel. Scott-Elliot was still confused and under the impression that Mary Coggle was his wife. Clearly unaware of the danger he was in - which testified to the convincing acting skills of the villainous three - paid the bill, thanked the proprietor for 'a very nice stay' and left with the others about nine-thirty. It was their intention to drive further north, looking for a suitably remote spot to murder the old man. By lunchtime, no such place had been found so the party called for a snack and a drink at a pub near Inverness.

After this, they sped south west to the deserted highlands near Loch Affric. It was here that Scott-Elliot asked to be allowed out of the car to urinate. It was then that the killers struck. Dragging him into some bushes away from the roadside, Fontaine started by trying to strangle him but he fought back with surprising strength. Kitto stepped in and tried to throttle him with a scarf while Fontaine ran back to the car to fetch the spade. Thrusting it towards Kitto, he told him to 'finish him off'. Kitto obeyed without protest dealing the old man a vicious blow to the head. It shattered his skull and within seconds he was dead.

Fontaine was to say later that the old man put up a tremendous fight.

'It was as though he was calling on the strength of his ancestors...' Fontaine recalled. 'He was a gentleman right to the very end.'

The two men quickly buried their victim in a shallow grave, covered it with any loose vegetation they could gather and then joined Mary Coggle in the car. Then they drove on towards Inverness before heading back south. They stopped for a night at a hotel in Aviemore, where they dined well. Kitto and Coggle, who were both drinking heavily, spent the night together but Fontaine, subdued and pre-occupied, distanced himself from his companions and drank alone in another bar.

The following morning, Thursday, 15 December, was spent in selling some of the Scott-Elliots' antiques in Perth. More were sold in Edinburgh the next day, leaving them with plenty of ready cash. Mary Coggle, however, had festooned herself in Mrs Scott-Elliot's expensive belongings - in addition to the fur coat, she was wearing her diamond rings, gold necklaces and carried her crocodile skin handbag. This displeased Fontaine. He found her flashy, coarse manner and inebriation offensive - she was also, he felt, drawing attention to the group by being loud and grossly overdressed. She was also making phone calls to her friends and talking too much. It was only a matter of time before she bragged about the proceeds of the murders and their arrest would surely follow. Fontaine had already begun to view Coggle as a threat to his survival and therefore expendable. Now he was sure.

They returned to Middle Farm Cottage on Friday, 16 December, and Fontaine told Mary Coggle that it was essential that they rid themselves of anything connected with the Scott-Elliots - including the fur coat, another expensive one made of Persian lamb and the jewels. Coggle, relishing the luxury of exquisite things for once in her life, refused to hand them over. A fierce argument flared up, in which Michael Kitto sided with Fontaine. Coggle eventually, but very reluctantly, agreed to the sale of the jewellery - but still refused to give up either of the coats.

Fontaine seethed with anger. Realising this, and perhaps hoping to appease him, at two o'clock in the morning, Mary Coggle asked Fontaine, of all things, to make love to her on the mink coat. Why Fontaine agreed to such an eccentric coupling is difficult to fathom - unless, of course, he hoped a satisfactory performance might pave the way for him to persuade her to relinquish the mink coat.

It was a wasted effort, however, for later that day, further arguments ensued and at one stage Fontaine switched on the electric fire and threatened to burn the mink coat. Mary Coggle flew at him and his temper snapped. He picked up a poker and brought it crashing down onto her head. At this point, Michael Kitto joined in, holding onto her thin arms, preventing her from struggling, as Fontaine attacked her once more with a poker. Finally, when she was near to death, they suffocated her by putting a plastic bag over her head. This done, the two men went for a drink in Carlisle, before organising the disposal of the woman's body - the third in the space of one week.

The next day, Sunday, 18 December, Fontaine and Kitto drove back across the border and dumped Mary Coggle's body in a stream in countryside near Lockerbie. Despite dressing the corpse in men's clothing in an attempt to frustrate identification, the disposal of Mary Coggle's body was uncharacteristically careless. There was no attempt to conceal the body. Surprisingly, however, it was not discovered until Christmas Day, by which time, Fontaine and Kitto were staying with Violet and her family, near Stoke on Trent.

During the intervening two weeks, Fontaine and Kitto had made several trips to the Scott-Elliots' apartment in London, which they had systematically stripped, selling everything of value, mostly to dealers in the Midlands, and netting many thousands of pounds. With the proceeds, they lived in lavish style, staying at the best hotels and spending freely. They also made trips to see various friends and family members, no doubt bearing expensive gifts for the festive season.

One such trip led to Fontaine's fifth and final murder. On Saturday, 14 January, 1978, the two men travelled to Lytham St Annes, in Lancashire, to visit Fontaine's stepfather. His brother, Donald, now thirty-six, was also there. He had just been released from prison after serving three years for house-breaking and, for some reason, Fontaine brought him back to his cottage. Why he should do this is not known for Fontaine despised Donald; he loathed his unkempt appearance and considered him totally lacking in purpose or refinement. Unable to accept the close kinship with such a specimen, he always swore that they had different fathers. Even sister Violet commented later that 'while Roy's criminal career largely revolved around stealing things he knew had real value, Donald was unintelligent. I would never condone Roy's thieving but at least he had guts whereas Donald was a snivelling little small-time crook and also very mean.'[51]

Why then did Fontaine take him back to Middle Farm Cottage? Was he simply showing off the proceeds of his latest theft to his kid brother or had he already made up his mind that his next victim would be the unfortunate Donald?

By this time, the pair of killers had exchanged the silver-grey Ford Cortina for a red Granada but Fontaine was disturbed by the registration number - YGE 999 R. He had a premonition that the number 999 would be unlucky so, on their way back to the cottage, he collected a new set of plates which had been ordered earlier. He had no way of knowing that, bizarrely, it would be the new plates, not the old, that would bring about his downfall.

Now, with Donald in tow, Fontaine and Kitto spent money freely, mainly on dining out and drinking heavily, Fontaine treating himself to his favourite hand-rolled Havanas. Donald, himself a convicted thief, knew, of course, that his brother must have acquired his money illegally - unfortunately, instead of just accepting the fact, he started asking too many questions and, once more under threat of exposure, Fontaine decided to kill.

On Sunday, 15 December, pretending to include Donald in plans for

51 From '*The Monster Butler*' Norman Lucas and Philip Davies.

his next robbery, Fontaine said it would involve tying someone up. Eager to prove himself in the eyes of his big brother, Donald bragged that he could tie someone up so well he could guarantee they would never escape - all he needed was a six inch piece of string.

Like a lamb to the slaughter, he cut six inches off some pyjama cord and urged his companions to tie his thumbs together behind his back. Kitto obliged and, after Donald had laid face down on the floor, did as he was told by pulling his legs under his arms. The sight of his brother trussed up like a chicken must have given Fontaine extreme satisfaction. Swiftly, he bent down and pushed a chloroform-soaked cloth into his face. But Donald fought back, struggling violently. When he finally lost consciousness, Fontaine and Kitto carried him into the bath and held his head under the water until they were sure he was dead.[52] This done, he was hidden in the boot of the car as it sped towards the highlands in search of a suitable burial ground.

The two killers, with Donald's body still in the boot, stopped the night at the Blenheim Arms Hotel, in North Berwick, booking two rooms as usual under false names. Perhaps by now their evil work had begun to reflect in their faces - whatever it was, something alerted the hotel manager, Norman Wight. He thought it odd that the two men had little luggage - only a small holdall, a jacket, a shirt on a hanger and one overcoat between them.

He said later: 'I don't know why I became suspicious. It's just one of those things you learn in the trade. The pair were respectable enough, well-dressed and well-spoken - but somehow their appearances seemed only superficial. They told me they were spending a short holiday in Scotland before emigrating to Australia.'

He was sufficiently suspicious to telephone the local police who sent two officers to investigate. Making a routine check of the tax disc on the hired Granada, they saw straight away that the details did not correspond with the car's registration plates and decided to

52 The post-mortem examination of Donald Hall's body revealed that he was already dead from the effects of the chloroform. The first case of murder by liquid chloroform was that of Adelaide Bartlett in 1886 – see author's book, *In the Interests of Science: Adelaide Bartlett and the Pimlico Poisoning.* Death by chloroform is usually associated with suicide or accidental death.

make further enquiries.

Inside the hotel dining room they found Fontaine and Kitto drinking brandy after an excellent meal. Arresting them on suspicion of fraud concerning the registration papers on the car, they took them to the North Berwick Police Station for questioning. Fontaine gave his name as Roy Thomson Hall, antique dealer, whilst Kitto said his name was John Blackman, from North London. An officer was sent to retrieve the car from the hotel forecourt; he drove it back to the station, unaware that there was a body in the boot.

Meanwhile, a body search carried out on Fontaine and Kitto revealed a number of items that could be traced to the Scott-Elliots but the police still had no idea that the murders of five people were involved. Nor had Fontaine any intention of waiting for them to find out. In desperation, he squeezed through a lavatory window at the police station and escaped.

Within a few minutes of walking free, Fontaine, nattily dressed in a blazer and flannels, came across a young woman willing to help. Already drenched by heavy rain, he told her his wife had been involved in an accident and was in a hospital in Dunbar; he soon persuaded her to drive him to the home of a taxi driver. For the next three hours, while the police were searching for him, Fontaine was being driven around the countryside of East Lothian by an unsuspecting cabbie. It was not until late that night that police made a thorough search of the red Granada and found the body of Donald Hall in the boot. In the meantime, Fontaine's luck ran out - after asking the cabbie to take him to Edinburgh, the taxi was stopped at a police road block on the A1 motorway and he was recaptured - but such was his own peculiar code of ethics that he insisted on paying the cabbie the money owing on his fare.

When arrested, Fontaine was carrying £326 in cash, several items belonging to the Scott-Elliots and a quantity of Librium tablets. The police had no way of knowing, however, that he had a further supply of barbiturates hidden in his rectum. When, a little later, he was given a glass of water, he managed to extract some of the tablets and swallow them. He was subsequently rushed to Edinburgh Royal

Infirmary where they managed to save his life but, two days later, he tried to kill himself again with a back-up supply of drugs concealed in the same way.

While he was recovering, the police network was set into action. Detective Superintendent Ray Adams of Chelsea CID was very anxious to speak to Fontaine about the disappearance of the Scott-Elliots. News also came in that various items of silver bearing the Scott-Elliot crest had been sold in the Stoke-on-Trent area and in other parts of the Midlands.

As for Michael Kitto, with Fontaine in the hospital, he was left to face the questioning alone and soon confessed to complicity in the murder, not only of the body in the car, but of the other three victims. At Middle Farm Cottage the police found the bottle of chloroform used on Donald Hall and a number of items, including firearms, that could be identified as belonging to Walter Scott-Elliot. From Kitto's statement, they were able to identify the body found on Christmas morning as that of Mary Coggle. Blood stains inside the cottage were found to be compatible with that of Mary Coggle's and some of the fingerprints found were also identified as belonging to her. Others were found to be those of Mr Scott-Elliot and Donald Hall and their killers, Fontaine and Kitto.

Michael Kitto fully co-operated in the search for the remaining bodies; he was able to lead them to the grave of Scott-Elliot, which had been disturbed by feral animals, and even managed to locate the poker Fontaine had used to kill Mary Coggle. He could not remember, however, the exact spot where they had buried Mrs Scott-Elliot. Once he had recovered from his second suicide attempt, Fontaine was questioned at length. Realising that it was futile to deny his part in the murders, he also confessed to the killing of David Wright. He told the police where to find Wright's body but a subsequent search was unsuccessful. On 21 January, a bitterly cold and stormy day, Fontaine was taken to Lady Hudson's estate so he could show them exactly where he had shot and buried his friend. Fontaine was seen to be badly affected by the task; it was, indeed, a bleak sight for heavy rain had uncovered much of the debris and part of the body was exposed.

It took much longer to find the grave of Mrs Scott-Elliot, even with Fontaine's co-operation, but eventually all five bodies were recovered and identified. Fontaine was sent for trial for the two murders carried out in Scotland - that of David Wright and Walter Scott-Elliot - the other three killings had taken place in England.[53] He pleaded Guilty to both charges at Edinburgh High Court on Tuesday, 2 May, 1978, under the name he hated so much - Archibald Thomson Hall.

The presiding judge was Lord Wylie, and throughout the two hour hearing, the public gallery remained tightly packed with spectators. Many of them had waited for hours to get a seat in court, anxious to see the man the headlines were calling 'The Monster Butler' or 'The Evil Servant'. Yet, if they were expecting an evil-looking renegade, they were disappointed for Fontaine arrived in court wearing a beautifully-cut grey suit complete with a white handkerchief precisely folded in the breast pocket.

The prosecuting counsel, the Advocate-Depute, Mr Colin McEachran, revealed to the court Fontaine's history of mental instability; he confirmed that two psychiatrists, who had examined him after his arrest, agreed that he possessed a psychopathic personality and, although he felt no remorse for the killings, he was not insane and therefore fit to plead. Fontaine's statement was read to the court and they heard that he had decided to kill David Wright because he was tired of being blackmailed and also feared that, after trying to shoot him in the bedroom without success, another attempt would be made on his life.

On trial with Fontaine was Michael Kitto who pleaded Guilty to complicity in the murder of Walter Scott-Elliot. His defence counsel sought to present him as easily led, a man dominated by Fontaine, the latter being the mastermind behind all the robberies and the killings. As Fontaine had pleaded Guilty there was no defence and

53 The fact that Fontaine was to stand trial for another three murders was not disclosed at the Edinburgh trial. It was inadmissible evidence. Press coverage led to a Contempt of Court issue and an attempt by the Defence to defer the trial.

the jurors retired to consider their verdicts. They found both men guilty as charged. Lord Wylie sentenced Fontaine to a minimum of fifteen years' imprisonment.

Many of the spectators present that day must have expected Roy Fontaine, immaculate and seemingly composed, to make some dramatic gesture at this moment, knowing that every eye in court was focused on him - but, perversely, he said nothing, merely allowing himself to be led away in handcuffs, the slightest hint of a smirk on his face.

Michael Kitto, on the other hand, quipped with reporters as he passed the press benches:

'Life begins at forty,' he said, with a broad grin.

Six months later, on 1 November, 1978, both men stood in the dock at the Old Bailey, further charged with the murders of Mrs Dorothy Scott-Elliot, Mary Coggle and Donald Hall. Fontaine prepared to meet his nemesis in a smart dark blue suit, complete with white handkerchief. Every seat in the public gallery was taken but a swift look told him that his sister, Violet, was not among the spectators. She had been too upset to attend. Whilst Fontaine pleaded Guilty to killing Mary Coggle and Donald Hall, he put up a plea of manslaughter only in the case of Mrs Scott-Elliot.[54]

Michael Kitto, dressed more casually in a tweed suit, admitted the murder of Mary Coggle but pleaded Guilty to manslaughter in the case of Donald Hall and Mrs Scott-Elliot. Presiding over the trial was the Recorder of the City of London, Mr James Miskin, QC. The prosecution was led by Mr Michael Corkery, QC, who told the court of the events leading to the murders and the robbery at 22 Richmond Court, Chelsea. Again, as in Edinburgh High Court, the hearing was short, lasting less than three hours, and both men were found guilty as charged. Asked if either prisoner had anything to say

54 The charge of the first degree murder of Mrs Scott-Elliot, which was contested, was left on the Court File as both men pleaded Guilty to killing Mary Coggle. A further specimen charge of stealing Tudor silver coins from 22, Richmond Court, remained on file. The police also investigated the possibility of a sixth murder victim but Fontaine was not charged with any further offences.

before sentence was passed, they both declined.

The judge dealt first with Michael Kitto. Whilst recognising that Fontaine was the main instigator of the violence, he reminded him that he, too, had played his 'vile part' in the killings. He sentenced Kitto to life imprisonment and recommended that he serve a minimum of fifteen years. When the judge had finished speaking, Kitto said: 'Thank you, sir.'

As for Roy Fontaine, the judge had this to say:

> Having regard to your cold-blooded behaviour and undoubted leadership in these dreadful matters, I have no hesitation in recommending to the Home Secretary that you shall not be considered for parole during the rest of your natural life save in the case of serious infirmity.

These chilling words marked the end of the line for Roy Fontaine. His hands manacled, the dapper butler bowed briefly to the judge as he left the dock.

'Jesus Christ,' he was heard to mutter under his breath, before turning to smirk at the assembled press.

After his conviction, Fontaine was sent to Hull Prison but constantly petitioned the authorities to transfer him to a Scottish prison where, he said, 'as a lifer I will be able to have the small luxuries like my television, radio, newspapers and books and settle down.'

His request, however, was rejected. By way of protest, Fontaine – known by his real name, Archibald Hall, whilst in the prison system - went on hunger strike on 10 July, the following year and his weight plummeted from thirteen stones to six. He was transferred to Wakefield Prison in Yorkshire where he continued to protest, but stayed alive by taking liquids and some light food before finally giving up.

Successive Home Secretaries stipulated that Fontaine must serve a whole life tariff and he became the country's oldest serving prisoner. In 1995, the *Observer* published a letter from Fontaine in which he requested the right to die. He had, apparently, made several unsuccessful suicide attempts. In 1999, he published his autobiography, *A Perfect Gentleman*, and in 2002, he died, aged 78, after suffering a stroke in Kingston Prison, Portsmouth, Hampshire.

One cannot help but suppose that, had Roy Fontaine chosen to apply all his intelligence, ingenuity and resilience to legitimate enterprise, he could have become, quite legally, a very rich man. Undoubtedly, with his ability to communicate and his manipulative skills, he could have been successful in a number of entrepreneurial schemes that might have had a beneficial effect, not just on him, but on society as a whole. Instead, he chose to cheat and lie and eventually, to kill.

In common with all such case histories, there are always the elements of chance, the inevitable 'if only syndrome'. If only, for instance, he had been able to run away from Kirtleton Hall on the night David Wright tried to kill him. If only Lady Hudson hadn't entrusted him with the dogs and if only he'd had the heart to abandon them. And, if only Dorothy Scott-Elliot had stayed in the clinic another night and not returned to the apartment, she would not have been killed. Had she not been inadvertently killed, there would have been no reason to cover his tracks by killing her husband. As for Mary Coggle, if only she hadn't been so greedy and tried to hang on to the fur coat, she could have been alive today.

But the killing of Donald Hall was something else. It seems to have been an act of senseless violence on Fontaine's part - the act of vicious sibling rivalry out of control. Perhaps, having already killed four people, extinguishing the life of a much-hated brother, one whose life he considered to have no value, seemed almost mandatory and of little significance.

In common, too, with many other criminals, Roy Fontaine's personality was complex and at core, self-destructive - almost as if he was driven to even more outrageous crimes and yet knowing that he would eventually be caught. When, after his arrest for murder, his sister, Violet, begged him for some sort of explanation, he merely shrugged and put it down to fate. Yet she, and other members of his family, saw another, more positive and kindly side to his nature - and his friends and associates saw him as a gregarious and amusing companion.

His female friends, finding him a charming and generous lover, seemed to have remained loyal for many years. He was also a sentimental man, fond of children and animals and one who said that the only time he was happy when he was working at Kirtleton Hall for Lady Hudson. He even expressed the wish to have his ashes scattered over the estate though whether this would have met with her Ladyship's approval is doubtful for it was said that after Fontaine's arrest she always concealed a pistol under her pillow at night.

Yet, although he professed to liking the old lady so much, he would have willingly robbed her had he not been thrown off guard by the unplanned killing of David Wright. Likewise, despite the kinder elements in his character, he was also a compulsive thief with little thought for his victims. He was a prolific thief, certainly, but not a particularly successful one, as his years of imprisonment will testify - and eventually a ruthless killer.

With all his attributes, he could have so easily fitted into society, made a success of his life and perhaps found some lasting fulfilment. So what was it in this man's psyche that made him seek out that extra challenge, the heart-pounding threat of sudden exposure, the nail-biting uncertainty of fraud and impersonation? Clearly this heightened element of risk brought him tremendous excitement, like a very powerful drug that he couldn't resist returning to time and time again, until it finally, inevitably, destroyed him.

Bibliography

The Monster Butler. Norman Lucas and Philip Davies.
(Weidenfeld & Nicholson, 1990)

The Butler Did It. Paul Pender.
(Mainstream Publishing Company, 2012)

The Secret of the Babbacombe Murder. Mike Holgate.
(Peninsular Press. 1995)

The Babbacombe Murder. Frank Keyse.
(Carreg Lwyd, 1988)

John 'Babbacombe' Lee - His Own Story. John Lee.
(Devon Books, 1985)

The Papin Sisters. Rachel Edwards and Keith Reader.
(Oxford University Press, 2001)

Murder At The Priory; The Mysterious Poisoning of Charles Bravo.
Bernard Taylor and Kate Clarke. (Grafton 1988)

Death At The Priory. James Ruddick.
(Atlantic Books, 2001)

Executioner: Pierrepoint. An Autobiography. Albert Pierrepoint.
(Harrap 1974)

My Experiences as an Executioner. James Berry.
Introduction by Jonathan Goodman. (David & Charles Reprints, 1972)

Executioner: The Chronicles of a Victorian Hangman. Stewart Evans.
(Sutton Publishing Limited 2004)

A Perfect Gentleman. Roy Hall with Trevor Anthony Holt .
(Blake Publishing Ltd 1999)

Encyclopaedia of Murder. Colin Wilson & Patricia Pitman.
(Arthur Barker, 1961)

Murder In The West Country. intro. Colin Wilson.
(Bossiney Books, 1975)

The Murder Guide. Brian Lane.
(Robinson Publishing, 1991)

Look For The Woman. Jay Robert Nash.
(M. Evans & Company, Inc. New York, 1981)

Murder 'Whatdunnit'. J. H.H. Gaute and Robin Odell.
(Harrap Limited, 1982)

The Trial of Kate Webster. ed. E.O'Donnell. Notable British Trials.
(William Hodge & Company Ltd. 1925)

Studies in Ferocity: A Book of Human Monsters.
The Case of the Papin Sisters. Raymond Rudorff.
(Neville Spearman, 1968)

Newspapers and Periodicals

The Torquay Directory
Lloyd's Weekly News
The Penny Illustrated Paper
The Western Morning News
The Gloucester Journal
The Hereford Times
The Pall Mall Gazette
The World
The Balham Mystery
The Daily Telegraph
The Daily News
The Times
The News of the World
The Daily Mirror
The Exeter Gazette
The Observer

Index